Journal of a Voyage with Bering

1741–1742

GEORG WILHELM STELLER

Journal of a Voyage
with Bering
1741–1742

EDITED AND WITH AN INTRODUCTION BY

O. W. Frost

TRANSLATED BY

Margritt A. Engel and O. W. Frost

Stanford University Press
Stanford, California

Stanford University Press
Stanford, California
© 1988 by the Board of Trustees
of the Leland Stanford Junior University
Printed in the United States of America

Original printing 1988
Last date below indicates year of this printing:
02 01 00 99 98 97 96 95 94 93

CIP data appear at the end of the book

Research for this book was partially funded
under a grant from the Alaska Humanities Forum
and the National Endowment for the Humanities

Published with the assistance of the Alaska
Humanities Forum and the National Endowment
for the Humanities

Acknowledgments

WE WISH TO ACKNOWLEDGE the assistance given by individuals, institutions, and funding organizations. Karen E. Willmore coauthored with Frost a research report entitled *Description of Unpublished Steller Papers in Smithsonian Archives and the Library of Congress* (1983) and produced with Engel the typed German text in *Steller's Manuscript Journal: Facsimile Edition and Transliteration* (1984). These two studies, as preliminary steps to the present work, place Willmore preeminently among those whose counsel is here gratefully acknowledged.

John F. Thilenius, research wildlife biologist of the Forestry Sciences Laboratory, Juneau, Alaska, and Edgar P. Bailey, field biologist of the U.S. Fish and Wildlife Service, Homer, Alaska, both generously shared with Frost their firsthand knowledge of the biology of Bering expedition landing sites in Alaska and their personal commitment to the preservation of wilderness values in these locales. Thilenius led Frost and John L. Mattson, archeologist of the Chugach National Forest, to Kayak and Wingham islands via helicopter from Cordova, Alaska, for a four-day field investigation in July 1984; and Bailey guided Frost to the Bering expedition landing sites on the Shumagin Islands via a fishing vessel chartered by the U.S. Fish and Wildlife Service during the spring and summer of 1985. The Service has used Frost's identification and description of the Shumagin sites as a basis for seeking formal historic site status through the National Register of Historic Places.

Alaska Pacific University granted Frost a full-year sabbatical in 1984–85 to pursue Steller studies and also travel and research funds to utilize archives and rare book collections at the Smithsonian, the Library of Congress, and Yale University. The Alaska Historical Commission awarded three small research grants and offered encouragement through William S. Hanable, executive director, and Joan Antonson, historian. Finally, the Alaska Humanities Forum provided funds for field research on Kayak and Wingham islands, for this translation of Steller's journal, for travel to use the archives of Stanford University's Hoover Institution, and for trips to Alaska coastal communities for discussion of public issues arising from the identification of Bering expedition landing sites. The Forum's executive director, Gary H. Holthaus, has been helpful at every turn.

Paul Psoinos of Stanford University Press, with unfailing graciousness and thoroughness, assisted most generously in our joint efforts to achieve clarity and accuracy. In particular, he helped improve our translations of Steller's, Markgraf's, and Gesner's Latin, and called attention to an instance of Steller's borrowing from Propertius.

It is not possible to cite all those who have in various ways assisted in the preparation of this book, but certain persons stand out: Andrew Gronholdt, Aleut historian of Sand Point, Alaska; Janet R. Klein and John L. Martin of Homer, Alaska; V. Louise Kellogg of Palmer, Alaska; Robert Fortuine, M.D., John F. C. Johnson, David McCargo, Susan D. Morton, John L. Mattson, and Eva Trautmann of Anchorage; Marvin W. Falk of Fairbanks; Rose and Robert Arvidson, Dolores Crowley, Ken Hill, Pete Mickelson, and Andrew Smallwood of Cordova, Alaska; Sheila Nickerson, Juneau; Carol Urness, Minneapolis, Minnesota; Elizabeth P. Crownhart-Vaughan, Portland, Oregon; Eric W. Nye, Laramie, Wyoming; L. Lewis Johnson, Poughkeepsie, New York; Olga M. Griminger, Highland Park, New Jersey; Alix O'Grady, Victoria, B.C., Canada; and John Massey Stewart, London, England. Debts of another kind are due our supportive spouses, Mary B. Frost and August W. Engel.

O.W.F.
M.A.E.

Contents

Illustrations

Introduction

Introduction

NINETEEN NINETY-ONE marks the 250th anniversary of the European discovery of the northwest coast of America. This event, undertaken under Russian sponsorship, is the beginning of Alaska's recorded history. It is most fully and dramatically described in the journal kept by Georg Wilhelm Steller (1709–46), the German naturalist and academician who in 1741–42, as physician and mineralogist, accompanied Captain-Commander Vitus Jonassen Bering aboard the *St. Peter* on an unforgettable voyage. The journal is presented here in the first English translation based completely on a surviving copy of Steller's manuscript, which was written in German and dated 1743. A source document of invaluable historical importance, it is also a narrative of bitter human conflict, of nature as an overwhelming adversary, and of deliverance from death for scarcely more than half the crew. Through all the hardship and despair of the return voyage, Steller emerges as a dutiful, courageous man whose healing arts and organizational skills restored body and spirit, and whose scientific genius—embracing biology, ethnography, and medicine—was eminently practical and instantly applicable.

Steller's Writings

The three books published posthumously under Steller's name were hastily written between 1740 and 1743. The zoological treatise *De bestiis marinis* (1751), the ethnographic study *Beschreibung von dem Lande Kamtschatka* (1774), and Steller's *Tagebuch* or journal (1781, 1793), even taken together, represent but a small fraction of his total production during the last eight years of his life. *De bestiis marinis* (Of marine beasts) enjoyed almost immediate fame among European scientists. Written on Bering Island early in 1742, it is the record of Steller's observations of four large North Pacific sea mammals—the sea otter, the fur seal, the sea lion, and the hitherto unknown North Pacific sea cow (*Hydrodamalis gigas*). Soon after this treatise appeared in 1751 in the second volume of *Novi Commentarii Academiae Scientiarum Imperialis Petropolitanae*, the Russian Academy's journal of research reports, it appeared serially in German in a Hamburg periodical and was published as a small book in Halle in 1753 under the title *Ausführliche Beschreibung von sonderbaren Meerthieren* (Detailed description of extraordinary sea animals). Nearly a century and a half later, it made its only appearance in English as the "Beasts of the Sea" in a partial translation from the Latin by Walter Miller and Jennie Emerson Miller in Part 3 of *The Fur Seals and Fur-Seal Islands of the North Pacific Ocean* (1899), edited by David Starr Jordan. Here the interest was primarily in Steller's sea cow, which became extinct in 1768. Steller was the first—and only—scientist ever to describe this elephantine sea mammal.

Steller's field reports for his most ambitious work, a study of the Kamchadals (also called Itelmen) on the Kamchatka Peninsula, were first utilized by Stepan P. Krasheninnikov in his deservedly much-praised descriptive account of Kamchatka, which was published in Russian in St. Petersburg in 1755. Unfortunately, Krasheninnikov, who was on Kamchatka as a student of the Russian Academy for several years before he briefly came under Steller's supervision, died in 1755 before his book was ready for the printer, and probably for this reason his debt to Steller has never been fully acknowledged. But in 1774 Steller's work was published in Frankfurt and Leipzig as a 384-page book, edited by "J. B. S." (Jean Benoît Scherer) and entitled *Beschreibung von dem Lande Kamtschatka* (Description of Kamchatka). Although Krasheninnikov's work has been reissued three times in Russian (most recently in 1949) and fully translated into both French (1770) and English (1972), Steller's *Kamchatka* remains undeservedly little known and accessible today only to readers of German.

The journal, surviving in manuscript for half a century, was reorganized, largely rewritten, and published in two installments by Peter Simon Pallas, professor of natural history of the Imperial Academy of Sciences at St. Petersburg. The first installment (1781) was actually the journal's appendix on the physical geography of Bering Island, to which Pallas added several sections describing animal life from the journal proper. The second installment (1793) contained the remainder of the journal. Both appeared in St. Petersburg and Leipzig among documents collected by Pallas and issued as *Neue nordische Beyträge zur physikalischen und geographischen Erd- und Völkerbeschreibung, Naturgeschichte und Ökonomie* (New northern contributions to physical and cultural geography, natural history, and agriculture). Simultaneously, the journal without the appendix was printed as a small book by the same publisher.

Translations of the journal have been published only once in Russian (1928) and twice in English, first in summarized selections in 1803 in the fourth edition of William Coxe's *Account of the Russian Discoveries Between Asia and America* and more recently in 1925 in volume 2 of Frank A. Golder's *Bering's Voyages*, a collection of translated documents pertaining principally to the Bering voyage of 1741–42. Both English translations are based on Pallas's text, although Golder's work footnotes many variants from the 1743 manuscript.

Bering's Voyages was reprinted in 1968, and a limited facsimile edition in German of all three books by Steller was reprinted in 1974 in Stuttgart in a single volume with a general introduction by Hanno Beck. Thus, although all three major surviving works have appeared in both the eighteenth and the twentieth centuries in German, none has been published in a French translation, and only one—the journal—in the twentieth century in Russian and English.

Steller's correspondence is as yet largely uncollected, and his letters to his wife in St. Petersburg, last known to be in Scherer's possession, and to his older brother Johann Augustin in Germany are apparently lost. What remain are chiefly letters to fellow academician Johann Georg Gmelin in Siberia, published in 1861 in *Joannis Georgii Gmelini, Reliquiae quae supersunt commercii epistolici cum Carolo Linnaeo, Alberto Hallero, Guilielmo Stellero, et al.* (Johann Georg Gmelin, Fragments remaining of correspondence with Carolus Linnaeus, Albert Haller, Wilhelm Steller et al.), edited by G. H. T. Plieninger; letters and memorandums in German and Russian to officials in St. Petersburg, published in 1870 in P. P. Pekarskii's four-volume history of the Imperial Academy of Sciences and at various times in other Russian sources; and English translations of much of this correspondence provided, sometimes in full, in Leonhard Stejneger's *Georg Wilhelm Steller: The Pioneer of Alaskan Natural History* (1936).

Much of Steller's phenomenal output of scientific papers in Latin was irretrievably lost in transit between outposts in Siberia and St. Petersburg or from private collections once they reached the Russian capital. Five lists of North Pacific plants and seeds, totaling 126 manuscript pages, are available in a cache of photocopied documents Golder deposited in 1917 in the Library of Congress. One of these, Steller's list of plants gathered chiefly on Cape St. Elias (Kayak Island) in the Gulf of Alaska, is reprinted fully (but not trans-

FIG. 1. Leonhard Stejneger (1851–1943), biologist, Smithsonian Institution. (Courtesy of the Smithsonian Institution, photo no. 85-5538)

lated into English) in an appendix to Stejneger's biography of Steller. But it is clear from Steller's report to the Senate, dated November 16, 1742, that he also prepared a paper on North American birds and fish and another on Bering Island birds and fish. Moreover, in 1747, Krasheninnikov compiled a list of 62 manuscript titles delivered to the Academy by Steller's traveling companion, the illustrator Johann Christian Berckhan; the titles are printed in full in Pekarskii's history of the Academy (1:613–16). Those by Steller total 635 manuscript pages. They concern Siberian flora and fauna and include *De bestiis marinis* and one paper on fish and another on bird nests and eggs published in 1753 and 1758 respectively in *Novi Commentarii*. These 62 manuscripts are presumably still available in Academy archives in Leningrad. But Krasheninnikov's compilation omits many titles Steller himself refers to as his own in his three books; and Johann Augustin Stöller, in a biographical sketch of his brother, lists five Latin titles of scientific works already lost by 1747.

Indeed, during the eighteenth century, Academy control over Steller material must frequently have been relaxed. In 1746, at Steller's death, his unfinished work on the flora of Perm mysteriously disappeared. By 1750, Linnaeus in Sweden had obtained some actual plant specimens Steller collected on Kamchatka. By 1774, Scherer had secured copies of Steller's journal and Kamchatkan material, apparently from academician Johann Eberhard Fischer, and had the latter published in Germany without authorization from the Russian government. Finally, by 1784, Pallas had supplied Thomas Pennant, in London, with a list of flora Steller collected in America and Kamchatka, a list Pennant published in his *Arctic Zoology* (1:cxiv–cxvi, cxlvi).

Because Steller's own extant writings are mostly inaccessible, it is far easier to read about Steller than to read him. Chiefly through Stejneger's monumental pioneering work as translator and biographer, others have introduced Steller to a wider reading public—Ernest Gruening in his *State of Alaska* (1954), Margaret E. Bell in *Touched with Fire* (1960), Ann Sutton and Myron Sutton in *Steller of the North* (1961), and Corey Ford in *Where the Sea Breaks Its Back* (1966). These all concern the mature Steller, the naturalist who accompanied Bering.

Stejneger's biography has three limitations. It discusses Steller's achievements in biology but not in ethnography and medicine. It ignores the influences on him of Lutheran Pietism. Most seriously, it avoids the comprehensive study of Steller's character. Nowhere does Stejneger portray fully the intense, indomitable personality of the journal, the independent, solitary figure with an alert intelligence, a stubborn single-mindedness, and a hair-trigger disposition to judge and to act, driven by an implacable, almost reckless determination to do his duty for God and emperor, whatever the obstacles, but withal a fundamentally compassionate, modest, and cheerful individual. Stejneger's work is notably a meticulously researched compilation of factual information about Steller and about people and places associated with him. Before Steller's departure for Kamchatka and the Pacific, Stejneger presents only glimpses of his subject in a succession of settings—at home in Windsheim (1709–29), 34 miles west of Nuremberg; at the neighboring universities of Wittenberg (1729–31) and Halle (1731–34); briefly in Berlin (August 1734) to take an examination; and finally in St. Petersburg (1734–38) and eastward to Kamchatka (1738–40) to begin his career. Through all these moves and the first 31 of his 37 years, Steller remains an elusive and shadowy figure.

The fault is not altogether Stejneger's. In his surviving writings, Steller rarely reflects on these early years. Virtually no personal correspondence belonging to this period is available, and indeed it appears likely that there was never much of it, even to his older brother Johann Augustin (called Augustin), who preceded him at Halle in 1725–26 and lived as a physician in the vicinity of both Wittenberg and Halle during his younger brother's university years. In 1747 Augustin wrote "Zuverlässige Nachricht von dem merkwürdigen Leben und Reisen Herrn Georg Wilhelm Stöllers" (Reliable information about the remarkable life and travels of Georg Wilhelm Stöller), published in Leipzig in a fancifully titled, short-lived periodical, *Ergetzungen der vernünftigen Seele aus der Sittenlehre und der Gelehrsamkeit überhaupt* (Amusements for the rational soul from moral philosophy and learning in general). Augustin's account of his brother's years in Germany may be fairly reliable, but his presentation of Steller's last years in Russia is sketchy at best. Augustin simply lost touch.

Steller's Preparatory Years

For Georg Wilhelm Steller, life became a pilgrimage, and his path lay north and east to Russia and the Pacific. Once there, he gradually slipped away from his family and origins. When he left Germany in 1734, he was still "Stöller," but he soon adopted "Steller," a modification more easily pronounced by non-Germans. In 1737, in the Russian capital, he married Brigitta-Helena, the young widow of Daniel Gottlieb Messerschmidt, in a public assembly, an event his family in Germany learned about only ten years later, after his death. By 1741, his allegiance to Russia, as personified in its monarch, was fervent and unwavering, and Russia was the "fatherland" to which he returned from America. His burial in 1746 within Russia's vast eastern frontier seems entirely appropriate, for the work he accomplished there was the culmination of what he lived for—to visit unknown, faraway lands, to discover and describe the peoples and natural wonders to be seen there, and, by the grace of God, to use his science and his faith to serve Russia and its peoples.

When and where his professional career began to take definite direction is difficult to say, for almost nothing is known about the shaping of a vocational commitment during his childhood and adolescence in Windsheim. His father, Jacob, was a musician from Nuremburg who taught music in Windsheim's Latin school and played the organ and led the choir in St. Kilian's (Lutheran) Church. Of his mother, nothing is known but her maiden name (Susanna Louysa Baumann), the year of her marriage (1702), the name of her home town (Crailsheim), and the fact that she bore ten children, of whom Augustin was the first (1703) and Georg Wilhelm the fourth (March 10, 1709). We can only assume that Lutheran influences through parents, church, and school were primarily orthodox: Augustin first chose orthodox Leipzig before going to reformist Halle to study medicine, and Georg Wilhelm went to Luther's Wittenberg to study theology. But after two years there on a Windsheim scholarship, he shopped around, visiting both Leipzig and Jena before settling on Halle, the seedbed and mission center of a new and rapidly spreading Lutheran movement known as Pietism. Begun by Philip Jacob Spener and August Hermann Francke, Pietism emphasized religious practice based not on Luther's "faith alone" but on faith as manifested in fellowship, charity, and mission. From its founding in 1694, Halle was the intellectual center of Pietism, and Spener and Francke influenced the selection of staff and the practices of the university.

Why Halle? Had Augustin recommended it? Was he better able to support himself there as a private tutor in the city and as a student teacher in Halle's famed orphanage schools, now that his scholarship from Windsheim had ended? Did he find a superb opportunity there to pursue a growing interest in biology, as well as theological studies? Was he attracted by the university's religious practices, or did he recognize in Halle the starting point of a spiritual and scientific journey? Perhaps he chose Halle for all these reasons.

Who or what prompted Steller's decision to seek a career in the natural sciences and medicine rather than in the Lutheran ministry? Augustin was almost surely a major influence. In "Zuverlässige Nachricht" (p. 367), Augustin wrote that Steller at Wittenberg "did not forget the interest of his early years, namely, the knowledge and exploration of natural things. He was particularly interested in herbal science, which he pursued most eagerly on his own, following the text [*De materia medica*, written ca. A.D. 50] of Dioscorides and some newer ones. Even though he then had not yet decided to specialize in medicine, he nevertheless attended lectures in dissection." At the same time, Steller was becoming skilled as a preacher "in and around Wittenberg as well as in the county Barby" (ibid.), where Augustin was then living. The two brothers usually met on these occasions and discussed medical texts, medical schools, and medicine as a career. Perhaps Steller's copy of Pedanios Dioscorides' text came from Augustin's own library.

In any event, Halle was Steller's starting point for his pilgrimage. Here, as Augustin relates, Steller "dedicated himself once again most seriously to the sciences . . . but now primarily the healing arts" (p. 368). At the same time, he continued his theological studies and added a third major subject—philosophy, or *Weltweisheit* (world-wisdom) as Augustin significantly calls it, a late-seventeenth-century descriptive term to distinguish what can be learned from history or experience, that is, philosophy, as opposed to *Gottesgelehrtheit* (God-learning), revelation, or theology. In philosophy, Steller no doubt read the works of such thinkers as he later names in his *Kamchatka* (p. 246): Girolamo Cardano, Hugo Grotius, Samuel von Pufendorf, and Johann Franz Budde.

Cardano, in his *De varietate rerum* (1557), was a harbinger of Darwinian evolution in seeing all creation as development and all animals as existing for their own sake, but he also speculated (much too narrowly) that all human differences arise from environmental factors. Grotius, in his *De veritate religionis Christianae* (1627), espoused the universality of divine grace, decrying doctrines over which Lutherans and Calvinists quarreled, and advocated the application of history and philology to the study of Scripture. Pufendorf, in his *De jure naturae et gentium* (1672), defined knowledge as coming from three sources, reason in natural law, civil statutes in civil law, and revelation in moral theology. Budde—a professor of moral theology at Halle from 1694 to 1705—upheld both Grotius and Pufendorf in their recognition of a law of nature ordained by God.

These and similar thinkers were attractive to many Pietists because, by expanding conceptions of God and the world, they at least by inference disapproved of the doctrinal disputes engendered by a strict adherence to Lutheran orthodoxy. It is instructive to recall that, in these fractious times dominated by religious controversy, a "mixed marriage" was one between a Lutheran and a Calvinist and that in 1690 the University of Leipzig forbade Christian Thomasius to write or to lecture because he defended both Pietism and such marriages. Thomasius later joined Francke in launching the University of Halle and there became best known as a critic of witchcraft trials and a leader of the German Enlightenment.

Renowned for its teaching of both theology and philosophy, the University of Halle fostered an academic freedom unusual for its time, as well as a highly individualistic pursuit of truth across established disciplines and schools, a potent network of influence and support, and an uncompromising commitment to scholarship and social service. As the head of the university, the king of Prussia in Berlin acted on all faculty appointments and set salaries. As in other German universities, the professoriate ruled, with the rectorship rotating annually among the professors. However, Halle was unique in having Pietism as its standard and in its tie to a thriving, independent, and private Pietist institution.

The faculty worked with Francke—and, on his death in 1727, with his son Gotthilf—in establishing and expanding the orphanage schools, notably in the selection of university students to serve as teachers in the schools through *Freytische* (free bed and board), an arrangement that recruited many able students like Steller who otherwise could not have afforded a university education. Although each of the four faculties—theology, philosophy, law, and medicine— was largely autonomous, the cohesion among the faculties was extraordinary because of a shared commitment to Pietist objectives. As Johanna Geyer-Kordesch has remarked, "Persuasion must have mattered, as did conviction, because the records show that financial gain (in terms of salary) was not guaranteed in Halle" (p. 191).

But just as Pietism signified a break with Lutheran orthodoxy, *Weltweisheit* (philosophy newly defined) signified a break with Pietism both inside and outside Lutheranism. Thomasius broke with Francke, first over Francke's condemnation of Frau Thomasius's stylish Easter finery and later over questions of pedagogy in the orphanage schools. In 1721, another renowned Halle scholar, Christian von Wolff—the first university professor to teach Leibniz's and Newton's calculus and, as a rationalist in philosophy, no Pietist—stung most of his colleagues by declaring, in a formal address entitled "On the Practical Philosophy of the Chinese," that the attainment of high ethical standards and a great civilization did not in the least depend on Christian revelation. The theology faculty, outraged, branded Wolff a heretic but could not effect his removal. Only when Wolff made the mistake of appealing to Berlin for relief from his critics was he summarily ousted by the king. Perhaps it was a Pietist who suggested that Wolff's "determinism" implied that Prussian soldiers who deserted could not be punished because they could not help deserting! Wolff was given 48 hours to leave Prussia—or be hanged. He left, only to return with great honor to Halle in 1740 in calmer times as one of the foremost philosophers in Europe.

For Wolff *Weltweisheit* was, at any rate, historical and global, utilizing cultural information about distant places. Steller's own curiosity in strange sub-Arctic cultures was aroused by two seventeenth-century travelers whom he mentioned in his *Kamchatka* (p. 246): John Scheffer, who reported on the Lapps in his *History of Lapland* (1674), and Adam Olearius, who commented on the Samoyeds and Greenland Eskimos in digressions in his *Vermehrte neue Beschreibung der muscowitischen und persischen Reysen* (1656). Olearius in particular began a German tradition of ethnographic study in Russia, commenting on church and state, food and housing, marriage and family, and crime and punishment, occasionally mixing fancy with fact and betraying the bias of a moralizing German Lutheran. Employed as a scholar in a trade mission sent by the Duke of Holstein to Russia and Persia, Olearius first visited Moscow in 1634 and returned in 1636, 1639, and 1643.

The tradition was advanced by the University of Halle through its ties with Russia under Peter the Great—and the traffic went in both directions. Laurence Blumentrost, Peter's physician and the first president of the newly created Imperial Academy of Sciences in St. Petersburg, had studied medicine at Halle as well as at Oxford and Leiden. Wolff was actively recruited (unsuccessfully) for Peter's Academy, first when Blumentrost returned to Halle in 1719 and two years later when Blumentrost's assistant, Johann Daniel Schumacher, arrived. By this time, Peter had contracted with Daniel Gottlieb Messerschmidt, a graduate of Halle in medicine, to explore western and central Siberia to investigate, as Alexander Vucinich puts it in his *Science in Russian Culture* (p. 59), "the area's geography, natural history, medicine, medicinal plants, epidemic diseases, historical documents and antiquities, and 'everything deserving attention,'" a pioneering assignment carried out between 1720 and 1727, with no little distinction. In addition to being a physician, Messerschmidt knew several Eastern languages and possessed mapmaking skills. He discovered copper, iron, and silver, compared native languages and brought back many plant and animal specimens for Peter's *Kunstkammer*, or museum of natural science and ethnography. In 1731, the very year Steller matriculated at Halle, Messerschmidt had settled in retirement, recently married, in St. Petersburg. The year before, Bering had returned to the same city after his first Great Northern Expedition into the Arctic Ocean, begun in the summer of 1728. Having failed on that voyage to sight the American continent, he was now proposing a second expedition, which became much expanded to include charting the northern coast of Siberia, visiting Japan as well as America, and preparing a thorough inventory of flora, fauna, minerals, and peoples within eastern Siberia and along the coasts of the North Pacific. Thus knowledge of the world was still expanding under the aegis of Peter's successors, and Halle with its Russian connections was a strategic place for Steller to be.

Two professors who facilitated Steller's departure for Russia were on different faculties. Recruited by Francke, Friedrich Hoffmann dominated medicine at Halle from 1694 until his death nearly fifty years later, with the exception of the years 1708–12, and eight months in 1734 spent in Berlin as royal physician. Hoffmann was so well known in Europe that, on his reputation alone, Halle achieved renown for medicine as for theology and philosophy. Both Blumentrost and Messerschmidt had come from afar, from Moscow and Danzig, respectively, to receive training specifically from him. But it is ironic that by 1734 Hoffmann, already 74, had personally selected Steller, who was probably eager to go to Russia, to become a future member of the medical faculty at Halle for the express purpose of assuming responsibility for botany or herbal science, in those days an adjunct to medicine. In "Zuverlässige Nachricht" (pp. 368–69), Augustin wrote that his brother began "to lecture publicly on herbal science. His opening lecture, held May 1, 1732 . . . was fortunate to receive much applause and [his lecture series had] a consistently large audience." But, says Augustin, "it was just this that led to problems. Other scholars became jealous of his steadily increasing audience, and attempts were made to thwart his efforts in all manner of ways and to make them difficult and irksome." It was in this dilemma, says Augustin, that Hoffmann, "who esteemed [Steller] highly because of his abilities and who supported him for the good of the school in many ways, thereupon counseled him to travel to Berlin and let himself be examined by the local medical board and promised to do his part to obtain for him a faculty position in botany."

Hoffmann was in a good position to help, for over the years he had maintained close ties with the royal court, the Berlin Academy, and specifically with Georg Ernst Stahl, an eminent medical friend and former colleague at Halle. Indeed, these two, sharing a common Pietist commitment but a divergent approach to the study and practice of medicine, had from 1694 to 1715, when Stahl left for Berlin, made Halle the pre-eminent center for medical studies among German universities, supplanting Jena, where both men had achieved M.D. degrees. To Hoffmann, the human body was strictly material, and its ailments predictably responsive to given medication, whereas for Stahl, mental and emotional influences were paramount factors in medical treatment. At Berlin, Stahl was court physician and president of the *collegium medicum* and was responsible for regulating the practice of medicine in Prussia. He founded the first German *theatrum anatomicum* and a charity hospital for teaching purposes. When Stahl died suddenly early in 1734, Hoffmann was called to Berlin to replace him until a successor could be named. Thus Hoffmann was in Berlin, and had been there for some months, when Steller arrived in August 1734.

It would not be surprising, then, if Hoffmann were ignorant of Steller's plan to go to Russia and of the assistance already given him to get there through the good offices of Gotthilf August Francke, who had connections to officials in the Russian Orthodox church. The Francke name was already immortalized by the *Franckeschen Stiftungen*, or Francke Charitable Foundation, which in Halle supported not only the orphanage and a number of schools for rich and poor alike, but also a bookstore, publishing house, pharmacy, and homes for widows, the elderly, and even "strolling beggars." In 1733, the schools enrolled more than 2,000 students and provided their teachers both room and board in the six-story orphan house, the largest structure in Halle. Even though Steller as a teacher was once sharply criticized for mediocre lessons, poor delivery, and insufficient stress on piety (in archival records examined by Stejneger, *Georg Wilhelm Steller*, p. 37), there can be no doubt that he supported the schools' objective of preparing youth for godly and useful lives and himself became "ein Pietist aus Halle," to quote Eduard Winter (p. 233). Steller was by this time highly motivated and self-directed, having, like his Halle mentors, much to accomplish and being constantly too aware of God's wrath ever to tolerate laziness, cursing, gambling, and promiscuity. He was probably an acceptable candidate to the younger Francke, and it seems likely, as Winter suggests (p. 328), that Steller left Halle for Berlin with one or more letters of introduction to Russian Orthodox churchmen in St. Petersburg.

In "Zuverlässige Nachricht" (pp. 369–70), Augustin explained that his brother, on being examined in Berlin by the distinguished botanist of the Royal Academy, Michael Matthias Ludolf, and receiving from him a "very laudable certificate," was unable to obtain the desired faculty appointment at Halle because the king of Prussia, Friedrich Wilhelm, was too ill to consider it. As a result, Augustin said (in a very awkward construction) that "the intention that [his brother] had had before, namely to go to Russia, was therefore aroused once more in him." Stejneger, who accepted this version of events, suggested (p. 61) the unlikely circumstance of a later chance meeting in St. Petersburg between Steller and Theophan Prokopovitch, the archbishop of Novgorod, Russia's highest churchman and a resident of St. Petersburg. The story is that Steller, penniless and newly arrived, went to an apothecary garden on the outskirts of the city, where the archbishop "was in the habit of almost daily taking his outdoor exercise." They almost literally bumped into each other, and the archbishop, instantly drawn to the newcomer, generously invited him to stay at his residence.

Surely, given Steller's admitted "insatiable desire to visit foreign lands" (see Preface of translation), acquired probably by the time he left Halle, Berlin must have been but a stepping-stone en route to the Russian Empire. By 1734, he would know, first, that Academy Professors Gerhard F. Müller and Gmelin, the one from nearby Leipzig and the other from Tübingen, were following Bering across Eurasia and, second, that any opportunity he would have to join the second Great Northern Expedition would be enhanced by certification in his dual competencies in natural history and medicine. Ludolf, then, was yet another facilitator of his objective to reach Russia.

In any event, probably through letters of introduction, Steller had the good fortune to be employed in 1734 as physician to the archbishop's household staff, and by 1736, when the churchman died, he had received notification of appointment to the Academy as an adjunct in natural history with orders to serve as a member of the Bering expedition's scientific contingent. One should not be surprised that Steller, in his twenties, had much of the discipline and direction he shows in the journal in recounting the hardships of his thirty-first and thirty-second years. As a man constantly on the move, from Windsheim to Wittenberg to Halle to St. Petersburg, one suspects that Steller left little to chance and purposefully shaped his destiny, following Messerschmidt's footsteps from Halle, volunteering his services to Academy botany professor Johann Amman to help set up and catalog the Academy's new botanical garden, visiting Messerschmidt until he died in 1735, and two years later even marrying his young widow when she promised to go with him to Kamchatka. Steller was seemingly always leaving and not coming back—leaving family in Germany, colleagues at learned institutions, and (most bitterly as it turned out) his new wife when she turned back at Moscow. He was ever outward bound from home and centers of culture to new East Asian frontiers and finally to the unknown lands northeast of Kamchatka.

On the Great Northern Expedition during the last nine years of his short life, Steller succeeded, it would seem, far better against the elements and the native inhabitants than against a Russian bureaucracy in Siberia that mindlessly sidetracked him and hastened his death just as St. Petersburg and a deserved renown were within reach. On November 12, 1746 (Old Style), he died of a sudden fever in Tiumen, Siberia, while en route to St. Petersburg after twice being detained in Irkutsk on the malicious charge of arbitrarily and without authority releasing seventeen Kamchadal prisoners accused of rebellion. Steller speedily exonerated himself, asserting that the natives were Christians loyal to the state and that the charge had been trumped up by a personal enemy. But in death his grave was robbed, his body mutilated by stray dogs, and (years later) the site of his grave eroded away by the Tura River.

Steller's Journal as a Literary Document

No contemporary picture or description of Steller's physical appearance has survived. Yet at age 31, he suddenly appears as a full-blown, compelling personality in his autobiographical journal, and this journal is responsible for Steller's sudden resurrection in the twentieth century.

The journal's appeal lies not so much in its story of the events along the way between Kamchatka and America, or even in the momentous sighting of the mysterious northwest coast of that continent itself. Rather, it is the calamities of the return voyage that engage our attention—the scurvy, storms, shipwreck, Bering's death, overwintering on a large, treeless, uninhabited island a mere hundred miles from the Kamchatkan coast, and finally getting back, in August 1742, to home port in a little vessel built from timbers of Bering's wrecked ship.

Steller, of course, could not have predicted the popular twentieth-century interest in the story of his life and in the voyage his journal describes. He simply intended the journal to serve as an introduction to a larger work concerning the natural history of Russia's eastern frontier—Kamchatka, Bering Island, and other Siberian locales.

The journal is well organized. Steller included a preface to give his narration historical perspective and to explain his own involvement in the voyage. Then he related only the important events of the outward voyage, a period of a month and a half. Later, in concluding his story, he again related only the important events of the stay on Bering Island and the return to Kamchatka, a period of eight months. Finally, he appended a description of Bering Island, evidently left incomplete since he expressly intended to include a description of flora and fauna in it. Within this frame of preface / introduction and conclusion / appendix, he narrated day-by-day happenings only between July 16 and November 13, 1741 (O.S.), or during the four months between the sighting of America and the first week on Bering Island. In devoting more than half his narrative to a fourth of the trip, Steller highlighted a series of disasters that culminated in a crew decimated by scurvy and a ship battered by storms and left to drift onto an unknown coast. At the start of this period, Steller was persona non grata and found his advice as the ship's physician, tragically, almost totally ignored.

The journal is of literary interest as an interior monologue and confessional statement by one who had much to contribute to the success of the voyage and who was nevertheless repeatedly rebuffed and ridiculed. Keeping the journal was, in large measure, therapy for Steller. Sarcastic comments made publicly about him by his shipmates could be put to rest privately through the medium of his journal, and his failure to produce a full report about America and the Americans could be judged within the context of a voyage that allowed him to set foot on only two islands for a part of each of three days and not on the American mainland at all. The journal, then, is both an apology and a reproach, and through it Steller makes good on the promise he made solemnly aboard ship off Cape St. Elias to report Bering's conduct to higher authorities "in terms it deserved."

Steller was decidedly out of his element aboard Bering's ship. As a former Halle university student become academician, he was no doubt accustomed to open discussion of issues and reasoned discourse based on available knowledge. Sven Waxell, Bering's lieutenant and routinely in charge of the ship, was, however, not inclined to recognize any expert testimony outside the naval chain of command. Moreover, he and other officers probably felt not a little threatened by Steller, who had—or seemed to have—influence over Bering as

Bering's cabinmate. Even Bering at times might have been intimidated by Steller's university training in natural sciences and theology and by his knowledge through books and field experience (see, for example, Chapter 1). For Steller was seemingly interested in everyone and everything. He was constantly alert, formulating tentative conclusions from observed data and most conscientiously and earnestly seeking to contribute to the success of Bering's mission.

On Bering Island, Steller quickly assumed a decisive and unobtrusive leadership. Bering was deathly ill. Waxell also seemed close to death. The dead had to be buried, the sick nursed and fed, Arctic foxes fended off, shelters prepared, game hunted, driftwood collected, and exploration begun. Steller led by example, building underground shelters, organizing households, initiating a democratic regime devoid of most social distinctions, and fostering observance of holidays kept in more civilized environments. His healing was both medical and pastoral. Salad greens and fresh meat from sea otter, ptarmigan, seals, whale, and the sea cow prevailed over the scurvy. Cheering words like "God will help!" countered misery and depression, and a constant good humor encouraged camaraderie and united effort. Even so, Steller's role in the deliverance of 46 survivors of an original complement of 78 is easily underestimated because of his genuine modesty. That many of his companions regarded him as responsible for saving their lives is apparent in Müller's later history of the voyage. As a fellow academician who knew Steller and interviewed survivors of the voyage, Müller reported (*Bering's Voyages*, p. 120) that of the nearly 900 sea otter pelts brought back to Kamchatka from Bering Island and divided up, nearly 300 became Steller's property. Some he purchased, but many were given him as tokens of gratitude.

The journal also has literary merit in its highly quotable satirical commentary, its occasional, brief dialogues, and its frequent vivid imagery. Moreover, it can be appreciated as a pilgrimage story, as a life journey represented by a sea voyage, with a protagonist ever loyal to God and God's imperial representative on earth, passing through scorn, destruction, and death to a joyous physical and spiritual deliverance. That this protagonist at times reveals himself as excruciatingly human in his hurts and in his assignment of blame does not diminish his triumph and fulfillment in the end. Like Job he suffered, and like Job he gained his reward. (Steller, however, gave little thought to "reward." He moved on to continue his work.) He was not so much Bunyan's gullible Christian needing an Evangelist, Hopeful, or Faithful to keep on the straight and narrow way, as he was—especially on Bering Island—a Greatheart leading a fellowship of the weak and infirm with little or no regard for dogma or religious differences. Steller, Pietist from Halle, assumed that all his companions, whether Lutheran or Russian Orthodox, shared a faith in a providential God, and his concern was not so much the definition of faith as the practice of faith. Steller is also surprisingly modern in his appeal to reason, his dedication to exploration in this world, and his practice of democratic ideals in an open society. At the same time, he stands very much in his century in his view of an ordered world controlled by a just God mirrored by divinely appointed higher authority at national levels.

Endlessly fascinating, this Steller. Ever old and new, lucid and obscure, contradictory, unforgiving, and even dead wrong at times but also for the most part perceptive, compassionate, and indisputably right.

Steller as Physician and Botanist

Ever in a hurry, circling half the globe, and never in a position to prepare his manuscripts for publication, Steller had too much to do in too little time. He explored, collected, described, speculated, and moved on to do more of the same. Others after him gained reputation from the use of his information —Gmelin in *Flora Sibirica* (1747–69), Linnaeus (Linné) in *Plantae rariores Camschatcenses* (1750), Krasheninnikov in his history and description of Kamchatka (1755), Peter Simon Pallas in *Flora Rossica* (1784), and Thomas Pennant in *Arctic Zoology* (1784–85). A free spirit, contracted for scientific services on one of the last great land-and-sea expeditions sponsored by a national government, Steller is remembered today as little more than a name—as a naturalist under Bering who was the first to describe hundreds of plants and such creatures as the Steller's jay, the Steller's sea eagle, and the now-extinct Steller's sea cow. His independent discovery of remedies against scurvy, antedating James Lind's landmark "Treatise of the Scurvy" (1753) by a dozen years, is highlighted in this edition two and a half centuries after his life.

Steller was a new breed of naturalist. Unlike Gmelin and other academicians who traveled in Siberia with entourages befitting their dignity—including assistants, servants, and cooks, select wines, large wardrobes, and small libraries—Steller preferred to travel light to cover great distances with few helpers and with minimal provisions. Gmelin marveled at him (*Reise durch Sibirien*, 3: 175–78). Steller drank from a single cup and ate food that he prepared himself from a single plate. Any clothes, any boots, that served a purpose would do. In his self-sufficiency, his love of nature, his predilection for preaching, his reputation as a loner, his respect for aboriginal peoples, and his zest for science, he anticipates Henry David Thoreau and John Muir by more than a century.

Like theirs, his science was chiefly self-taught. Collecting his own botanical specimens around Wittenberg and Halle, he followed the example of Dioscorides, who reportedly made his herbal studies while serving in Nero's armies. It was for this independent botanizing that Hoffmann recognized the potential contribution Steller could make on the Halle medical faculty. All three medical professors there, Hoffmann himself and Stahl's two disciples, Michael Alberti and Johann Juncker, were trained in anatomy and chemistry. Steller learned his botany both from Dioscorides and from three widely used pre-Linnaean catalogs of European plants: Gaspard Bauhin's *Pinax theatri botanici* (1623), listing 6,000 species according to structural affinities (that is, by genera) and using a basically binomial nomenclature; Joseph Pitton de Tournefort's *Institutiones rei herbariae* (1700), dividing 8,000 species illustrated by woodcuts into 22 classes according to the form of the corolla; and John Ray's *Historia generalis plantarum* (1686–1704), organizing 18,655 species into 33 classes with comprehensive yet succinct descriptions.

Dioscorides' *De materia medica* is eminently practical, organizing 600 plants according to their value as food, seasonings, or medicines. Bauhin used three new tools for plant classification—botanical gardens, herbaria, and, for his own plant discoveries published in his *Prodromus theatri botanici* (1620), engraved illustrations—bringing order from the disorder of various names for the same plant. Many of his names for species were adopted by Ray and Linnaeus. In Bauhin, Steller had an admirable model for classification, nomenclature, and description. Indeed, in Bauhin, botany, as a science independent of medicine though (like chemistry) contributing to it, reached a high plateau. Tournefort and Ray simply added more European species and offered alternatives to Bauhin's classification system. Steller, as plant hunter, was on the crest of a great wave circling the earth in all directions from Europe at a time when Linnaeus was offering a simpler, more dependable taxonomy based on sex characteristics.

With the notable exception of Ray, early botanists were typically physicians. Conflicts often developed as botanist-physicians set their priorities. In St. Petersburg, Steller continued his passion for plant collecting, so much so that the archbishop teased him with Latin verses, which Stejneger translates as follows (*Georg Wilhelm Steller*, p. 68):

> While the good Steller goes searching for medical
> plants for the sick,
> The dutiful patient departs this life by a lingering death;
> Past are the funeral rites and dried the tears of the comrades;
> Goods, which he left, were divided according to law.

> Steller, still being away, is blamed by every person
> Lovingly clinging to life—why, I shall never know!

These lines are not so much a gentle reproach for long absences from his duties as the archbishop's resident physician (as Stejneger supposes, pp. 67–68) as they are a jesting tribute to a dedicated botanist (whose interests incidentally extended far beyond medical plants) intent on helping Amman set up the Academy's botanical garden. The archbishop could appreciate this preoccupation and be amused, even as those ailing in his service irritated Steller by their complaints. Important work was in progress (in 1739 Amman published his *Stirpium rariorum icones et descriptiones*, for which Linnaeus complimented him), and greater work lay ahead. Steller had set his priorities.

Steller's plant collecting continued in every locale he visited between St. Petersburg and Kayak Island, Alaska, from 1738 to 1746. His surviving plant lists, together with references to lists now lost, include:

> Catal. plant. ad Obium [Ob River] 1738
> Flora Ircutiensi [Irkutsk] 1734 [1,100 plants, 90 pp.]
> Cat. plant. a Iacutia Ochotium [between Iakutsk and Okhotsk]
> 1740 [20 pp.]
> Flor. Ochotensem [lost]
> Catalogus plantarum intra sex horas [chiefly from Kayak Island,
> Alaska] 1741 [143 plants, 11 pp.]
> Catalogus seminum [chiefly from Nagai Island, Alaska] 1741
> [seeds of 25 plants, 7 pp.]
> Descriptiones plantarum rariorum in insula Beringi [Bering
> Island] 1742 [54 plants, 76 pp.]
> Mantissa plantarum minus aut plane incognitarum [n.d., 12 plants,
> 14 pp.]
> Flora Kamtschatica [lost]
> Catalog. plant. ad Lenam [Lena River, n.d., 5 pp.]

They also include the Flora of Perm (1746) and these additional items listed by Krasheninnikov in 1747 and translated from the Russian (Pekarskii, 1: 614):

> Description of sea grasses, 7 pp.
> Plants and seeds of Kamchatka and America, 47 pp.
> Plants collected on Kamchatka in 1743, 3 pp.
> Seeds gathered on Kamchatka in 1743, 1½ pp.
> Seeds gathered near Kiakhta, 1739, 3 half-sheets
> Seeds gathered near Irkutsk and Lake Baikal, 4 pp.

Among the hundreds of plants unknown in Europe and first described by Steller, one he found on Kayak Island on July 20, 1741 (O.S.), is especially memorable in the history of plant collecting. It is the wonderful salmonberry, unique to the northwest coast, and both plentiful and delicious on uninhabited Kayak Island even today. Steller called it *Rubus americanus* (now *R. spectabilis*). It reminded him of both the raspberry (*R. idaeus*) and the European moschatel, or, as he calls it, *Moschata*. Evidently he started this description on the beach of the island, after refreshing himself with tea made from the water of the stream at the landing site. He completed it aboard ship after Bering refused passage for the salmonberry specimens Steller brought with him from the island (see Chapter 2). Here is a rendering of his Latin:

Rubus americanus: erect, not bristly, with a red, ovoid fruit, and a very large, very delicately serrate, scarlet perianth. The fruit occurs quite profusely on Cape St. Elias: larger than a moschatel drupe, glabrous, ovoid; doubtless of superb flavor, since the fruit was not yet fully ripe. The bush is up to 3 or 4 cubits [4.5 or 6 feet] tall; the leaves resemble the raspberry's; the perianth is finely serrate at the edges, and deep scarlet on the upper side. I wanted to take some bushes with me, that they might go with other specimens to St. Petersburg; but the seaman's stupendous curiosity refused help once promised, and the space, and with a great guffaw ventured to set aside containers that very gentle hands had most gladly collected. Verily, the seaman knows winds, the shepherd sheep.

The salmonberry is bristly, but as Steller viewed the top of this plant at eye level, the acicular prickles of the lower stem were not perhaps readily apparent.

Steller's reflective, concluding statements underscore both his predicament and his self-assurance. His botany was incidental to his assignment as mineralogist and physician. The naval officers, who know wind, let his good advice, grounded in his knowledge of natural history, go to the four winds. Under these circumstances, what could he accomplish? Only reluctantly had Bering let him go ashore with the water carriers; hence, even minerals had a low priority. There remained his pastoral role; it was Müller who wrote, "Steller was a doctor who at the same time ministered to the spirit" (*Bering's Voyages*, p. 115). His last statement, *verum satis navita de ventis, enarrat pastor oves* (reminiscent of Propertius, *Elegies*, II, i, 43–44), proclaims his broader role: he is the pastor as physician and counselor; and his sheep are both plants and seamen. Seamen may reject plants and the prescription-giver, but there is here also implicitly the recognition that the pastor knows their needs better than they do.

It took the *St. Peter* six weeks (June 4 to July 20, O. S.) to go from Asia to America and another six weeks (July 21 to August 30, O.S.) to go from Kayak Island to Nagai Island in the Shumagins, where once again the expedition stopped—again, not for science but for water. Otherwise, circumstances had changed. Instead of the beautiful forests of Kayak Island, extending to the seashore, the Shumagins seemed a treeless desert. Moreover, an epidemic of scurvy hung over the *St. Peter*. Bering, confined to his cabin, could scarcely walk. Five men were too ill to work, and sixteen more were affected by the disease. Again, Steller went ashore with the water carriers and spent a day, August 30, collecting plants and seeds. He was disturbed, however, that his medical advice was disregarded, first by the mate, who had his men fill barrels with water from a pond that Steller tested and found salty, and later by Lieutenant Waxell, to whom he had sent a sample of good spring water. Also, he was probably alarmed that the sailor Nikita Shumagin had died ashore in the afternoon. Instead of spending the night on the island as he had planned (he had, he tells us, already prepared shelter), he returned to the ship to reason with Bering and Waxell about the water and also to request "a few men to gather up as many antiscorbutic plants as we would need." But, wrote Steller, "the gentlemen scorned even this proposal, so valuable to themselves and for which they should have thanked me" (see Chapter 4).

Steller did not explain that he had learned the value of these plants from the native peoples of northeast Asia or that the officers might have scorned him out of ignorance, for scurvy was then very much a mystery, even to ship's physicians.

Steller was miffed: "I regretted my good opinion," he writes, "and resolved, in the future, to look after the saving of myself alone, without the loss of one word more." What he did was the opposite. With his friend, Friedrich Plenisner, the surveyor, and no doubt with his hunter, Thoma Lepekhin, he spent much of the next day, August 31, gathering *Cochlearia* (*C. officinalis*, now called scurvy grass) and *Lapathum* (possibly *Rumex graminifolius*, or dock).

That very night and the remainder of the days spent in the Shumagin Islands, from August 31 to September 6 (O.S.), Steller must have begun the "ministrations, under divine grace," that abruptly transformed his situation as persona non grata aboard the *St. Peter* and marked probably the first time in the history of nautical medicine that a ship's physician successfully treated scurvy. Steller modestly remarked: "By giving him raw scurvy grass, I managed to bring the Captain-Commander—so bedridden with scurvy that he had already lost the use of his limbs—so far within eight days that he was able to get out of bed and on deck and to feel as vigorous as he had been at the beginning of the voyage. Likewise, the *Lapathum* I prescribed to be eaten raw for three days firmed up again the teeth of most seamen" (see Chapter 4). That Steller, as miracle worker, was suddenly regarded with respect and esteem—this plant gatherer much ridiculed and ignored all the way from Kayak Island to the Shumagins—is apparent in Steller's selection as a member of Waxell's party to visit the newly found Aleuts. Steller related this circumstance very simply: "Thereupon, after a short discussion, the boat was lowered in which I, along with Lieutenant Waxell, the Koriak interpreter, and nine sailors and soldiers, decided to go ashore" (see Chapter 5). Off Kayak Island, Steller had had to argue bitterly with Bering before being permitted to go ashore at all. Off Nagai, he was slyly invited to go ashore with the water carriers; he knew very well that the honor of investigating a fire seen in the night and presumably of being the first to find the native Americans would go to Bering's fleet master Sofron Khitrov and his party. But now, on September 4 (O.S.), off Bird Island in the outer Shumagins, he was to share the honors with Waxell.

As for scurvy, Steller's achievement preceded Dr. James Lind's controlled dietetic tests by only six years. As a surgeon of a British ship in the Channel fleet over which Lord George Anson was admiral in 1747, Lind took twelve scurvy patients with similar symptoms and fed them the same diet except for the various items he wished to test as possible scurvy remedies, such as cider, vinegar, seawater, and citrus fruit. The results seemed conclusive. As Lind wrote (p. 21), "The consequence was that the most sudden and visible good effects were perceived from the use of the oranges and lemons; one of those who had taken them being at the end of six days fit for duty." Lind's "Treatise of the Scurvy," published in 1753, was scarcely noticed. Captain James Cook was among those apparently unaware of it. Cook operated on his own theory that any green vegetable promoted health. He was one of the first sea captains to forage for fresh vegetables at every opportunity on long voyages. It was not until 1795 that the administration of Mediterranean lemon juice was mandated in the British navy, replaced by West Indies lime juice in the mid-nineteenth century.

Meanwhile, news of Steller's success did not reach Russian-sponsored expeditions in the North Pacific. As late as 1789–90, during the voyages under the command of Captain Joseph Billings, ship's physicians were still resorting to that universal panacea, bloodletting, to combat scurvy. By 1803, however, another captain sailing under Russian auspices, A. J. von Krusenstern, had learned about wild garlic on Kamchatka. At Petropavlovsk, he picked up three barrels of it, calling it both "a perfect antiscorbutic, and a most admirable substitute for sourkraut [*sic*]." He also noted that "the water in which this wild garlic is preserved, and which may be renewed daily, affords a wholesome and not unpleasant beverage" (*Voyage Round the World*, 1:215).

Despite Bering's rejection of Steller's plant specimens, it would appear that through Steller's "ministrations," and those of Lind, Cook, Krusenstern, and others, the curse of the scurvy was finally overcome by the very medium once scorned—plants. Whether sweet or sour, these plants became prized as seamen slowly learned that their lives could depend on them.

Steller as Zoologist and Ethnographer

Compared with botany and medicine, zoology and ethnography were still infant sciences in early-eighteenth-century Europe—witness the continuing popularity of Conrad Gesner's *Historia animalium* (1551–58) and of Olearius's accounts of sub-Arctic peoples. Gesner did not discriminate between myth and reality, mixing whale and unicorn, sphinx and rhinoceros. He gathered into his encyclopedic work every animal reported anywhere at any time and provided woodcuts to make them fascinating and memorable. A century later, Olearius also entertained his readers with fact and fancy, not about animals but about human beings. He related (on good authority, of course) that Samoyeds feed on human flesh, "even that of their deceased friends," and that Greenland Eskimo women "are not troubled with womens [*sic*] monthly diseases" (pp. 67, 71). With models like Bauhin's *Pinax* and Hoffmann's anatomy lectures, Steller justifiably complained about "imperfect histories . . . swarming with fables and false theories . . . in which the writers of natural history saw only through a lattice what they might have seen with their own eyes" ("Beasts of the Sea," p. 196).

Herein lay much of Steller's contribution: he traveled great distances to observe closely strange and wonderful creatures; and, as a conscientious anatomist, he described objectively in minute detail even the genitals and sexual behavior of both sea cows and Kamchadals. Indeed, he alone recorded the life history of the North Pacific manatee or sea cow (*Hydrodamalis gigas*) before it became extinct in 1768 in its last known habitat in the Commander Islands. When Steller was in Kamchatka, during 1740–44, the Kamchadals were rapidly being assimilated into cossack society. What Steller and Krasheninnikov wrote about these demoralized people—their religion, history, language, customs, clothing, and diet—is wholly unique; later commentaries on their culture are comparatively quite fragmentary. Steller in particular viewed the Kamchadals sympathetically, admiring their thorough knowledge of their natural environment and decrying Russian exploitation and abuse. Their only hope, he believed, was in Christianity, and he pleaded for additional Russian Orthodox missionary teachers.

Steller himself was much indebted to the Kamchadals and their neighbors. From them he learned remedies for scurvy, various food resources, and the benefits of underground winter dwellings. This knowledge acquired on Kamchatka indisputably saved many of Bering's crew on uninhabited Bering Island and possibly even the expedition itself. From native peoples of northeast Asia, he also learned about geographical and trade relationships between Asia and America. Unlike Bering, Steller had complete confidence in this information, and it is hardly surprising that his sympathy extended to the "Americans" (Eskimos and Aleuts), who, he was convinced, were related to the Kamchadals because of similar cultural characteristics. In proposing an Asian and specifically a Mongolian origin for Americans, he was the first to hit on a view almost universally accepted today.

His extremely brief exposure to these Americans, for which he bitterly blamed Bering, is of considerable historical importance. It enabled Kaj Birket-Smith and Frederica de Laguna to identify the underground cache Steller found on Kayak Island as Chugach Eskimo rather than Eyak. Moreover, his extended description of the Aleut in the Shumagin Islands has provided a pre-contact base from which Lev S. Berg, Waldemar Jochelson, and Lydia T. Black have been able to document cultural change, especially from the last half of the eighteenth century when Russian hunters began to overrun the Aleutians and south-coastal Alaska, seeking the precious sea otter pelts Steller and his companions brought back from Bering Island.

The range of Steller's interests in ethnography is evident in both his journal and in his *Beschreibung von dem Lande Kamtschatka*. His interests in natural sciences (other than in botany) are seen in the *Beschreibung*, in *De bestiis marinis*, and in Krasheninnikov's 1747 list of Steller's papers, which was published in Pekarskii's history of the Imperial Academy of Sciences. This last is translated here from the Russian (1:614–16):

> Incomplete list of minerals, 4 pp.
> List of minerals found near Irkutsk, $2\frac{1}{2}$ pp.
> History of minerals, 21 pp.
> Description of sea animals, 26 pp.
> Description of some winter animals, 2 pp.
> Rough-draft description of some animals, 11 pp.
> Rough-draft description of sea and land animals, 18 pp.
> Description of birds' nests and eggs, 6 pp.
> Various observations concerning description of birds, 2 pp.

> Observations concerning birds' nests and eggs, 4 pp.
> Descriptions of birds, 1743, 32 pp.
> Rough-draft dissertation on fish, 19 pp.
> General observations on the begetting of fish, 5 pp.
> Description of fish, 1743 and 1744, 44 pp.
> Observations concerning the histories of various fish, 11 pp.
> Rough-draft dissertation on various fish, 56 pp.
> Description of the "omul" [type of salmon] fish, 3 pp.
> Rough-draft description of birds, 29½ pp. (On the first page is a
>   diary of a trip from Bolsheretsk to Avacha.)
> Rough-draft description of spiders and other insects, 17 pp.
> Description of insects, 1740, 28 pp.
> Vocabulary of various languages, 12 pp.
> Description of Koriaks, 5 pp.
> Additions to the history of the Kamchadals
> Description on catching various animals, 21 pp.
> List of insects, 32 pp.

Had Steller lived longer, this list would probably also include findings related to paleontology and geomorphology. In "Beasts of the Sea" (pp. 181–82), he wrote that he was eager to visit the mouth of the Kolyma River on the Arctic Ocean, where a skeleton of a mammoth had been discovered. He also wanted to explore deserts. It is unlikely, then, that Steller could ever have become a Darwin, comfortably settled on a large estate in domestic tranquillity, rewriting manuscripts based on youthful travels and teasing startling new scientific revelations out of them. Instead, Steller would have remained, by his own preference, a scientist in the field, continuing to bridge eons and oceans. He explains his motivation and his quest in "Beasts of the Sea" (pp. 181–82): "As long as things escape us and perish unknown with our consent, and through our silence are counted as fabulous—things which may be seen with little labor in the very land where we, with all our inquisitiveness, live—it is not strange these things, which we are prevented from observing by the great sea that lies between, have remained to the present time unknown and unexplored." This testimony is also a statement of his achievement: he crossed the sea to Kamchatka and to America and, despite great difficulties, reported precisely what he saw.

Editions and Translations of the Journal

The English translation of Steller's journal presented here is made solely from the *Fraktur* (old German alphabet) manuscript written in two or three

FIG. 2. Frank Alfred Golder (1877–1929), professor of history, Stanford University. (Courtesy of the Hoover Institution, Stanford University)

different hands, reproduced on 221 half-page negative photostats, 7×6 inches, and deposited in 1917 in the Library of Congress by Frank Golder. This was issued in 1984 in 30 copies as "Steller's Journal: The Manuscript Text" (Alaska Historical Commission Studies in History, no. 114), edited by O. W. Frost with the eighteenth-century handwritten copy converted to typed copy by Margritt A. Engel and Karen E. Willmore. Golder found the manuscript copy in the archives of the Academy of Sciences in Petrograd (formerly St. Petersburg).

The relationship of this copy to the original in Steller's own hand, now apparently lost, is impossible to determine. On August 18, 1746 (O. S.), Steller entrusted his journal and other manuscripts to fellow adjunct Johann Eberhard Fischer, who was returning to St. Petersburg ahead of Steller. Fischer still had the manuscript in his own possession as late as 1769, when Pallas borrowed it to have a copy made. Sometime before Fischer died in 1771, Scherer evidently also borrowed the manuscript, for he had about half of it translated into French and he quotes a page and a half of the German in a biographical essay on Steller included in his published edition of Steller's *Beschreibung*. The

FIG. 3. Peter Simon Pallas (1741–1811), professor
of natural history, Imperial Academy of Sciences, St.
Petersburg. (Courtesy of the Smithsonian Institution, photo no. 85-5539; reprinted from Stejneger,
Georg Wilhelm Steller, 488)

complete copy Golder found may antedate the copy Pallas had made—one
with two missing pages Pallas later had translated back into German from a
manuscript Russian translation made by Vasilii I. Lebedev in 1764.

In any case, the restoration of a complete, authentic text of Steller's journal
is impossible without the original manuscript. Copyists make mistakes, occasionally misreading words and numbers or omitting a word or phrase.
Many eighteenth-century translators, such as Scherer and Coxe, frequently
summarized or altogether omitted passages that may seem tiresome or incomprehensible. Of all the versions of Steller's journal, Golder's copy seems most
nearly complete and accurate; therefore, we present it in its entirety and report
in the notes variants in Scherer's translation and in Pallas's published text.

Unlike Scherer, Pallas brought outstanding scientific credentials to the task of introducing Steller. As president of the Imperial Academy of Sciences in St. Petersburg, and compiler of *Flora Rossica*, he was one of the most influential natural historians of the late eighteenth century. Like Steller, he was born in Germany and educated at the University of Halle. A fellow of the British Royal Society, he participated in Russian expeditions into Siberia and organized others that, under Captain Joseph Billings, crossed the North Pacific, and he published in Latin and German a vast accumulation of scientific information originating with Messerschmidt, Gmelin, and Steller.

Pallas's first installment of the journal, issued in 1781, is entitled "Topographische und physikalische Beschreibung der Beringinsel, welche im östlichen Weltmeer an der Küste von Kamtschatka liegt" (Topographical and physical description of Bering Island, which lies in the eastern sea off the coast of Kamchatka). It appeared in the first volume of a journal Pallas edited called *Neue nordische Beyträge zur physikalischen und geographischen Erd- und Völkerbeschreibung, Naturgeschichte und Ökonomie* (New northern contributions to physical and cultural geography, natural history, and agriculture), published by Johann Zacharias Logan in St. Petersburg and Leipzig. The second installment, published in 1793 and appearing in the fifth and sixth volumes of the same journal, is entitled "Reise von Kamtschatka nach Amerika mit dem Commandeur-Capitän Bering" (Voyage from Kamchatka to America with Captain-Commander Bering). Unlike Scherer, Pallas was authorized by the Russian government to edit and publish Steller material. Moreover, as professor of natural history at the Academy, he was well qualified for his task: his factual prefaces, illuminating notes, and interpretations of the text are important contributions to Steller studies.

For the twentieth-century translator, however, Pallas's text presents serious problems. By comparing the surviving manuscript text of Steller's journal with Pallas's text of the same document, one discovers that Pallas took editorial liberties no longer universally acceptable. He "improved" the German of the manuscript journal by rewriting much of the entire journal. He freely reorganized large segments of the text, attempted to correct errors and misconceptions, censored politically sensitive language, omitted passages, and added others either of his own invention or from other Steller manuscripts.

Pallas's reorganization of Steller's manuscript journal resulted from his decision to publish the appended description of Bering Island separately and, at the same time, to complete Steller's evident design of including flora and fauna as well as geology and geography with this description. Consequently, Pallas more than doubled the length of the text by adding (1) information about the Arctic fox from an unidentified source—possibly from another

Steller manuscript; (2) major sections on the sea otter and North Pacific sea cow quarried from the journal proper and, interjecting between these two sections, an exposition by Steller—obviously out of place here—on the methods used by Kamchadals and Kurile Islanders in hunting the sea otter; and (3) several concluding paragraphs on birds, fish, and plants, with the last probably extracted from lists Steller prepared in Latin from researches on Kayak Island, the Shumagins, and Bering Island. One result of this reorganization is, quite simply, a jumble. Another is that the appendix takes on the appearance of an important separate work more or less equivalent to the journal narrative itself. Finally, Pallas introduced major dislocations into the journal narrative when, on its publication in 1793 in both periodical and book form, he omitted the sea otter and sea cow sections he had already used.

Just as amazing is Pallas's way of "correcting" Steller's geography (see comments of W. L. G. Joerg in Golder, *Bering's Voyages* 2: 78*n*, 174*n*418). Having last seen the American mainland north of the outer Shumagin Islands, Steller and other expedition members assumed that the mainland continued westward north of the Aleutian Islands' arc nearly all the way to Bering Island, from which Steller supposed the same mainland could be seen to the northeast. This misconception of the position of America in relation to Asia had been corrected by 1793 with the charting of North Pacific waters by Russian navigators and Captain James Cook.

Pallas, of course, was well aware of these developments. His own fieldwork in Siberia under Russian auspices had not taken him to either Bering Island or America, but he had access to new Russian and English maps of the Bering Sea region. Moreover, he was chiefly concerned not with Steller as an author with a distinctive personality and style of writing but with Steller as a scientist who had gathered important new information. He understood that Steller's papers were state property and reflected on the Russian Empire, which had financed and directed the expedition in which Steller had participated. He was also aware of the rivalries among European nations with political and commercial interests in the Pacific and of Russia's long-standing policy of secrecy regarding Bering's voyage to America. Pallas, then, would not knowingly act independently of Russian pride and national interest in publishing Steller, and he does seem (1) to belittle Steller's geography—as if other members of the second Bering expedition had some better idea of the subject—and (2) to minimize the irritating frequency with which Steller brings up the subject. Pallas's objectives explain to some extent his apparently erratic editing of Steller's manuscript journal concerning questions of geography: he expressed impatience with Steller in a footnote; he omitted altogether an erroneous phrase of

Steller's; and he altered Steller's meaning in an unsuccessful attempt to make Steller's geography conform to contemporary knowledge.

Pallas's problems with North Pacific geography are clearly revealed in his footnotes. Steller observed that, from the first Shumagin Island landing site (on Nagai Island), "das feste Land sahe man in Norden und westen ohngefähr 10 Meilen davon entfernet" (the mainland was visible in the north and the west about ten miles away). Pallas rearranged the wording to read: "In Norden und Westen sahe man das feste Land ohngefähr zehn Meilen davon entfernt." In his footnote to this observation, he complained: "Steller glaubte, seiner einmal gefassten Meynung nach überall festes Land zu sehen, wo vermuthlich nahe an oder hintereinander liegende Inseln einen Anschein davon gaben" (Steller, once his idea became fixed, thought he saw the mainland everywhere, where probably islands close together or behind each other gave the appearance of it). But in this instance Pallas was mistaken. On a clear day, the Alaska Peninsula is visible in the directions and at approximately the distance (46 English miles) Steller indicated.

What did Pallas delete? At a later point in the narrative, Steller discussed distances from Kamchatka. Bering Island is, he said, only "20 Meilen," or 92 English miles, directly east of Kamchatka; to this statement Steller added "das feste Land aber 40" (but the mainland 40), which, indeed, is not true. Pallas deleted this phrase as if it never existed.

Finally, Pallas directly changed Steller's meaning. For example, Steller wrote of high mountains seen northeast of Bering Island and added: "hielte ich dafür nach dieser Breite, dass es kein anderes als das americanische feste land seyn könnte, angesehen dieses eine Insel, davon man auf Kamtschatka keine Nachricht hat" (I thought according to this latitude that it could be none other than the American mainland, considering that this is an island of which nothing is known on Kamchatka). In his revision, Pallas deliberately reversed the meaning: "Nach der Breite in der wir uns befanden, halte ich dafür, dass dieses nicht als ein Theil von Amerika, sondern als eine andre, auf Kamtschatka unbekannte Insel angesehen werden müsse" (According to the latitude in which we found ourselves, I think that this must not be considered a part of America, but another island unknown on Kamchatka). In a footnote Pallas identified the mountains as those of Copper Island. Actually, there are no islands visible to the northeast; Copper Island is to the southeast. If Steller's geography of the North Pacific was flawed, so was Pallas's—and much less excusably.

If Pallas confused Steller's geography, he dealt with politics by the simple expedient of deleting any potentially offensive phrase. So out went "in Russischen Diensten" (in Russian service) in Steller's criticism of the second Great Northern Expedition: "Und hatte ich hier zum ersten mahle die betrübte Gelegenheit in Russischen Diensten zu sehen wie es Zugehe, dass bey aller angewandten Mühe und grosen Kosten, auch darreichung aller nöthigen HülfsMittel die grösten und nüzlichsten Unternehmungen am Ende viel mahl kleiner, was das Interesse anbelanget, als sie Anfangs im project aufgerissen waren" (For the first time in Russian service, I had the sad opportunity to see how—despite all the expended effort and great expenditures and the outfitting with all necessary resources—potentially the greatest and most beneficial undertakings many times fail to live up to expectations). Pallas's deletion did not substantially alter Steller's criticism; it merely softened it by not drawing attention to the author's—and editor's—non-Russian origin.

Although the Pallas text may have served the interests of the late eighteenth century, it should not represent Steller in the late twentieth century. The two previous English translations are based on Pallas's publications of 1781 and 1793. Coxe's 1803 rendering is sketchy; Stejneger's translation of 1925 is not only competent and complete but also most enlightening with its copious footnotes concerning Steller's scientific nomenclature and variants of the manuscript text. It is indeed a remarkable work of scholarship, whose documentation adds significantly to that in Pallas. It is unfortunately a scrupulously accurate literal rendering of Pallas's "improved" text.

This first complete and modernized English translation of the manuscript text utilizes much of the learning of Pallas and Stejneger while endeavoring to preserve both the sense and the spirit of the manuscript Steller produced within a year of his return from America. Like Pallas, we repunctuate, reparagraph, delete repetitious phrases, break up some sentences of paragraph length, and make complete sentences of sentence fragments. Moreover, to enhance the readability of the text, we editorially provide chapter headings. In several instances, we correct obvious errors, as in dating, and document these changes in notes. We cite, also in notes, Steller's use of foreign words and phrases, especially those in Latin and Russian; however, we retain in the text many such words and phrases that are not readily translatable.

Steller's language (or the copyists'!) in the manuscript journal is often idiosyncratic, not to say cryptic. His prose in one place can be breathless and obscure, or in another will run together thoughts that clearly belong to different stages of composition (revealed, for example, in an unnatural shift of verb tenses). In the occasional particularly vexed passage, we have sought to favor accuracy over elegance, preferring the fact of the text to mere imputation of its meaning; and throughout we have aimed to recreate the special fiber of

Steller's original while neither insisting upon nor denying altogether his sometimes remarkable peculiarities.

Nevertheless, we admit that our English is more polished than Steller's German, but Steller himself probably would not object. In *De bestiis marinis*, he writes: "As to the style and arrangement of matter, the pressure of duties does not permit me to spend too much time in perfecting any one thing, unless I am to allow many things to go to waste on my hands. I therefore set out my porridge in carefully made earthen vessels. If the vessel is an offense to any one, he will perform for me and others a most friendly service if he will pour it all into a gold or silver urn" ("Beasts of the Sea," p. 208).

Chronology

DATES IN STELLER'S JOURNAL are Old Style (O.S.), based on the Julian rather than the Gregorian calendar. For example, July 20, 1741, is Steller's date for the Bering expedition landing on St. Elias (Kayak) Island. The Gregorian calendar or New Style (N.S.) date is eleven days later, July 31, 1741. (Actually, it is August 1, 1741, because the expedition made no allowance for crossing the International Date Line.) Moreover, dates are based on civil rather than astronomical time, as in the log book of the *St. Peter*; that is, Steller's return to the ship at 8:00 P.M. fell, according to his time, within July 20; but in the ship's log it was July 21, since the nautical day is from noon to noon, not from midnight to midnight.

In the following chronology of events related to Steller's life and work, all dates belonging to the German period are New Style, all dates belonging to the Russian are Old Style (Russia did not adopt the Gregorian calendar until 1900), and all dates concerning Bering's voyage to America are based on civil time.

GERMAN PERIOD

1709   March 10. Birth of Georg Wilhelm Stöller (Steller), Windsheim, Franconia.

1729   September. Matriculation at University of Wittenberg as a student of theology.

1731   April 23. Matriculation at University of Halle as a student of theology.

1732   May 1. Delivery of the first of a series of private lectures in botany at the University of Halle.

1734   August. Certification in botany at the Royal Academy of Sciences, Berlin.

RUSSIAN PERIOD

November-December. Arrival in St. Petersburg and appointment as physician to the household staff of Theophan Prokopovitch, archbishop of Novgorod and primate of the Russian Orthodox Church.

1737   January 24. Appointment as an adjunct in natural history at the Imperial Academy of Sciences, St. Petersburg, and acceptance into the academic section of the Great Northern Expedition.

Marriage to Brigitta-Helena Messerschmidt "in a public assembly," probably near the end of the year.

1738   January. Departure for Kamchatka.

1739   January 20. Arrival at Eniseisk in Siberia and first meeting there with Gerhard F. Müller and Johann G. Gmelin, Academy professors.

1740   September. Arrival at Bolsheretsk, Kamchatka, and first meeting with Stepan P. Krasheninnikov, Academy student.

1741   February 17. Receipt of letter from Vitus Bering, who asked Steller to meet him at the port of St. Peter and St. Paul on Avacha Bay.

March 20. Arrival on Avacha Bay.

May 4. Meeting of sea council in which the decision was made to sail SE by E from Avacha Bay to seek Company Land.

VOYAGE WITH BERING

June 4. Departure of the *St. Peter* and *St. Paul* from Avacha Bay.

June 20. Separation of the two ships in fog.

July 15. *St. Paul*, under Captain Chirikov, sighted America off present-day Southeast Alaska.

July 16. *St. Peter*, under Captain-Commander Bering, sighted America from the present-day Gulf of Alaska.

July 20. About 10:30 A.M. First successful landing of the Bering expedition in America on Cape St. Elias (Kayak Island). Farther east, Chirikov had attempted a landing on July 18, but his boat with its party of 11 men did not return.

1741 July 21. *St. Peter* began return voyage.

July 27. *St. Paul*, having lost both its boats and their crews, began return voyage.

August 30. *St. Peter* stopped for water in a bay of islands and suffered a first death from scurvy. Buried ashore, Nikita Shumagin gave his name to the island group.

September 5. About 4:00 P.M. First meeting between Europeans and Alaska Natives (Aleuts), occurring at anchorage of *St. Peter* in the Shumagin Islands.

September 9. About 10:00 A.M. *St. Paul* met with Aleuts off present-day Adak Island.

October 12. Arrival of *St. Paul* in Avacha Bay.

November 6. *St. Peter* ran aground on uninhabited Bering Island, only 100 miles from Kamchatka.

December 8. Death of Bering. Waxell assumed command.

1742 January. After 32 deaths, scurvy was checked on Bering Island by a diet of fresh sea-mammal meat.

August 14. Departure from Bering Island on rebuilt smaller ship.

August 27. Arrival of *St. Peter*'s 46 survivors in Avacha Bay.

LAST YEARS IN SIBERIA

November 16. Date of Steller's report concerning the voyage to America, addressed to the High Senate at St. Petersburg.

1743 Date of Steller's manuscript journal.

1744 January 31. Date of official letter from the Academy, recalling Steller from Kamchatka.

April. Steller arrived at Anadyrsk after a winter journey from Bolsheretsk; he returned to Bolsheretsk via Karaga Island.

1745 December. Arrest on the basis of a trumped-up charge from which Steller was exonerated at Irkutsk.

1746 August 16. Arrest at Solikamsk on the same charge.

October. Release at Tara while en route to Irkutsk for second trial.

November 12. Death from a sudden fever at Tiumen in Siberia while en route to St. Petersburg.

PUBLICATIONS

1747 Biography of Steller by Johann Augustin Stöller.

1751 *Of Marine Beasts*, published in Latin, St. Petersburg.

1774 *Description of Kamchatka*, published in German, Frankfurt and Leipzig.

1793 Peter Simon Pallas's edition of Steller's journal, issued in St. Petersburg.

1925 First complete English translation of Steller's journal by Leonhard Stejneger, based on Pallas's edition.

1936 Stejneger's biography of Steller.

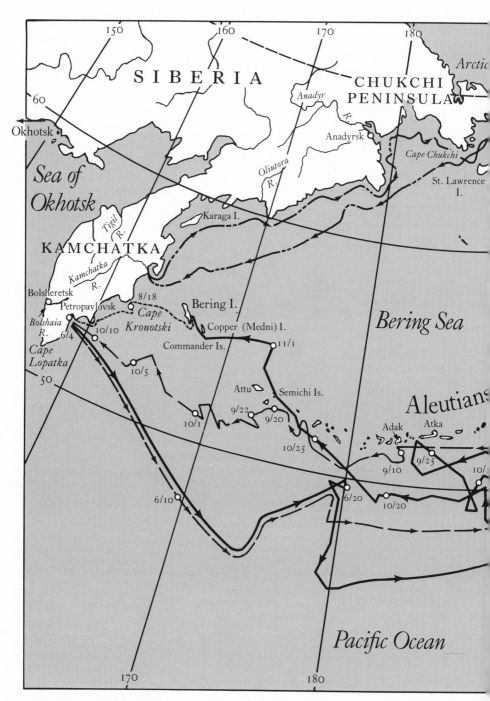

FIG. 4. Russian exploration in the far Northern Pacific, 1728–42. In this map and those that follow, dates shown are Old Style.

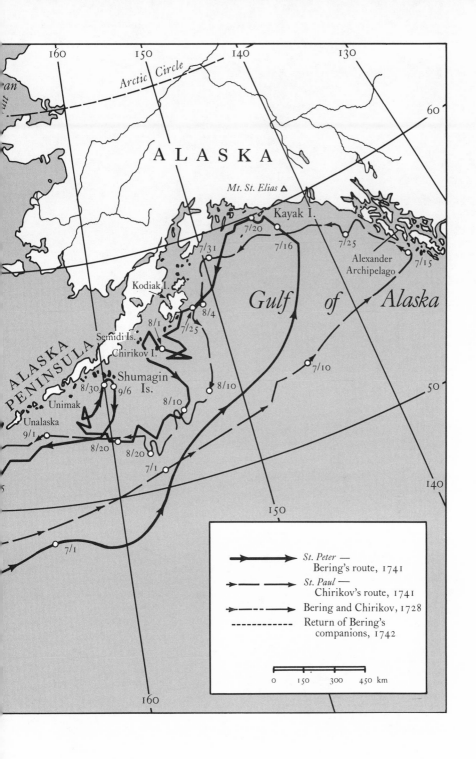

ALASKA

Mt. St. Elias △

Kayak I.

7/20

7/16

7/25

7/15

Alexander
Archipelago

Kodiak I.

Gulf   of   Alaska

8/4

8/1

7/25

7/10

Semidi Is.

Chirikov I.

ALASKA
PENINSULA

Shumagin
Is.

8/10

8/30

9/6

8/10

Unimak

8/20

Unalaska

9/1

8/20

8/20

7/1

50

140

150

7/1

160

7/1

	St. Peter — Bering's route, 1741
	St. Paul — Chirikov's route, 1741
	Bering and Chirikov, 1728
	Return of Bering's companions, 1742

0   150   300   450 km

Journal of a Voyage with Bering
1741–1742

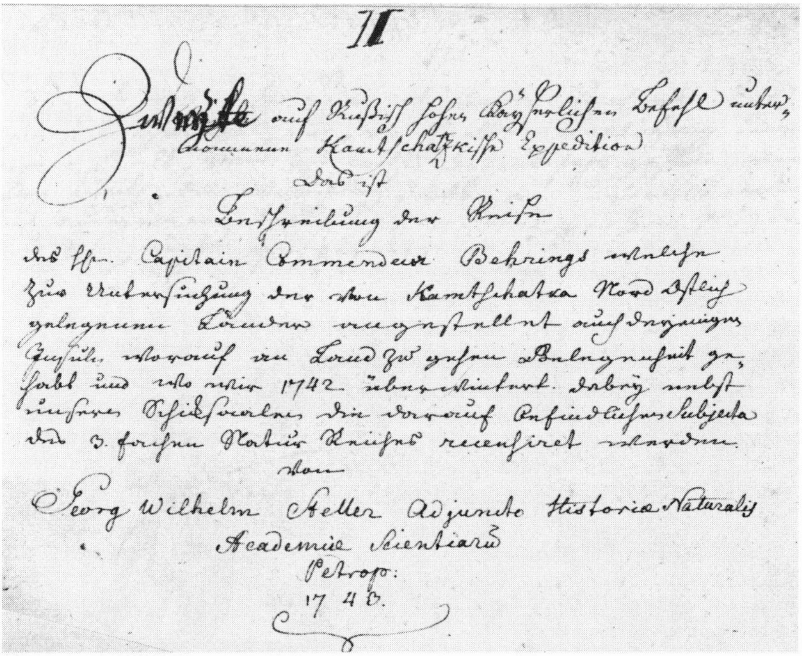

FIG. 5. Title page, Steller's manuscript journal. (From the American Geographical Society Collection)

Second Kamchatka Expedition
undertaken upon His Imperial Majesty's Command
or
Description of the Voyage of the late Captain-Commander Bering
for
The Exploration of Lands Northeast of Kamchatka
and of
The Island on which we chanced to land
and on which we overwintered in 1742,
what happened to us,
and
the plants, animals, and minerals[1] found there

By
Georg Wilhelm Steller
Adjunct in Natural History of the St. Petersburg
Academy of Sciences
1743

Preface

*N*ow that I have set foot again on the blessed soil of Russia and recovered from a difficult voyage of fourteen months to explore the coast
of America to the northeast, having on it often lost the hope to live and
to be able to serve Russia further, I feel obliged to precede other
information[1] with a short, impartial, and true account of the voyage and
what happened to us on it.

In 1725, Peter I, great monarch of most glorious memory, was persuaded by the discovery of Kamchatka and by the urging of the Parisian
Academy of Sciences to find out how far distant to the east America is
from the most extreme northeast borders of Kamchatka, or whether
America in the north is not closest to Cape Chukchi (called Promontorium Tabin by the ancients),[2] or even if—as many speculate—Cape
Chukchi does not form a land bridge to America. Accordingly, in
1725, he sent Captain Bering and other officers there to investigate.

If the ship *Gabriel* had on the first attempt sailed, on a northeasterly
or easterly course, from the 51st to 61st degree[3] of north latitude, or as
far as the Kamchatkan coast stretches from Lopatka[4] to Cape Chukchi,
it would have been so easy, without further cost and delay, to land on
the American islands 20 to 30 miles away or on the American continent
at 50, 60, or 70 miles away.[5] But the gentlemen in command contented
themselves with a short exploration of Kamchatka from Lopatka to
Serdtse Kamen,[6] which is not Cape Chukchi—not by a long shot!—by
going on a northerly course along the coast without losing sight of the
land except when it was obscured by fog. Thus, the double purpose of

the voyage was not in the least achieved, for, if America were so close to Asia, the cossacks in their *baidars* would have landed there. On various occasions, they had already passed that way from the mouth of the Anadyr, just as in 1732, on the *Gabriel*, the geodesist Gvozdev[7] with some cossacks had gone much farther, up to 66 degrees, north latitude.

And then on Captain Bering's return, the curious world was entertained with only a map and a deficient account about Kamchatka (a place already well known), and a few verbal statements by Anadyr cossacks to the effect that the said Cape Chukchi was indeed separated from America by the ocean, whereas on the 51st parallel, opposite Lopatka, several islands rich in resources were said to stretch toward Japan, where the cossacks had in the past ventured, with a few geodesists, in very poor craft, and explored thirteen islands.

On Captain Bering's return to Moscow in 1730, it was immediately realized how little the Tsar's purpose had been achieved and how much hope still remained that the American mainland was close by. Besides, there was much interest in having dependable information about the lands lying from Lopatka to Japan. Out of this hope and interest developed the second great expedition, so costly and difficult because of the long route, the distant destination, and the troublesome transport of food and materials. Perhaps it would have been less costly and difficult if the undertaking had been based on an unbiased and scrupulous summary of those distant Asian regions and their actual conditions, the more so since these had become known on the first expedition.

I pass over the ten years of continuing preparations for this voyage, the endless other difficulties, expenses, and destruction of men and beasts occurring between 1733 and 1741, as well as the circumstances and results of Captain Spangberg's separate voyage,[8] that have nothing to do with my purpose. I turn solely to what concerns the voyage of the Captain-Commander (and Captain Chirikov[9] as long as both packet boats kept together at sea) and to what happened from June 5, 1741, when we sailed out of the port of St. Peter and St. Paul[10] in Avacha, to August 26, 1742, when we reached this port again. But since it is known how I was sent out in 1738 from St. Petersburg only to Kamchatka to investigate plants, animals, and minerals and was not in the least to participate in the endeavors of the officers, I shall briefly explain how I nevertheless got into their company.

In 1740, through a petition sent to the High Governing Senate, I humbly requested permission to accompany Captain Spangberg on another impending voyage to Japan so that—considering the great costs already incurred—I could be charged with collecting thorough information about the islands along the route as well as about Japan itself.

But when Captain-Commander Bering learned of my insatiable desire to visit foreign lands and to investigate their conditions and curiosities, he sent me a special letter in February 1741, from the port of St. Peter and St. Paul, in which he requested that I come to him so that he could discuss various matters with me.

I could see right away that I was to be persuaded to join the expedition to America, and I did not waste much time: with a *sluzhiv* I took off by dogteam to meet him.[11]

As soon as I arrived, he presented me with many reasons for the necessary and useful services I could perform[12] and how well my undertaking would be received in high places if I were to decide to become his traveling companion.

I answered that I had no orders to go to America and that I personally did not dare make that decision, especially because I had already requested permission from the High Governing Senate to travel to Japan. I added that this decision to go to America could be considered a very bold and thoughtless infraction if the American voyage became prolonged and I were not available on receipt of an order to go to Japan.

But the Captain-Commander assured me that he would assume full responsibility and also petitioned the High Senate on my behalf. Besides, he also promised to give me every possible opportunity to achieve something worthwhile and, if need be, to give me as many men as necessary since I had to leave those under my supervision behind.[13]

Later, after holding a conference with all officers of the expedition, he also sent me an official letter making me a public offer, albeit only concerning the accurate observation of minerals.

I therefore decided to accept the invitation in view of the fact that the investigation of Kamchatka would in no way suffer. I now hope that everyone will the more graciously receive news of my venture, the more sincerely it was devoid of all self-interest and was based on the common good and the special interest of Her High Imperial Majesty's Academy of Sciences and on my own most humble sense of duty. Nor do I expect to be punished for doing something without orders, because the long distance did not allow me to send in a preliminary proposal and to wait for orders to undertake a matter that could wait a few days for a decision at my own discretion but not for orders from afar.[14]

For this reason I also expect a gracious pardon beforehand, even though after a fourteen-months' absence and a six-months' sea voyage that was overly prolonged, miserable, and dangerous, I returned with few results and useful discoveries,[15] not through any fault of mine but because the Captain-Commander kept his promise to me so poorly that I was shown the mainland only from a distance and was finally put ashore for a few hours on three islands[16] with great reluctance, as if I were a delinquent, without any help and with a lot of sarcastic comment in return for my honest zeal. Also, because the Captain-Commander did not accept the least advice from me[17]—he had too much regard for his own opinion, when the aftermath and divine judgment showed only too clearly how different my reasoning was from his unfounded presumption and how great the respect I held for him, despite the greatest vexation, for his services and the advantage resulting from them.

The chagrin over having been delayed so long in Siberia and over having to stay there even longer was the incentive for now doing all at once in one summer what, according to any reasonable calculation, of necessity requires two.

It was taken into consideration that often at the beginning of July the coasts of Kamchatka between 56 and 51 degrees are covered with ice.[18] Because this drift ice was wrongly believed to come from the channel between Cape Chukchi and America, even though above the mouth of the Anadyr River to the northeast it is never observed, and from the Anadyr to the Oliutora very rarely, whereas it is seen every year from Uka or Ukinsk Bay to the mouth of the Kamchatka River and from there to Lopatka, nothing else is to be concluded but the following:

1. That this is river ice from America;[19]

2. That in this region the land must be closest where every year drift ice is regularly noticed;

3. That it always occurs with easterly winds and is usually driven to Kamchatka the third day after a wind arises, so that the land in that region must be closest straight to the east;

4. That when 56 degrees, north latitude, is passed going to the

north, no drift ice is seen and hence no more hindrance from it is to be feared.[20]

Nevertheless, it was erroneously supposed that ice might hinder the progress of exploration if in June or July ships should be turned to the north to make a landing and begin exploration across from Cape Chukchi, where everyone assumed land was closest.

Therefore, it was decided to proceed on a gradual course between east and south so that after a change in longitude of about 20 degrees from Avacha we would reach 46 to 45 degrees, north latitude, where the land discovered by the Dutch Company[21] was supposed to be. From there, they were sure, it would be easier to discover America or more specifically the coasts of America extending to the west reported by Juan de Gama[22] to be in the vicinity.

But if no landfall were made on this course, it was decided to continue further on a course between east and north and then gradually proceed up to the north because it was hoped that by then, the middle of July, the sea would be clear of all ice and no time would be lost. In the event a landfall were made, the American coast should be followed to the north until the parallels of 64 to 66 degrees, north latitude, were reached, where the extreme northeast point of Asia or Cape Chukchi is located. From there we should proceed to the west, and after determining the distance between the two continents in the north, preparations should be made to return to port. However, considering wind and distance, the necessary precaution was decided on that the coast be followed only until there was still time to reach Avacha by the end of September, leaving any remaining exploration for another year and a second voyage.

The fact is, indeed, that Captain-Commander Bering was firmly resolved to spend a winter in America and to finish from there in the springtime before returning to home port what could not be finished in one season because of the short summer and great distance. This plan would not only have prevented the decimation of the crew from scurvy and exposure during an overextended fall voyage and have resulted in acquisition of accurate knowledge about the condition of the American continent and its people, but it would also have permitted the efficient and advantageous conclusion of the whole design.

However, Master Khitrov's[23] two mishaps made this plan impossible from the start. It was his fault that, first, an entire ready supply of biscuits for both packet boats was lost in 1740 in Okhotsk[24] at the mouth of the Okhota River, and, through the other mishap, the provisions destined for Avacha in place of the first remained on the Bolshaia River.[25] Their eventual transport in winter by dogsled prompted the Koriaks[26] on the Tigil[27] to rebel before a beginning had even been made. To deliver to the port five puds of supplies for each seaman, Koriaks were to be driven to the *ostrog* from 500 to 600 versts away, whereby they got the idea that something else was afoot, especially since cossacks of the sea command, charged with driving them out of their homes, treated them in a totally unchristian and cruel manner and burdened them with many unnecessary additional jobs.

In such circumstances, the Captain-Commander and the other officers probably saw themselves forced to decide on two separate voyages to carry out the entire project,[28] especially since the investigation of the rebellion and the obstacles caused by the constant drunkenness of the Kamchatkan commander Kolesov[29] delayed departure from the port of St. Peter and St. Paul until the beginning of June, when otherwise May was suitable and previously scheduled for it.

1. Outward Voyage

*F*inally, toward the end of May, everything essential for the voyage had been organized,[1] and on May 29 the two packet boats *St. Peter* and *St. Paul* left the port and anchored in the roadstead of the bay to await winds favorable for final departure.

On the *St. Peter* were

> Captain-Commander Bering as chief
> Lieutenant Waxell
> Fleet Master Khitrov
> Mate Hesselberg
> Second Mate Iushin
> Assistant Surgeon Betge
> Assistant Constable Roselius
> Guard Marine Sint
> Boatswain Nils Jansen
> Assistant Navigator Khotiaintsov
> Commissary Lagunov
> Trumpeter
> Surveyor Plenisner

the remaining seamen, soldiers, and five sons of Kamchatkan cossacks as apprentice seamen, an interpreter, and men assumed to be familiar with all places along the Kamchatkan coast, among whom was one as rifleman in my service;[2] in all, including the lieutenant's son,[3] 76 persons.[4]

On the other packet boat, the *St. Paul*, were

> Captain Aleksei Chirikov
> Lieutenant Chikhachev
> Lieutenant Plautin
> Professor of Astronomy Delisle de la Croyère
> Fleet Master Dementiev
> Mate Elagin
> One guard marine
> Commissary
> Assistant Surgeon Lau

in all, with seamen, soldiers, and sons of Kamchatkan cossacks, 76 men.

June 4: about nine o'clock, we finally sailed out of Avacha Bay into the ocean and set out on the actual voyage, with favorable winds and weather. We advanced with southwest and south-southwest winds, on an initial east-southeast and southeast-by-east course, so that after eight days, on June 11, we were 155 Dutch miles from Avacha at 46°47′N. The day after, that is, on June 12, we saw the first considerable signs of land lying to the south or southeast. In totally calm waters, we suddenly saw many different sea plants such as *Quercus marina*[5] floating around our vessel. We also saw gulls, terns,[6] and ducks, which are all land birds not usually seen on the sea or very far from land. From these signs it was, indeed, to be supposed that if we continued our initial course still further, we would soon reach land.

But just when it would have been most crucial to keep our objective most clearly in mind, the unreasonable behavior of our officers began. They mocked, ridiculed and cast to the winds whatever was said by anyone not a seaman as if with the rules of navigation all science and powers of reasoning were spontaneously acquired. And when this single day—so many vain excuses were afterwards made—could have decided the outcome of the entire business, we turned to the north. On this course we experienced our first little storm during which we also had our first calamity. In the fog and drizzle we lost the *St. Paul*, the other packet boat under Captain Chirikov's command. We never saw it again.

Even at this early time, a scheme was begun to tell the Captain-Commander, who remained constantly in his cabin, no more than was deemed expedient. So it happened that we had the other misfortune, that, when various men said they had seen land in the north—a not in-

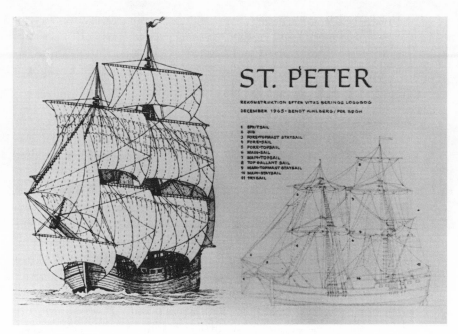

FIG. 6. Bering's ship the *St. Peter*, a drawing based on information in the logbook of the voyage of 1741–42. (Courtesy of the Vitus Berings Laug, Horsens, Denmark; Eva Trautmann; and the Cook Inlet Historical Society; reprinted from Shalkop, *Exploration in Alaska*, 110)

fallible yet very probable claim—the officers neither accepted nor even gave a thought to it, until on the return voyage, on September 24,[7] unexpectedly and to our alarm, land was sighted at 51 degrees—and the voices of regret were heard all too late! According to the ship's log, the land was where we lost Captain Chirikov.

Already back then, some had thought, after all, they had seen land, but that was considered simply a trifle because none of the naval officers themselves had seen it. For the officers, it was a greater honor to steer on and on toward land just so they could blow their own horns about how far they had been and how much they had—needlessly![8]—suffered.

Having searched several days in vain for the lost packet boat *St. Paul* but lost all hope of meeting it, we sailed south again from 50 to 46 degrees, hoping to find the *St. Paul* or Company Land on this course.

But we failed to find either, and had now for the second time in vain expected Company Land to appear in its "proper" place. It was therefore inescapably considered an imaginary land, a nonentity, an invention of the Nuremberg mapmakers:[9] either we or Captain Spangberg would necessarily have sailed over it had it been there!

It is as if those who were already suspect because of human errors could not err as badly in geography. One man, for example, placed our course off Canada[10] on a map of the world, and another argued vociferously with me that Canton is located at 45 degrees and the Maldive Islands are in the Mediterranean.[11]

So we began to give up altogether on Company Land even though there had been no other good reason to be so far south than to be seriously looking for it, and on June 26[12] we began in earnest to sail to the east and gradually up to the north so that we changed invariably from two to three degrees of longitude for each degree of latitude. Within a few days on this course, we again came to 52 degrees latitude, where we once more found numerous signs of a land close by to the north. We sailed along this land steadily for a little less than four weeks until July 16,[13] so that on that day, when we first saw land, we were at 59 degrees and some minutes, north latitude, and 59 degrees[14] longitude from Avacha and almost 500 Dutch miles away.

It should not be surprising that the events of a four-week voyage over such a great distance are so briefly discussed. The explanation is that while sailing on in constantly favorable wind and weather, we saw only sky and water and listened to the officers' *particulas exclamandi et admirandi*[15] about how we were so outrageously mistaken in believing that Kamchatka was separated from America by only a narrow channel, since we now found it so far away!

Besides, these same officers curtly and sarcastically refused all suggestions and proposals, however thoroughly reasoned and timely. Their overbearing and rather nasty treatment—they imagined that they were handling freight on rivers from Iakutsk to Okhotsk and were dealing with *sluzhivs* and poor exiles forced to toe the line and to keep their lips buttoned—was the reason that I and others kept our mouths shut, since everybody was told right out: "You do not understand. You are, after all, no seaman."

They, of course, have been in God's council chamber![16]

And considering all we had seen and could have discussed for the common good as well as for the public interest!

For the first time in Russian service,[17] I had the sad opportunity to see how—despite all the expended effort and great expenditures and the outfitting with all necessary resources—potentially the greatest and most beneficial undertakings many times fail to live up to expectations. Only through mutual and earnest harmony in consulting and acting by persons without special designs or interests can a small beginning grow to a great exploit and a modest advance be rewarded a thousandfold.[18]

But here it must be said that most of the officers had lived ten years in Siberia, each as he wished, and had acquired and maintained rank and honor from the ignorant rabble; or according to their own designs, they had totally forgotten themselves and by force of habit had deluded themselves into believing themselves highly insulted if anyone should say anything they did not know. Even Captain Spangberg is a clear example. He conducted himself toward members of the Academy of Sciences in such a way that it can well be said that he knew he was a captain but had not yet forgotten the lowest sailor's tricks.[19]

During this entire time, we had constant signs that we were running along land, which I want to present here for everyone's reasonable judgment, just as I put them in vain before the officers many times. We often saw species of seaweed and sometimes a great quantity at once floating from the north, especially *Quercus marina glandifera Bauhini*; the *Alga dentata Raji*; *Fuci membranacei calyciformes*—a species growing invariably two to three feet on rocks under the water—burst open, a sure sign that they were beached for a while, taken off by the tide, and carried thus far by the current; and *Fucus clavae effigie*, which is very common at two fathoms but grows nowhere around Kamchatka. Had it been floating in the sea for a long time, *Fucus lapathi sanguinei foliis Tourn.*, because of its tenderness, would have been torn by the waves or eagerly eaten by the sea animals, which we saw constantly in large numbers.[20] We also saw red and white stinging jellyfish,[21] which grow five to six feet under water, measured at low tide, on the rocky coast. As I myself observed in the Penzhin Sea,[22] they are never seen further than fifteen or twenty miles away from the coast at best. Often a large mass of a reed-like bent grass (*Gramen paniculatum arundinaceum, panicula densa spadicea*)[23] even came drifting along, an unmistakable sign of land because this plant grows everywhere on the seashore in Kamchatka as well as in America, and the clumps would long ago have been driven apart because of the plant's smooth stem had they not been brought here directly from land by the current. Not to mention several other types of plants found from day to day and hour to hour that I noted in my travel journal.

Now, whenever I presented such unmistakable signs to the officers, with reasonableness, the greatest modesty, and patience, and advised them to adjust the course northward to get us all to land sooner, the Captain-Commander himself always shared my opinion. But he saw himself outvoted by the other officers and, despite his character and authority, unnecessarily felt himself obliged to yield. Just like the other officers, he thought it ridiculous and contemptible to accept advice from me since I was no seaman. He therefore told me outright that I did not know how to draw valid conclusions about these things. The whole sea was overgrown with plants in many places. What was I going to say about that?

I assured him that I was very familiar with that subject and specifically with places around Cape Verde and Bermuda, the names of the plants, and why they could grow there. I told him that conditions differed, however, in northern regions where seawater was not affected in the same way by the sun and therefore had a different content. I also told him that *these* were the kinds of plants whose nature and habitat I knew quite well and that anybody could easily understand how they were being transported here.

Everybody thought it ridiculous and unbelievable that anyone should claim that currents existed in the sea at all, even though their movement was clearly visible, for the objects floating in the sea maintained a definite direction, often even opposite to that of the winds. For example, here we had southwest or southeast winds and saw different objects drifting toward us from the north. Because of this incredulity, necessary allowances that should have been made in the calculations because of the currents were not made on either the outward or the return voyage. As a result, many errors concerning the distance between the continents may have crept in from excessive cockiness, especially considering that afterwards, on the return trip, we saw with our own eyes how close we had been running along the land almost continuously and how full the sea was with islands and consequently with possible currents; the measurements taken had failed as well.

The frequent appearance of sea animals, unusual in the open ocean, was the other basis on which it could infallibly be concluded that we were along land and not far from it. It is known that the seal heart has both a so-called *foramen ovale* and the *ductus arteriosus Botalli* open, enabling the seal to remain under water a very long time, and that all fish-eating animals can obtain their food in all parts of the ocean far distant from land. It has nevertheless been observed that seals rarely go farther than ten miles from land and never more than twenty. Since we frequently sighted seals, it could easily have been guessed that land had to be near.

The constant appearance of the Kamchatkan sea beaver, or rather sea otter, provided still greater proof because this animal eats solely crustaceans and shellfish and because of the structure of its heart cannot stay under water more than two minutes[24] without breathing. So it must constantly stay close to shore because it cannot seek food at depths of 60 to 100 fathoms, nor would it find any there even if it could. Accordingly, we could be certain that we were along the shore, and I have always held this to be the strongest evidence that America is opposite Kamchatka to the east between 51 and 56 degrees. At this latitude, these animals are found only along Kamchatka in the aptly named Beaver Sea, neither farther south nor farther north. There is no apparent explanation for their not also being found at 57 or 58 degrees around Oliutora or at 48 or 49 degrees on the distant Kurile Islands, because they are found at almost 60 degrees at Cape St. Elias in America and even also at 10 or fewer degrees in Brazil where Markgraf describes them under the name of *Ilya*.[25] There is, however, a single explanation: This is no Asian but a veritable American animal, only a newcomer and stranger along Kamchatka.[26] Because of the great distance above 56 degrees in the north and because of its nature and the lack of food below 50 degrees in the south, it cannot cross the ocean in these places but only the so-called Beaver Sea, where it does not have a voyage of more than twenty miles from coast to coast in a straight line,[27] a route it can take within 36 hours without dying of hunger on the way.

Further, we saw at various times whole flocks of gulls sitting together on the water. These birds are found constantly close to the shore, especially in June, when the fish migrate from the sea toward the land and up the rivers, an occasion for plentiful food for the birds. Also, we always saw them fly to the north or northwest until they were out of sight, so that after a few hours' sail to the north, it would have been easy to find out if there was a reason or not why they flew in this direction— especially since the constant fog did not allow our eyes to roam more than a few miles—the winds being so favorable on the way out that we could not have wished better for carrying out our great plan.

I remain silent about several circumstances. Although other seafarers on such voyages of discovery (as is evident from their journals) endeavor to pay attention to all details and to profit from them, here the greatest and plainest signs and clearest reasons were put out of sight and thrown to the wind. Under these conditions we reached land six weeks after our departure from Avacha, although it could easily have been reached within three or four days on a northeast course and within twenty days on the course agreed on, if the officers had deigned to avail themselves of the aforesaid correct signs and traces of land. And it is true that on Thursday, July 16, we saw land for the first time, also that it had been decided that if it were not sighted by July 20, we would begin the return voyage to Avacha because our water supply was already more than half used up.

We did see land already on July 15, but because I had announced it and it was not so visible that it could be clearly delineated, it was, as usual, dismissed as something peculiar to me. But the next day, in very clear weather, it was sighted in the very same spot. At that location the land was highly elevated. A mountain range we saw extending inland was so high that out at sea it was clearly visible from 16 German miles. I do not remember having seen a higher mountain range in all of Siberia and Kamchatka.[28] The shoreline is everywhere much broken up— hence, there are many islands close to the mainland and innumerable bays and harbors along the shore.

Because I have undertaken to adhere to the truth and be impartial in all matters, I cannot but reflect on a circumstance that in high places might not be concealed and might be interpreted differently than it was in reality.

It can easily be imagined how glad we all were when we finally caught sight of land. Everybody hastened to congratulate the Captain-

Commander, to whom the fame of discovery would most redound. However, he not only reacted indifferently and without particular pleasure but in our very midst shrugged his shoulders while gazing at the land.

Had the Captain-Commander survived and later wanted to take action against his officers because of their conduct, some were prepared to interpret his indifferent behavior with evil intent. Yet the Captain-Commander had much better insight into the future than the other officers, and in the cabin he said to Plenisner[29] and me: "Now we think that we have found everything, and many are full of expectations like pregnant windbags![30] But they do not consider where we have reached land, how far we are from home, and what accidents may yet happen. Who knows whether the trade winds may not come up and prevent our return? We do not know this country. We are not supplied with provisions to keep us through the winter."

Now that we were near land, it was not a little amusing to hear conflicting passions, wild conceits about self and future rewards, and speeches full of passion. Some wanted to head for land immediately and seek a harbor; others protested that doing so would be very dangerous. Each and every one acted alone, and nobody made suggestions to the Captain-Commander. The discussion and sea council, which had been convened over trifles on land, was here not called to consider a matter of greatest importance at the climax of the ten years of the Kamchatka Expedition—and the only thing we agreed on was that we were shut up in a ship!

2. Cape St. Elias

Since those days after July 16 had more noteworthy events than any in the preceding six weeks, I continue by recording the events of each day.

On July 17, because of mild winds, we approached the land gradually. On Saturday, July 18, toward evening, we came close enough that we could clearly see beautiful forests close by the sea as well as great flatlands beneath the inland mountain range. The beach itself was flat, smooth, and, as far as we could see, sandy. But we passed the mainland on the right and sailed to the northwest to get around a tall island[1] consisting of a single mountain range and covered with nothing but coniferous forests. However, because of contrary winds, our sailing had to be done with constant tacking, which took all the following night. On Sunday, July 19,[2] we were opposite the northwest end of the island at a distance of two miles.

Again that morning we had a little controversy. On Saturday evening we had noticed a channel between the mainland and the island, and seeing it, I had the thought that a rather large river[3] flowed into it from the land since its current was noticeable two miles from shore and the difference in the water was clearly visible. It was also noticeable by the objects carried by the current and the taste-tested low salinity. We could therefore have tried to go into the channel, where we could have anchored as safely, if not more safely, than where it pleased higher authority to decide to anchor on Monday, July 20.[4] The mouth of the river probably would have been large enough and consequently deep enough to provide a harbor for our ship with its draft of nine feet.[5]

FIG. 7. Cape St. Elias (Kayak Island). (Courtesy of the U.S.D.A. Forest Service)

But the answer was, "Have you already been there and made sure?" when the most proper way to proceed in uncertainty is to do so from a semblance of reasons rather than haphazardly without any.

We spent Sunday tacking to get close to the island and into a large bay seen from a distance, and at the same time to get near the land. On Monday, July 20, this objective was achieved out of sheer terror[6] so that we came to anchor among nothing but islands.[7] The outermost had to be called Cape St. Elias since we came near it on St. Elias day. For they wanted to have a cape on the map, even though they were ever so clearly told that an island cannot be called a cape because a cape is a noteworthy projection of the mainland into the sea in a noteworthy direction of land toward a certain area. That's why in German it is called a *Vorgebürge*, in Russian a *nos*; which is to say, this "cape" would be a cut-off head[8] and a sliced-off nose.

Although the orderly conduct as well as the importance of the matter would have called for single-minded consideration of what to do and how to use the time and opportunity to best advantage, what to explore on shore and in what manner; also, if, considering time and provisions

63

and distance, we should continue to follow the coast or if it was too late and we should here pass the winter[9]—all of this was not considered worthy of calling a council, but everybody kept silent and did what he himself pleased. They were of one mind in only this, that we should take on fresh water. That's why I said, "We have come only to take American water to Asia."[10]

Besides, it was agreed to use the small yawl for transporting water and to turn over the larger one to Master Khitrov, together with sufficient crew and ammunition, to explore the country, an assignment for which he possessed the greatest aptitude. When I asked to be sent off at the same time as Master Khitrov since he did not, after all, know everything (Khitrov himself, knowing his strengths, also asked for my company), our request was denied, and at first the attempt was made to scare me with some gruesome murder stories.

But I answered that I had never acted like a woman, nor did I know any reason why I should not be permitted to go ashore. To get there was, after all, to follow my chief work, profession, and duty. Up to now I had served Her Majesty faithfully according to my ability and was willing to maintain the honor of my service for a long time yet. And I said that if for reasons contrary to the purpose of the voyage I was not to go, I would report such conduct in terms it deserved.[11]

I was then called a wild man who would not be kept from work even by a treat to chocolate, which was just then being prepared.

When I realized that I was to be forced against my will to inexcusable neglect of duty, I put aside all respect and uttered a particular prayer[12] by which the Captain-Commander was immediately mollified and let me go with the water carriers but without giving me the least help or a single person other than the cossack Thoma Lepekhin, whom I myself had brought along.

On my departure from the ship, the Captain-Commander attempted to find out if I could take a joke by having trumpets sounded after me. Without thanking him, I took the matter the way it had been ordered. But I have never been one to blow my own horn and would not have appreciated it if trumpets had been sounded in my honor.[13]

However, I now saw all too clearly why I had been persuaded to come along; namely, merely to fill a requirement in the instructions that no one else could, that is, the investigating of minerals by knowledgeable people, which for eight years Ekaterinburg[14] had forgotten to ask for. The assayer Hartepol, who had been in Okhotsk, could not have been taken along because he had been sent to Iakutsk to accompany Spangberg. I was also to lend the undertaking greater prestige, but in name only, and to be the ship's physician and the Captain-Commander's personal physician, since they realized they had only an assistant surgeon.

This day half the command remained aboard ship on watch and busied themselves with unloading the empty water barrels and with loading the refilled ones. I was dispatched with these water barrels to make watery observations, while they stayed on board to make windy ones.[15]

As soon as I was on land,[16] with the protection and assistance of one man, and realized that time was all too precious, I made the best of the situation and with all possible speed immediately headed for the mainland to get as close to it as I could[17] to discover people and habitations.[18]

I had gone scarcely one verst along the coast before I found in one spot[19] signs of people and what they were like. Under a tree I found an old piece of log hewn as a trough in which a few hours earlier[20] the savages, lacking kettles and dishes, had cooked meat with glowing stones according to Kamchatkan ways described elsewhere.[21] Where they had been sitting, bones lay scattered, some with meat remaining, that had the appearance of having been roasted at the fire. From the characteristics of the bones, I recognized that they were not from any sea animals but from land animals, and it seemed to me that these, according to their form and size, should most likely be considered reindeer bones,[22] even though I never afterwards managed to see such an animal, perhaps because this one had been brought here from the mainland. In addition to these bones there was leftover *iukola*, or dried fish, which in Kamchatka is consumed at all meals in place of our bread. Next to these leftover fish, very large Jacob's mussels eight inches in diameter were lying about in large quantities, as well as blue mussels or *musculi* as found in Kamchatka and undoubtedly eaten raw as is the custom here.[23] I likewise found lying in various shells, as in bowls, sweet grass over which water had previously been poured in order to extract the sweetness, which struck me as quite remarkable and led me to the following conclusions.

This rare grass was up to now thought to be unique to the Kamcha-

FIG. 8. Bering expedition landing site, Kayak Island, in inner bay (upper right) and shoreline Steller hiked (foreground) around the cape (Cape St. Peter). (Courtesy of U.S.D.A. Forest Service)

dals, is called *slatkaia trava*[24] by the Russians and *kattik* by the Kamchadals, and is a true species of *Sphondylium*.[25] The way of preparing it by cleaning the outer part with clamshells, as well as the way in which it is eaten, corresponds exactly with American practice.[26] On the other hand, this custom is unknown to the neighboring Tungus and Olenni Koriaks[27] living in Kamchatka. Nor was its discovery and use an absolute necessity; just as, lacking steel, they make fire without it. All this is almost certain proof that this invention comes from Kamchatka, and it follows that both nations have previously had traffic with each other, or that possibly this nation is one and the same with the Kamchadals and emigrated from them.[28]

Considering the distance of 500 miles between the two, it can be assumed that America continues farther to the west and, opposite Kamchatka, is much closer in the north than others, without any reason, have supposed. Otherwise, the possibility of a crossing could not very well be imagined since neither nation is equipped with capable seafaring craft now nor are there indications that better craft were previously available on Kamchatka. Be that as it may, most American objects and inventions are identical to Kamchatkan or Asian ones or little different.

Beside the tree, not far from the site of the fire, where there were still fresh embers, I also found a wooden fire starter. Lacking steel, just as on Kamchatka and elsewhere in America, the people customarily make fire by friction. But the tinder made on Kamchatka is different from the Americans', a species of algae, *fontinalis*,[29] which was bleached by the sun. I took along a sample to send back.

The felled trees lying about here and there were so cut up with many blunt blows that one can only surmise that they fell trees with stone or bone axes just as on Kamchatka and just like the old Germans in ancient times before the invention of iron—axes that now that their use has died out are considered thunderclubs.

After I had looked at these things briefly and made some notes, I continued on my way. Having traveled about three versts, I found a path[30] leading into the very thick, dark forest right by the shore.

I held a brief consultation with the cossack, who had a loaded gun besides a knife and ax, to decide what action we should take if we should meet one or more persons, and I ordered him to do nothing at all without my command. I was furnished with only a Iakut *palma*,[31] which was to serve for digging out rocks and plants.

I noticed right away that somebody had wanted to cover the path but had been hindered by our speedy arrival and had therefore made it all the more noticeable. We saw[32] many trees recently stripped of their bark[33] and surmised that it had been used for dwellings or *ambars*, which must be nearby, since wherever we looked there was no lack of beautiful woods. But since the path divided into several smaller ones leading into the woods, we explored some not too far into the forest and came, after half an hour, to a place strewn with cut grass.

I immediately cleared the grass away and underneath found a covering of rocks. When these were likewise put aside, we came to tree bark placed over poles in an oblong rectangle three fathoms long and two fathoms wide and found under it a dug-out cellar two fathoms deep in which the following items were present.[34]

1. *Lukoshki*, or receptacles made of bark, one and a half arshins

FIG. 9. Bark-stripped Sitka spruce, Kayak Island, and John F. C. Johnson, Chugach Eskimo ethnohistorian.

high, which were all filled with smoked fish of a Kamchatkan species of salmon, at Okhotsk called *nerka*[35] in Tungus and in Kamchatka by the common name *krasnaia ryba*,[36] that were so cleanly and well prepared that I have never seen any so good on Kamchatka; they also greatly excel the Kamchatkan in taste.

2. *Slatkaia trava*, from which liquor is distilled on Kamchatka.

3. Several kinds of grass, skinned like hemp; I took these for nettles, which grow here in abundance and perhaps are used as in Kamchatka to make fishnets.

4. The innermost bark of larch or spruce, rolled up and dried, which is eaten in times of emergency and hunger not only in Kamchatka but also throughout Siberia and even in Russia as far as Khlynov or Vyatka.[37]

5. Large bundles of straps made from seaweed, which by testing I found to be extraordinarily strong and firm. Among these I also found some arrows, which in size far surpassed the Kamchatkan ones and ap-

FIG. 10. Steller's impassable cliff (the present-day Sea-cave Rock).

proached the arrows of the Tungus and Tatars; they were scraped very smooth and painted black so that it might indeed be supposed that these people had iron instruments and knives.

Despite my fear of being surprised in the cellar, I searched everything thoroughly, but finding nothing further, I took, for proof of having been there, two bundles of fish, the arrows, a wooden fire starter, tinder, a bundle of straps from seaweed, bark, and grass, and sent them with my cossack to the place where the water was being loaded, with the command to take them to the Captain-Commander and ask for two or three persons to assist me further in exploring the region. I also had him warn the persons on shore not to feel too safe but to be well on their guard. I then covered the cellar as it had been and, now quite alone, pursued my purpose to further investigate plants, animals, and minerals until my cossack should return.

But after I had covered about six versts,[38] I came to a steep cliff that extended into the sea beyond the beach so far that it was impossible to go further. I resolved to climb the cliff, and after much exertion, got on it, but saw that the east side was steep as a wall and it was impossible to go on. I therefore walked south in the hope of getting to the other

69

FIG. 11. View from the hilltop Steller climbed, with Wingham Island (left) and snow covered mountains of the mainland (right).

side of the island, there along the shore to get to the channel to investigate my theory of the presence here of a river and harbor.[39] But when I was climbing down the hill,[40] which was very densely overgrown everywhere with a thick, dark woods, without finding a trace of a path so that I could not get through, I considered that it would be impossible for my cossack to find me, also that I was too far from the others in case something should happen, and that I could not get back before night, to say nothing of other dangers, which I would not have feared if I had had the slightest help from my companions.

I therefore climbed the hill and looked mournfully at the depressing limits set for my explorations, wistful about the behavior of those who held in their hands these important matters; for which actions, all have allowed themselves to be regaled with visions of money as well as honor. When I had come again to the top of the hill and turned my eyes to the mainland, at least to take a good look at the region on which I was not allowed to extend my efforts productively, I saw at a verst[41] from me smoke rising from a breezy knoll[42] covered with conifers, and I now

FIG. 12. Steller's hill viewed from the north, with "breezy knoll, covered with conifers" (center).

had the certain hope of meeting people and learning from them what I needed for a complete report.[43]

I therefore climbed down the hill with great haste and, loaded with my collections, headed back to the place where I had been put ashore. Here, through the men who were just then hurrying from shore to ship in the boat, I sent news to the Captain-Commander and asked him to let me have the small yawl and several men for a few hours. Meanwhile on the beach, utterly exhausted, I described the rarest plants,[44] which I was afraid would wilt, and revived myself by being able to check out the excellent water for tea.

After approximately an hour, I got the patriotic and gracious answer: I was to get my butt on board pronto,[45] or, without waiting, they would leave me stranded.

I thought, God gives us the place, time, and opportunity to do that which each is ordered to do, and through which one could recommend one's services in the highest quarters, and each in his station could give pleasure to our most gracious monarch after such long waiting and indescribable costs. Yet it is likely that at our departure we all saw Russia

71

for the last time, because I could simply not count on divine assistance on the trip back if winds and weather were to imitate our intentions and become so contrary as each was to the overall purpose and thereby to his own fortune.

But because there was no time to moralize but only to snatch together everything possible before our flight from shore, and because it was already toward evening, I sent my cossack out to shoot some rare birds that I had observed; whereas I went once again on a tour to the west[46] and at sunset returned with various information and collections (which I will treat more thoroughly in my observations at a later time)[47] and once again received strict orders: if I did not come to the ship this time, no further reflection would be accorded me.

With my collections I therefore went to the ship, where, to my great astonishment, I was treated to chocolate.

Although I tried hard not to tell anything to anyone except those who were capable of judging my efforts, I nevertheless showed some objects and communicated my ideas about several matters, of which, however, only one was accepted. That is to say, an iron kettle, a pound of tobacco, a Chinese pipe, and a piece of Chinese silk were sent to the cellar,[48] but in exchange it was plundered to such an extent that if in the future we were to return to this place, the people would flee from us just as they did this time. Or, since we had shown them hostility, they would be hostile in return, especially if they should use the tobacco for eating or drinking, since they might not know the true use of either the tobacco or the pipe, whereas at least a few knives or axes would have aroused greater insight since their use would have been quite obvious.

The answer was that they would look on such as a hostile sign, that war was being declared against them[49]—whereas from the tobacco, especially if they tried it out wrongly, they could conclude that we wanted to do them in. Also, we afterwards learned with what joy the Americans accepted some knives from Captain Chirikov and indicated that they would like several more.[50]

I was scarcely an hour on the ship when Master Khitrov with his party of about fifteen men returned in the large boat[51] and brought the following news.

1. Among the islands close to the mainland, he had come on a harbor[52] where the ship could stop without any danger.

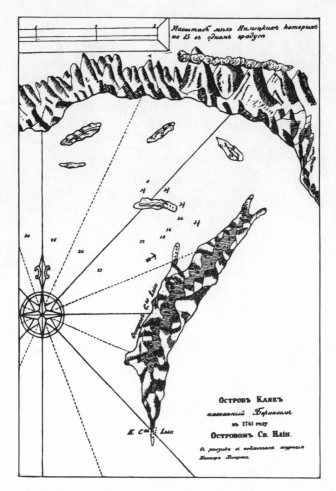

FIG. 13. Khitrov's sketch map of Cape St. Elias (Kayak Island), 1741. (Courtesy of the American Geographical Society; reprinted from Golder, *Bering's Voyages*, 2: 42)

2. He indeed had seen no people but had come upon a small habitation of wood,[53] whose interior walls were so smooth that it seemed as if they had been planed; therefore, it certainly seemed that the Americans had iron instruments and must know the use and preparation of iron.

Besides this report, he brought with him several artifacts.

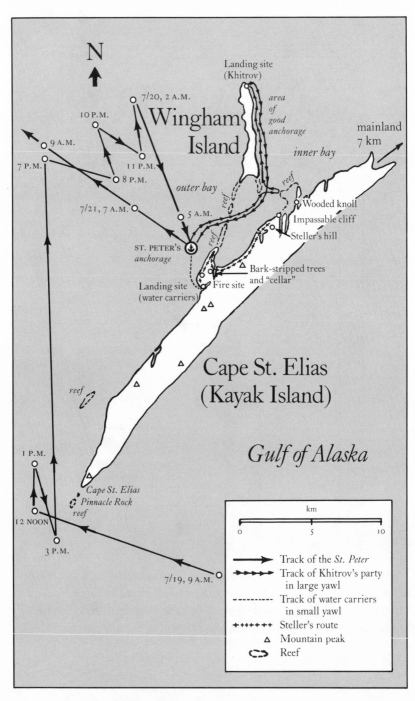

FIG. 14. Cape St. Elias (Kayak Island), 1741.

1. A wooden vessel[54] like those constructed in Russia of linden bark and used instead of a box;

2. A stone that perhaps, for lack of a better, had served as a whetstone, on which could be seen stripes of copper, from which I therefore concluded that their instruments—like those of the Kalmuks and Asian Tatars in Siberia in times past—must be of copper because the smelting of an iron ore so rich in copper requires more understanding and experience than could be expected from these people since it usually tears apart the best smelting ovens;

3. A hollow ball of hard-burned clay two inches in diameter, enclosing a stone that rattles when shaken, which I regard as a toy for small children;[55]

4. A tail from a black-gray fox;

5. A paddle from a canoe.

These things represent all we could do and find out, and not indeed from the mainland on which none of us set foot but only from an island that is three miles long and a half-mile wide,[56] the first and outermost from the mainland, which here forms a large bay studded with many islands, an island that is separated from the mainland by a channel that is not more than a half-mile wide.[57] The only reason no landing was attempted on the mainland was a sluggish stubbornness and cowardly fear[58] of a handful of unarmed and even more terrified savages, of whom neither friendly nor hostile action was to be assumed, and a cowardly longing for home, which the gentlemen probably considered excusable, especially if those in high authority reflected as little about the malcontents and their statements as did the officers themselves. The time spent for investigation bore an arithmetical relationship: the preparation for this ultimate purpose lasted ten years; twenty hours[59] were devoted to the matter itself.

Of the mainland we have a sketch on paper;[60] of the country itself we have only an imperfect notion based on assumptions drawn from what was found on the island.

What can be said from comparison and from investigation based on our perspective is summed up in the following points.

As far as climate is concerned, America is of a noticeably better character than the most extreme northeast part of Asia, although the land toward the sea, whether viewed close up or from afar, everywhere consists of amazingly high mountain ranges, most of whose peaks are covered with perpetual snow. Yet these mountains, compared with those of Asia, have a much better nature and character. Asian mountain ranges, long since bereft of their continuity, are throughout broken up and are therefore much too loose for the circulation of mineral gases, and lack all inner heat; accordingly they are also devoid of all precious metals, bare of all trees and plants, and only here and there among the rocks provided with a few hardy and low plants. The American mountain ranges, on the other hand, are firm, covered above their rock mantle not with moss but with good soil; therefore up to the highest peaks, they are densely overgrown with the most beautiful trees and on the ground provided with low grasses and all kinds of dry and succulent plants but not with water plants and mosses as in Asia.

The springs, of which I found so many, flow out of the valleys at the foot of the mountains, and not everywhere, as in Siberia, out of lakes, even on mountain summits.

The plants come out of the ground mostly of the same shape and size whether on mountain tops or lower places because of the equal distribution of interior heat and moisture, whereas in Asia they are so different that one would often make different species of a single plant if he did not observe the general distinction that the plant that at the foot of the mountain is scarcely two ells high will on the mountain appear hardly a half-foot high.

Whereas here at 60 degrees latitude the very beach itself is right from the waterline studded with the most beautiful forests, in Kamchatka at 51 degrees the willow and alder bushes first occur 20 versts from the sea, the birch forests not until 30 to 40 versts, to say nothing of resinous trees, which are not seen until 50 to 60 versts inland from the mouth of the Kamchatka River. In Asia at 62 degrees latitude, from Anadyrsk on, no tree is to be found for 300 to 400 versts inland.

And it is my opinion that, from here to the north as far as 70 or more degrees latitude, there is nothing but land, which, because it is protected and sheltered from the west, gives rise to this woodland fertility, whereas, on the other hand, the Kamchatka coast is utterly exposed to the north winds, especially on the Penzhin Sea. But the northern regions from Lopatka to Kamchatka,[61] although they are more northerly, are nevertheless also more fertile and have better woods even closer to the sea because they have the shelter of Cape Chukchi and of America, which lies northeast across the channel.

It is also because of this temperature that the fish go up the river from the sea earlier than in Kamchatka. On July 20,[62] we already found their fish supply stored, whereas in Kamchatka this day of St. Elias first signals the start of abundant fishing. That the plants that only begin to bloom in Kamchatka at this time already have ripe seed in this country is only partial evidence of its superior character, because in northern regions the longer days and the onset of great heat and its duration contribute to this end, as already observed in Iakutsk in 1740.

As far as minerals are concerned, anyone who considers how little one person can do on a small island in ten hours will easily recognize that my failure to have much to report is not attributable to my carelessness or laziness. Therefore I freely admit that I noted nothing but sand and gray rock, since it is also known that close to the beach Nature is not capable of or used to producing anything besides marcasite and pyrite products.

Of fruit-bearing bushes and plants, I met with only one new and elsewhere unknown species of raspberry,[63] growing in great abundance, but not yet fully ripe. Because of its exceptional size and peculiar and exquisite taste, this fruit would have well deserved that a few bushes of it be taken along in a box with soil to be sent to St. Petersburg to be further propagated. It is not my fault that space for it was begrudged, since I myself as a protester now took up too much space. But familiar berries,[64] such as *Chamaecerasus*, red and black whortleberries, scurvy berries, and *Empetrum*, were present just as plentifully as in Kamchatka.

Other plants[65] I have added at the end in a special register[66] that describes the rarest and most unique of those that are indigenous.

Concerning the animals present here that serve the inhabitants for food and clothing, there are seals,[67] sharks (*Canes charcharias*),[68] whales, and lots of sea otter, whose excrement I often found everywhere on the shore, which also shows that the inhabitants, with enough other food sufficiently supplied, must not be much concerned about them, because otherwise they would come ashore as infrequently as they do now in Kamchatka ever since the time when so many people developed such a liking for their pelts. Of land animals suitable for food, apart from what has above been conjectured about reindeer, I observed nothing but both black and red foxes, which I and others have seen at various times; also, they were not especially wild, perhaps because they are infrequently hunted.

Of birds, I observed only two familiar ones, namely ravens and magpies, whereas of strange and unknown ones, I saw more than ten different species, all of which were distinguished from European and Siberian species because of their quite distinctive brilliant color.

Luck, through my hunter, placed in my hands only a single specimen, which I remember having seen painted in vivid colors and written about in the newest description of Carolina plants and birds published in French and English not long ago in London and whose author's name[69] eludes me. This bird alone sufficiently convinced me that we were really in America, and I shall transmit the drawing of it next spring because I had to leave it behind in the harbor on my return on foot to the Bolshaia River.

After this short survey of the land discovered, I shall now continue the narrative of our voyage.

3. Sea Ape

*O*n the morning of July 21, two hours before daybreak, the Captain-Commander, contrary to his custom, got up, came on deck himself, and, without deliberating about it, gave orders to weigh anchor. Although Lieutenant Waxell earnestly requested that we remain at anchor long enough to fill all the barrels with water, since twenty were yet empty and nothing but a longing for home obliged us to return, the order was nevertheless carried out, and we ran out of the bay and gradually into the sea. It was considered reason enough that the wind was favorable for setting sail but contrary for going into the harbor. When a few days later a slight storm came up, there was not a little satisfaction that we were away from this bay and the shore.

Then the Captain-Commander offered his opinion as follows. Because August was drawing near and because we were unfamiliar with the country and the wind, we should be content for this year with this discovery and not follow the coast further or make the return voyage close to the land but on our earlier course. It was now safe to assume that the land continued farther to the west, but we did not know whether such land did not extend toward Kamchatka farther to the south. In that case, we might run on land blindly at night or in fog or, in the likely autumn storms, suffer disaster on islands in an unknown sea.

But because the matter was put before us only in conversation without submission to a council, and although I did not hear a reply to it, I could clearly tell from the later actions of Lieutenant Waxell and Master Khitrov that they had no use for this proposition. Consequently, until July

26 we always sailed offshore because they believed that the land should always be followed along the coast, although we could have made an attempt, after each one hundred miles, to go one or two degrees to the north.

Hence it happened that during the night of July 27 in a small storm we got bottom at 60 fathoms on a bank extending away from the land into the sea. The land was not seen. But if we had been running closer to shore, they could then have already realized the danger into which they later so often recklessly placed us all. They seemed to make no use of whatever experience they had in matters of the sea.

On July 28 and 29, we had continuously stormy, wet weather, and got indications of land from all kinds of drifting objects just as on the voyage out and constantly after and before we saw land, which was very often the case.

On July 30 and 31, as also on August 1, we had beautiful, clear weather, a calm sea, and a favorable southeast wind, and we advanced quite well. About one o'clock after midnight, we became aware, upon taking soundings,[1] that we were in four fathoms of water, though this fact was reported otherwise to the Captain-Commander. In calm weather, we finally got so far away from the land that we reached eighteen to twenty fathoms, where we dropped anchor and awaited daybreak.

On August 2 we were three versts away from a rather large, wooded island.[2] The weather was unusually pleasant and warm, sunshiny, and wholly calm. Toward noon a sea lion turned up by our ship and for more than half an hour continuously swam around it. I asked the Captain-Commander to let me go ashore for a few hours with the small boat to continue my business since wind and weather were so favorable. But we got into a little argument over the matter so that he called a council on that account, wherein it was settled that no one should reproach me in the future as if I, for my part, had not desired to manage my domain most zealously at each opportunity to the best of my ability. Everyone promised not to, and I let it go at that.

Toward evening I caught with a fishing rod two fish that are called *Scorpius marinus*,[3] which I described and preserved in alcohol, but which were lost with many other collections when the ship ran aground

SIMIA marina quædam,cuius iconem qualem à Ioan.Kentmanno accepi, hîc exhibeo. Is Si-
miæ marinæ nomine è Dania sibi allatam scribit. Pinnas tanquam uolans extendit, ut pictura
præ se fert:& inter duas in summo dorso pinnas aculeum retrò tendit,ceu Galeus centrines,os si-
mum habet,non ut Galei in longitudinem protensum rostrum,branchiarum foramina quina ap
parent,obliquo inter os & oculos descensu.Color ei uiridis toto corpore:sed in dorso magis fu-
scus,ad latera pallidus,dentes la i & continui.Reliqua satis apparent in icone:quæ cum ad
sceleton facta sit, in uiuo animali non omnia similiter se habere suspicamur, Te-
studineū inuolucrum si accederet,Aeliani hanc Simiam facerem;
quam in Mari rubro cartilaginei gene-
ris describit.

FIG. 15. Steller's sea ape. (Courtesy of the Beinecke Rare Book and Manuscript Library, Yale University; reprinted from Gesner, *Icones animalium*, 1:153)

in November. Toward evening we weighed anchor, and passing by the island, we went to sea to the west.

Toward noon the following day, on August 3, we sighted the mainland again at 56 degrees latitude in NNW1/2W about fourteen miles from us, yet very distinctly because of the very high, snow-covered mountains.[4] With easterly winds we sailed away from here to the south because in the west the land was in our way. We found ourselves in the previous bay since in the west and the north we had the mainland and in the east the island near which we had almost touched bottom[5] on August 1–2.

On August 4, when sailing to the south, we saw finally between south and west about two to three miles from us many high, large, and wooded islands,[6] so that we were surrounded by land. Wherever we wanted to get out, we found land in the way. So we wasted the winds, which at this time, until August 9, were mostly east or southeast and could have served us considerably on a straight course to Kamchatka, uselessly tacking back and forth in this bay, when we could have sailed several hundred miles with them.

During the time we spent close by the land, we constantly saw large numbers of fur seals, other seals,[7] sea otters, sea lions, and porpoises.[8] I frequently observed that as often as these sea animals allowed themselves to be seen, even in the greatest calm, shortly thereafter the weather changed, and the more frequently they appeared and the more movement they made, the more furious the storms were.

On August 10, we saw a very unusual and new animal, about which I shall write a short description[9] since I watched it for two whole hours.

The animal was about two ells long. The head was like a dog's head, the ears pointed and erect, and on the upper and lower lips on both sides whiskers hung down which made him look almost like a Chinaman. The eyes were large. The body was longish, round, and fat, but gradually became thinner toward the tail; the skin was covered thickly with hair, gray on the back, reddish white on the belly, but in the water it seemed to be entirely red and cow-colored. The tail, which was equipped with fins, was divided into two parts, the upper fin being two times as long as the lower one, just like on the sharks.[10]

However, I was not a little surprised that I could perceive neither forefeet as in marine amphibians nor fins in their place.

As for its body shape, for which there is no drawing, it corresponds in all respects to the picture that Gesner received from one of his correspondents[11] and in his *Historia animalium* calls *Simia marina Danica*.[12] At least our sea animal can by all rights be given this name because of both its resemblance to Gesner's *Simia* and its strange habits, quick movements, and playfulness.

For more than two hours it stayed with our ship, looking at us, one after the other, as if with admiration. It now and then came closer and often so close that it could have been touched with a pole. Then, as soon as we moved, it retired farther away.

It raised itself out of the water up to one-third of its length, like a human being, and often remained in this position for several minutes.

After it had observed us for almost half an hour, it shot like an arrow under our ship and came up again on the other side, but passed under the ship again to reappear in its first position. It repeated this maneuver back and forth about thirty times.

Now, when this animal spotted a large American seaweed, three to four fathoms long, which at the bottom was hollowed out like a bottle and from there to the outermost end became gradually more pointed like a phial, it shot toward it like an arrow, grabbed it with its mouth, and swam with it toward our vessel, and did such juggling tricks that one could not have asked for anything more comical from a monkey. Now and then it bit off a piece and ate it.

When I had observed it for a long time, I had a gun loaded and fired at this animal, intending to get possession of it to make an accurate description. But the shot missed. Although it was somewhat frightened, it reappeared right away and approached our ship gradually.

But when another shot at it was in vain, or perhaps only slightly wounded it, it retreated into the sea and did not come back. However, it was seen at various times in different parts of the sea.[13]

4. Shumagin Island

On August 11, when we were out of the bay, we gradually sailed to the west with a southeast wind.

But on August 12 it became calm, and on this day a council was held in which it was decided, because of the approaching autumn and the great distance, to set out immediately on the return voyage to Avacha without looking around any more to find out where the mainland might extend. Yet I can't deny that the council, together with what was decided in it, seemed very strange to me. That's because the immediate return trip was decided on, and the document drawn up for the record was signed, from the Captain-Commander on down to the boatswain's mate without—as was customary from the beginning—taking me in too.[1] And they just did not want to deviate from their old plan and go a few degrees farther south because of the contrary westerly winds but wanted to proceed on the Avacha parallel of 53 degrees to Avacha. Yet it could readily have been guessed that the land that had already been observed at 54 degrees could stretch even farther south,[2] which amounted to the same thing as wanting to follow the land steadily, still not making use of the closest way for the return voyage at a distance from the American continent. But that we were along the land and should assume it to run even farther south could clearly be deduced from the constant signs of animals and drifting objects; likewise the contrary wind was an indisputable witness of land lying ahead of us to the west. Without a doubt, other, more favorable winds could be expected at a latitude of

49 to 50 degrees, although we know of no instance of trade winds at such a latitude since trade winds have nowhere been observed above the tropics.

But although the Captain-Commander was of the same opinion as I, he would still not give an order accordingly, but only spoke about it and, without a response, let his opinion be utterly rejected.

If I now reasonably compare the purpose of the decision reached by their council with their actions, I must certainly conclude the following: "The gentlemen want to go home and by the shortest route but in the longest manner."

It is especially remarkable that never before had the wind so long and without change been contrary so constantly as from August 12. From August 13 to 17, the time was spent with constant tacking alternately toward the south and the north and advancing little by it.

On August 18, another amazing thing happened. About four o'clock in the morning, I heard someone on deck speak of land. I got up immediately and went out. But it had probably already been forbidden that anyone speak of having seen land, and that in a strange place, namely, in the south. Although the land that had been clearly visible before sunrise had later been covered by a fog, it could still be distinctly recognized, as could the fact that it was not far from us by the copious seaweed seen drifting from there. That the west wind all at once was stilled served, however, as further evidence that we were between America and some land in the south.[3]

I saw well enough why they wanted to hide this from me, that is, because the officers were already tired of reconnoitering the land. It was nevertheless uncalled for to leave it unexamined and not be able to put it on the map, having ascertained whether it existed or not.

But when I asked what land they thought this was, as doubtless it must be a large island (of which we had seen so many, having observed that America's shore is provided with as many islands in the west as in the east),[4] I received the answer: It must be Juan de Gama Land.[5]

I was not a little surprised by this answer since they considered it a land apart from America and did not know that up to now an unexplored American coast, reaching out from east to west in the north, had been called that. And I could therefore conclude how admirably they understood Delisle's large map, which they had so often from sheer ignorance maligned since they had such a wrong notion about this land. It also could not be over fifteen miles wide because otherwise on the voyage out we would of necessity have seen it, if not sailed over it. However, I will let it pass that the extent of the land was not ascertained, let alone noted on the map.

But I am very much surprised indeed that they could not guess the reason for the constant west wind, nor let themselves be persuaded by it to try a more southerly homeward course until, according to the reckoning, we should be opposite the open Vries Canal,[6] where other winds might be expected, the more so since the north and northeasterly winds I had for a long time observed on Kamchatka in the fall had also been found to be thus on the Captain-Commander's first voyage.

On August 19, at three o'clock after midnight, we got a favorable east wind, before which we sailed due west. Toward noon, however, it started to quiet down. The horizon cleared up so that we could recognize the mainland not indistinctly in the north while becoming more certain of its closeness once more because of the seaweed and other objects suddenly drifting from the shore to our ship and the many animals and land birds and even the changed water as one bit of evidence that experience had often confirmed.

Yet no one but I and several others would either believe or see it, although it was confirmed by the decreasing wind and even more by the way the wind changed according to the well-known rule and observation of seamen, namely, that as long as one stays by the land, day winds blow from the shore and night winds from the sea.

Nevertheless, we sailed somewhat more to the south, and when on August 20 we were so far away that neither the land itself nor the previous signs were visible, I was asked mockingly if I still saw land, although, when they spotted land even at 51 degrees latitude, I had not laughed at them for not being able to see farther than their disposition and experience permitted.

From August 20 to August 23, we tacked on the 53d parallel, and very often I saw whales, no longer singly but in pairs, moving along with and behind each other and pursuing each other, which gave me the idea that this time was destined for their mating period.

On August 24 and 25, we had a violent storm from the west.

FIG. 16. Bering expedition landing site, Nagai Island (right), with watering place (left), and Shumagin's likely burial site on grassy slope (background center).

We spent August 26 tacking. On August 27, the horizon was very clear. The air was cold and bright, the wind straight out of the west.

That day in a council it was suddenly decided, because of contrary winds and fear of a water shortage since only 26 full barrels were still on hand, to go on a northeast course toward land. This decision would not have been necessary if at Cape St. Elias we had filled the twenty empty barrels, which had then, for no reason, been left undone. The council had scarcely ended, the matter been resolved, and the document signed, when in the afternoon the wind suddenly changed, and accordingly at once the decision. But the ship had hardly been turned when the wind again blew from the west and, continuing steadily, not only forced us, indeed, to make up our minds to sail toward land but also made us actually go.

On August 28, we pursued the course toward land, and toward four o'clock in the evening we already saw various signs, namely, fur seals, a species of cod[7] found on banks at a depth of 90 fathoms at most, and a black gull.[8] Shortly afterwards we sighted land itself north by east al-

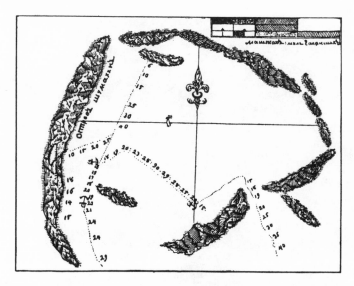

FIG. 17. Khitrov's sketch map of the "bay of islands," or outer Shumagins, 1741. (Courtesy of the American Geographic Society; reprinted from Golder, *Bering's Voyages*, 2:76)

though very indistinctly. But during the night we proceeded so far that on the morning of August 29 we could clearly see five islands[9] and from ten to twelve miles beyond them, the mainland.

These days the weather was very pleasant and very favorable for the purpose of approaching the islands to seek a harbor or shelter. At three o'clock in the afternoon, we reached the shore of the outermost[10] of these islands, which lay from north to south. Toward late evening, we anchored by a rocky and barren island[11] situated three versts to the east of this one.

In the early hours of August 30 began the execution of a twofold plan, that is, to look around for the nearest and most convenient spot from which we could get fresh water; then, because we had seen a fire burning in the night on the island north of us,[12] to send Master Khitrov there with a party to reconnoiter the place and to seek out people.

But so that the honor of the expected discovery might fall to the naval officers, they themselves alerted me and asked if I didn't want to go ashore. Even though I clearly saw their intention,[13] I nevertheless accepted their offer very kindly, and went ashore with the water carriers with the desire that both parties might find something useful, but there was little hope of that on a barren and miserable island.

I was scarcely ashore when I immediately endeavored to locate a watering place and found several springs with very good and safe water, but at the same time the seamen had selected the first and nearest puddle[14] and already begun the transport. However, I noted the following flaws in this water: namely, (1) that it was standing, chalky water, which I recognized right away by boiling tea and then by testing with soap; and (2) that, as I had observed on the beach, it rose and fell with the tide and therefore shared its salt, which immediately became apparent during boiling, unless one had totally lost one's taste.[15]

I thus proposed to use the spring water I had found,[16] of which I sent a sample to the ship together with an oral report, which besides information on the quality of the water contained the following: that by using the other water, scurvy would quickly increase, and because of its lime, the men would be dried up and debilitated, indeed, that this water after a short time aboard ship would increase in salinity from day to day and through standing finally become salt water. On the other hand, there was nothing of the sort to be feared from the spring water.

Although this was my proper business[17] and no seaman's affair and business, and although so much damage, even our eventual ruin, manifested itself from this decision, even this sincere advice, serving the conservation of my own life and health which had now fallen under foreign power, it was, from the old overbearing habit, contradicted right away and cast away with the answer: "Why shouldn't this water be good? The water is good. Just fill up with it!"[18]

When I received this answer and, meanwhile having found a watering place[19] even nearer than the preferred salty puddle, offered it in case the spring water did not please, they flatly refused, so that they might the better be able to deny me all understanding and knowledge in even a single matter. But since I was already used to such encounters, I did not concern myself further about this and began to reconnoiter the country. I noted the following: that this island on which I found myself was the largest among the eight[20] lying all around, approximately three to four German miles in length[21] and three, at the most four, versts in width from east to west. The mainland was visible in the north and west about ten miles away. It was nonetheless not settled whether this island

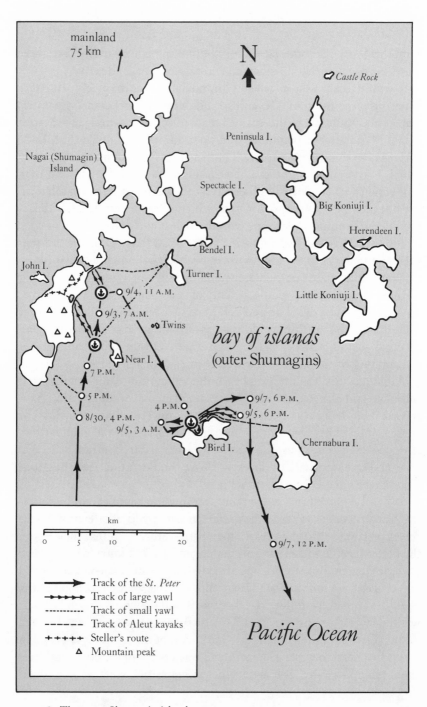

mainland
75 km

N

Castle Rock

Peninsula I.

Nagai (Shumagin)
Island

Spectacle I.

Big Koniuji I.

Herendeen I.

Bendel I.

John I.

Turner I.

Little Koniuji I.

○ 9/4, 11 A.M.

○ 9/3, 7 A.M.

Twins

bay of islands
(outer Shumagins)

Near I.

7 P.M.

5 P.M.

4 P.M. ○

○ 9/7, 6 P.M.

○ 9/5, 6 P.M.

○ 8/30, 4 P.M.

9/5, 3 A.M.

Chernabura I.

Bird I.

Pacific Ocean

km

0   5   10   20

○ 9/7, 12 P.M.

Track of the *St. Peter*

Track of large yawl

Track of small yawl

Track of Aleut kayaks

Steller's route

△ Mountain peak

FIG. 18. The outer Shumagin islands, 1741.

is not continuous with the mainland in the north and therefore a promontory, since we could not see the end of it there. This island, just like all the others, consists of nothing but lofty heights and solid rock overgrown with green. The stone is mostly a rough gray and yellowish rock, in some places a gray sandstone. There occurs also a black, thick slate. The shore is everywhere stony and rocky, with springs and small streams in abundance.

Of animals, I met a black fox[22] right away. I took it to be a dog, because it barked at me like a dog and was not shy at all. But after a closer look, I recognized my error, and thought that it should be killed by either Plenisner or my hunter to take as evidence. But both missed. We saw red foxes in various parts of the island.

Evrashkas, or small marmots,[23] are found in great abundance.

Besides these, I saw a track of an entirely unknown animal on the clayey beach of a lake. The track left in the clay was like a wolf's footprint, but its size and that of the claws suggested that it had to be another and much larger animal or a very large species of wolf.[24]

Water birds were there in great abundance, such as swans, two species of cormorants, auks, ducks, snipes, sandpipers, various gulls, divers, among them a very peculiar and unknown species, Greenland pigeons, sea parrots, and *michagatkas*.

But of land birds nothing whatsoever was seen except ravens, flycatchers, snowbirds, and ptarmigans.[25]

Of fish, we saw *malma* and *ramsha*.[26]

As far as plants, bushes, and trees are concerned, I observed on all the islands, of which in a circumference of six German miles eight could be counted, not a single other tree than the ones we had observed on exactly that latitude on the land sighted on August 4, which cannot be more than forty miles from here.

From here on, all of the islands as far as Kamchatka, at least those which we subsequently saw, are likewise barren and without any forests. Up to now I have not been able to find any other reasons for this except the following three:

1. These islands have a twofold position and a twofold characteristic. All the islands from here lie northeast–southwest from America. The islands in the channel and those situated near Kamchatka lie northwest–

southeast, and I have even noticed on the large as well as small rocks that, lengthwise, they have this same direction.

2. Their twofold characteristic is this, that altogether they are very long and have in comparison a totally disproportionate width. For example, Shumagin's Island is twenty to thirty versts long, two to three wide, Bering's Island thirty miles long, four, at most seven versts wide. All the islands, of which we observed seven[27] in number from here to Bering's Island, were just so constituted.

3. It follows from this that since their width is so very small anyway and open to the north and south from where the mightiest storms and winds blown over the land to its full length have the most opposite effects in warmth, cold, and wetness, neither tree nor bush can take root or grow.[28] Even the lowest bushes grow so crooked and tangled, one with the other, that it is impossible to find a straight stick two feet long in the entire region.

Likewise, it is observed in Kamchatka that those regions having a sufficient breadth of land between south and north are most fertile in woodlands and other necessities. On the other hand, the narrower the land gradually becomes, the more apparent is the change, for example, from the Bolshaia River to Lopatka. But opposite Karaga,[29] where the land is even narrower, and six degrees farther north, the area is quite differently constituted. The matter is even more obvious with respect to the islands lying in the channel since they are exposed without shelter in their narrowest parts to all the fierce winds that come into being between northeast and southwest.

However, I observed some islands that have the same position, length, and width but are different and have forests, for which the real reason is that they are close by the land and are sheltered to some extent by the mainland. An apparent reason for this is, I believe, that the mainland of America, or the coast stretching out from America toward the east, has a much larger width, but with a lesser width more to the west and a minimal width across from Kamchatka; that is to say, the northwest coast of America is formed just like northeastern Kamchatka of Asia.

For these reasons, then, the islands lying to the east can be wooded because of better shelter and the breadth of the land toward the north, and the westerly ones are barren because of opposite conditions, whether they are closer to Asia like the first, second, and third Kurile islands and the two islands[30] we saw on October 30, or nearer to America, like all those we observed in September and October.

As concerns the plants, other than the crooked willow brush, hardly more than two arshins high, I have added a special list[31] of them at the end. And I note only that most American plants and the rarest ones I described at Cape St. Elias and plants growing out of rocks were likewise present here. But I also encountered several in 1742 on Bering's Island and afterward in the fall in the same places on Kamchatka.

But concerning plants existing in valleys, bottom land, and moist places, they are, with the exception of a few, the same as those found in Europe, Asia, and America at the same latitude.

Excepting the lingonberries and black crowberries (or *shiksha*)[32] found here abundantly, the plants of greatest use to us were the magnificent antiscorbutic plants, such as *Cochlearia*, *Lapathum folio cubitali*, *Gentiana*, and other cresslike plants that I gathered only for my use and the Captain-Commander's.[33]

From the beginning, the medicine chest had been meagerly and miserably furnished, filled with the most useless medicines, almost nothing but plasters, ointments, oils, and other surgical supplies needed for four to five hundred men with wounds from great battles, but with nothing whatever needed on a sea voyage where scurvy and asthma are the chief complaints. Although I now brought up that fact and asked for a few men to gather up as many antiscorbutic plants as we would need, the gentlemen scorned even this proposal,[34] so valuable to themselves and for which they should have thanked me.

They rued it afterwards when we had scarcely four ablebodied men aboard. They implored me then for help, which I gave as best I could with bare hands, even though it was not in my job description and even though before they were in need they had scorned my advice. Ungrateful and coarse men though they were, my ministrations, under divine grace, very clearly caught their attention when, simply by giving him raw scurvy grass, I managed to bring the Captain-Commander—so bedridden with scurvy that he had already lost the use of his limbs—so far within eight days that he was able to get out of bed and on deck and

to feel as vigcrous as he had been at the beginning of the voyage. Likewise, the *Lapathum* I prescribed to be eaten raw for three days firmed
up again the teeth of most seamen.

Although I had already built a hut because of the evening's rain and
had wished to spend the night ashore, I decided to go on the ship to
bring up, emphatically and with the greatest modesty once more, my
opinion about the unhealthy water and the gathering of plants. But
when, concerning the water, I saw myself spurned and rudely contradicted and heard myself ordered to gather the plants as if I were a surgeon's apprentice subject to their command, and the matter that I recommended affecting their own interest, health, and lives was not
deemed worthy of the work of one or two persons, I regretted my good
opinion and resolved, in the future, to look after the saving of myself
alone,[35] without the loss of one word more.

With this intention, I went ashore again on the morning of August
31 to continue my work and with Plenisner to reconnoiter the land.

But toward evening, through a *sluzhiv*, we were called back to the
ship hurriedly with the announcement that in order not to leave anyone
stranded because of a suspected storm—of which back on shore we had
not had the slightest sign—all hands were to gather on the packet boat
in case the anchors should not hold in a rising storm, and because the
place where we were anchored, they said, was extremely dangerous,
which previously despite all opinions had been declared sheltered on all
sides.

Immediately we all ran in greatest haste more than a mile[36] to the
eastern coast of the island and discovered the situation to be as we had
been told. Also, because of the sick brought here the day before, who,
considering the high waves on the shore,[37] could scarcely be hauled into
the longboat, we found the confusion on shore so great that we decided
to wade waist-deep through the breakers to the boat and, trusting to
good luck, let ourselves be ferried in it.

This day, our first man, Shumagin by name, died just as soon as he
was brought ashore. He was buried there.[38] After him the island was
afterwards called Shumagin Island.

When after some worry we reached the ship, the greatest regret was
that Master Khitrov and his men were not present and that perchance
we might be forced to leave them ashore. I now thanked God that

through the crafty designs of the seamen I had been separated from his company.

But soon after our arrival a big fire was seen not far from the place where we had been taken into the boat, and I knew in consideration of the distance that Master Khitrov was staying at the lake[39] where I had suggested the second time that water be taken and where he had not long ago arrived.

In the worsening storm, the greatest luck for us was this: that although the storm had begun in the northeast, the wind had veered at once and changed to southwest, further west, and then northwest, where we were sheltered behind land and not subjected to such great danger. It was the greatest luck that in the storm at midnight the Captain-Commander did not let the anchor be needlessly cut off to allow another, considered more serviceable, to fall without reason in its place, because otherwise, in the darkening night and the usual confusion, we would surely have drifted against the rock and been wrecked.

I also learned this same evening that the officers had, though too late, changed their minds and, beginning to tremble in the face of death, sent ashore several barrels to take spring water for their own provision from the place I had pointed out. Fate, however, would let them partake of their biased stubbornness but not of the water, because out of haste and because the boat was being loaded with the sick, they unwillingly had to leave the barrels behind on the shore.

On September 1, the wind was still very strong, with continuous rain. The day was spent anxiously pondering how we could get away from the land and get the Master and his men on the ship. If he had either not gone at all or had returned sooner since he did not meet anyone, having also deprived us of the yawl and hindered us in transporting water just as at Cape St. Elias, we could have put out to sea with favorable winds and run more than 100 miles on our journey.

As it was, because of him we all had to be endangered at anchor near land without being able to avail ourselves of the auspicious winds lasting for five days afterwards. Everyone complained then that everything that this man tackled, from Okhotsk to the return voyage, took a harmful and unlucky course. Just as at Cape St. Elias, through his long and fruitless absence, it was his fault that we did without the boat for transporting water and had to sail to land this second time, for which he had also been the first adviser.[40] Generally, it was remarked after this that he was very quick and eager to give bold advice but left the doing to others,[41] and in facing trouble he was without resolution and purpose, but only whined and tried to hide.

On September 2, we got a southeast wind, and the large boat with eight men was sent ashore to bring Master Khitrov and his party aboard ship. During that time the anchor was weighed, and with the southeasterly wind we sailed farther to the north up along the shore to take on the oncoming boat more conveniently; there we dropped anchor.[42]

It rained and blew very hard this day. So, for greater safety, the second anchor was dropped. But toward evening we suddenly got a storm blowing violently from the southeast, and a third anchor was also kept ready in case one of the other two anchor cables should break.

But, God be thanked, the wind shifted to the southwest shortly thereafter so that we lay sheltered, and it became more still. But the boat remained ashore through the night.

On September 3, for the whole day, the weather was pleasant and calm, the wind remaining southwesterly. Moreover, toward morning came the added pleasure of getting the boat with Master Khitrov and all our men back on board without losing a single one. The little yawl, however, together with some needed materials, was needlessly left ashore as a souvenir.[43]

Both anchors were therefore weighed, and with southwesterly winds we sailed around the rock,[44] and since in the south we could not sail out into the sea from the bay, we went to the outermost island[45] located in the southeast.

The Master, who with the rest was extraordinarily pleased by his deliverance and made joyful by the welcome, took the sounding lead in hand and at the first attempt left it at the bottom of the sea.[46] Ordinary seamen took it as an evil omen, recalling that just a year had passed since through his skill provisions had been lost at the mouth of the Okhota River.

At two o'clock in the afternoon we dropped anchor behind[47] this outermost island two versts from shore.

5. Meeting Americans

On September 4, likewise in calm weather, we tried to put out to sea around the western side of this island[1] but found ourselves obliged, because of impossible westerly winds, to go back eastward to the other place. Toward four o'clock in the evening, we were fortunate finally to return once again to the previous spot, where we dropped anchor. Here the event occurred through which, unexpectedly and without searching, we got to see Americans.[2]

We had just dropped anchor when, from the cliff[3] lying south of us, we heard a loud noise, which at first we took for the roaring of a sea lion. (We did not expect any trace of human beings on this miserable island twenty miles away from the mainland.) But soon we saw two small boats being paddled from the shore to our ship. We all awaited them with the greatest eagerness and utter amazement to mark most carefully the boats' mountings, shape, and design.

When they were still half a verst away, the two men in the boats, while paddling steadily, began to deliver a long, uninterrupted oration to us in a high-pitched voice, not a word of which any of our interpreters could understand. We took it for either a prayer or a conjuration, the incantation of shamans or a ceremony welcoming us as friends,[4] since both customs are in use on Kamchatka and in the Kurile Islands, as may be seen in more detail in my *Historical Description of the Kuriles*.[5] As they paddled closer and closer, shouting continually, they began to speak to us with pauses between statements. But since no one could understand their language, we beckoned them with our hands

FIG. 19. Waxell's drawing of an Aleut with a stick of spruce with two falcon wings attached. The inscription reads, "An American in a sealskin boat." (Courtesy of the Smithsonian Institution, photo no. 85-5537; reprinted from Golder, *Bering's Voyages*, I: 149)

to come closer without fear. But they pointed their hands toward the shore to signify that we should come to them there. They also pointed to their mouths and scooped up seawater to signify that we could have food and water with them. But we beckoned to them rather to come to us. When we called *nitschi* back to them, which in Baron Lahontan's description of America means "water,"[6] they repeated it many times and pointed again to the shore to indicate undoubtedly that water was available there.

Nonetheless, one of them came quite close to us. However, before he approached us altogether, he stuck his hand into his bosom, took some iron- or lead-colored shiny earth and painted himself with it from the wings of his nose across the cheeks in the shape of two pears, and stuffed his nostrils full of grass; the wings of his nose on both sides were pierced by fine pieces of bone. Then he took a stick of spruce wood[7] lying behind him on top of the skinboat, painted red like a billiard cue and three arshins long. On this he stuck two falcon wings and bound them fast with baleen, showed it to us, and then, laughing, threw it toward our ship into the water. I cannot tell if it was meant as a sacrifice or a sign of friendship.[8] Then, for our part, we bound two Chinese tobacco pipes and Chinese glass beads to a small piece of board, and threw it in exchange to them. He picked it up, looked at it a bit, and handed it over to his companion, who put it on top of his boat. Then he became somewhat braver, came still closer to us, yet with the greatest caution, bound a whole falcon to another stick, and presented it to our Koriak interpreter, to receive from us a piece of Chinese silk and a mirror. But it was not his intention at all that we should take the bird for ourselves; rather, he wanted us to put the piece of silk between the bird's claws so that it wouldn't get wet. But when the interpreter held on to the stick and pulled the American, who held the other end in his hands, together with his boat to our vessel, he let go of the stick, and it remained in our hands. Then he got frightened and paddled a little to the side; nor did he want to come so close again. So we threw the mirror and silk to him; with that they paddled toward the shore, signaling us that we should follow so that they might give us food and drink. The whole time these two Americans remained with us, their companions on shore did not quit calling constantly and shouting in high voices, without our being able to figure out their intention.

Thereupon, after a short discussion, the boat was lowered in which I, along with Lieutenant Waxell, the Koriak interpreter, and nine sailors and soldiers, decided to go ashore. We supplied ourselves with plenty of firearms and sabers, however, and covered them all with sailcloth to cause no suspicion. We also took along biscuits, brandy, and other trifles to be able to give them gifts. Considering all these preparations, it was the greatest misfortune that we could not get ashore[9] because the beach was very rocky, the water increasingly turbulent, and the wind and the waves so heavy that only with the greatest difficulty could we keep the boat from being dashed to pieces. From the place where their boats and our presents lay without great regard strewn here and there on the beach, all the people on our approach, men as well as women (who because of the sameness of their dress could hardly be distinguished from one another), came full of amazement and friendliness toward us, not failing to beckon us constantly ashore.

But when we saw that it was hopeless for us all to get ashore, we had our interpreter and two others undress and wade through the water[10] to them to inspect a thing or two. They received the interpreter and the others in quite a friendly manner and led them by the arm very respect-fully, as if they were very important people, to the place where they had been sitting, presented them with a piece of whale blubber, and talked some with them, although neither group understood the other. In the process they often pointed over the hill, perhaps to indicate that they had come here only for our sake but that they had their homes on the other side of the hill; later, on sailing out to sea to the east around the island, we saw some huts in the distance.

But half of them remained standing by us, looked at us fixedly, and with frequent gestures invited us to join them. But when we gave them to understand by all sorts of signs how impossible it was for us to join them on land, one of them got into his boat,[11] which he had lifted with one hand and carried to the water under his arm, and came paddling to us. We welcomed him with a cup of brandy, which, imitating our ex-ample, he smartly drank up. But immediately he spat it out again, act-ing strangely about it, and did not seem at all amused by this supposed trick.

Although I had advised against this as well as against tobacco and pipes, they supposed nevertheless that the Americans had the stomachs of our seamen and tried to make up for one annoyance with a new one. They presented him with a lighted pipe of tobacco, which he, to be sure, accepted, but, displeased, he paddled away. The smartest Euro-pean would do the same if he were treated to the fly agaric,[12] rotten fish soup, and willow bark that the Kamchadals fancy so delicious.

But when the water rose up more and more along with the wind,[13] we called our people to the boat. These poor people, however, wanted their company a while longer and did not at all want to let them go to the boat. They especially showed a very great liking for our Koriak in-terpreter, whose speech and looks fully resembled theirs. At first they presented them with more whale blubber and iron-colored paint, but since they would not let themselves be moved by gifts, they tried to hold on to them by force,[14] gripping them by the arms and forcefully keeping

FIG. 20. Bering expedition landing site, Bird Island, showing the cliff rimming the inner bay into which the Russians fired three muskets over the heads of Aleuts. Abandoned fox farm cabin in foreground. (Courtesy of Edgar P. Bailey)

them away from the boat. The other party, however, took hold of the line to our boat, perhaps not out of malicious intent but pure naivete because they were unable to perceive our danger; they wanted to haul the boat with its occupants on shore, where it would have been wrecked on the rocks, and thus they brought us into the same confusion and danger. But because there was now no time to be lost in trying to keep them from their purpose with sweet talk[15] and since they were not about to let the line out of their hands by any gentle means, we immediately fired three loaded muskets[16] over their heads at the cliff.[17]

When they heard it, they all looked so stunned that, as if struck by thunder,[18] they all fell to the ground and let go of everything in their hands.

Right away our men ran through the water and luckily made it into the boat.

As funny as it was to behold their dismay, it was yet more curious that they all stood up again and scolded us that we had repaid their good-will so poorly, and with their hands they bade us be gone speedily since they wanted us no more. Some of them, in standing up, grabbed stones and held them in their hands. But we had to cut the anchor line quickly from the boat (it was caught on a rock) and returned rather displeased to the packet boat because we could not observe what we wished, but had, on the contrary, encountered what we had not expected.

We had, however, no sooner arrived on the ship than a violent storm rose from the south, and we thanked God both that we were on the ship and that it was so well sheltered from the storm. Shortly thereafter it also began to rain, and it lasted all through the night. Our Americans, on the other hand, lit a fire on shore and made us think this night about what had happened.

Here I must mention some circumstances that I observed in the space of the quarter hour[19] that we were along the beach.

The American boats are about two fathoms long, two feet high, and two feet wide on the deck, in front pointed toward the nose, but aft cornered and smooth. In appearance, the body is of poles fitted to each other at both ends but spread apart on the inside by crosspieces. On the outside, this body is covered with skins, perhaps of seals,[20] and colored black-brown. On the top, it is level; on both sides toward the keel, slanted. A shoe or keel appears to be put on underneath and at the bow is bound to the body by a vertical piece of wood or bone that serves as a bridge on which the upper surface rests.

About two arshins from the rear is a round opening, around all of which a piece of whale gut is sewn. Its outermost edge has a hollow seam made fast by a string pulled through it, by means of which it can be pulled tight or loosened like a purse. As soon as the American has seated himself in the opening with his feet stretched forward under the deck, he pulls this seam around his body like a bag and fastens it by a slipknot to keep any water from getting in. At the back lie one or more round red sticks pointed at the end and bound together, all formed in the same way as the one we got from them—for what purpose I cannot guess, unless they are used to repair the boat if something on the frame should break.[21]

The American sticks his right hand in the opening of the boat, holding the paddles in the other, and because it is so light carries it from the land to the water, and seats and fastens himself in it. For paddling, he makes use of a thick stick several fathoms long which on both ends is equipped with a blade the width of a hand. With this paddle, he strikes the water alternately to the right and to the left and in this way propels his boat with great agility even among the highest waves.

On the whole, this kind of boat is very little or not at all different from that used by the Samoyeds[22] and by the Americans in New Denmark.[23]

As concerns their persons—I counted nine people on the shore, mostly young or middle-aged—they are of average height, strong, and stocky, but rather well proportioned and fleshy on arms and legs. The hair on their heads is glossy black and hangs perfectly straight around the head. The face is brownish, a little flat and squashed. The nose is likewise flattened, yet not especially wide or large. The eyes are as black as coal, the lips thick and turned up. Moreover, they have short necks, broad shoulders, and a thick yet not paunchy torso.

They all wear sleeved shirts that reach to the calves of the legs; they are of whale gut sewn together with very subtle seams. Some have the shirt tied below the navel with a string, but others wear it loose.

Two among them were wearing boots and pants, both made after the Kamchadal fashion of seal skin and dyed brown-red with alder bark. Two had, in a sheath on their belt, in the fashion of Russian peasants, a long iron knife of very poor workmanship, which may be their own and no European fabrication. Although I asked to trade for one of their knives, by offering two, three, or more of ours in exchange (it was a matter of some consequence to me because in the event it was not their own work, it could possibly be ascertained from a mark engraved on it where they got it and with what European nation they were in commerce), an exchange did not occur, even though we had in our stores several hundred knives. From a distance, I observed very exactly the quality of this knife, when one of the Americans unsheathed it and cut a bladder in two with it, and I saw that it was of iron and also that it did not resemble any European workmanship.[24]

For this reason, it can be concluded not only that the Americans have iron ore, of which on Kamchatka there are few or no traces, but also that they know how to smelt and prepare it.[25] Nevertheless, the following reasons seem to contradict this opinion: First, if they know how to fabricate knives, how could it yet be obscure to them how to make an ax or a similar instrument for felling trees? But I learned from the trees on Cape St. Elias, which had been felled and slashed by many blunt blows, that the Americans make use of stone or bone axes like the Kamchadals, although at the same time their smoothly produced arrows as well as the well-built hut would suggest something altogether different, that at least they have to have knives, be they of iron or copper. Second, I have it from completely reliable reports that the Chukchi trade with America from the second Chukchi island.[26] Although right now, because of a misunderstanding, they themselves have refrained from this trade for several years, it is being continued by those living on the islands. The most important goods are knives and axes, which the Chukchi acquire through trade at a very high price from the Russians at Anadyrsk and then barter for a price many times higher to the Americans for sea otter, marten, and foxes, of which some have been taken to Russia by way of Anadyrsk. If the Americans did smelt iron themselves and could make said products, why should they acquire them from others at greater expense?

It is, nevertheless, very odd that the cossacks on the Anadyr River traded with the Americans before the Kamchatka Expedition collected any information about the country itself. But there is a double cause for this on the part of the cossacks: (1) their self-interest and the perjury of the commanders; and (2) fear, because anyone who in these distant places announces anything unfamiliar to benefit the Empire is forced to carry out the plan himself and instead of reaping gratitude is ruined by the loss of all his goods and property. For their part, the officers are too haughty to converse with common folk in a friendly manner, and when something is discovered, they are too negligent and disbelieving.

On my arrival in Kamchatka in 1740, I immediately made a diligent effort to obtain such information, questioning all arrivals, traders, and cossacks in the most friendly way; where it would not come out by fair means, I made them confess with brandy, the pleasant torture. But when I had bribed so many for such information that I could prove with more than twenty valid reasons where the land was nearest and where a voyage should be taken, and informed the Captain-Commander of everything, my manifold efforts were deemed unworthy even of being placed before the other officers in a council, and the entire official judgment consisted in this statement: "People talk much. Who believes cossacks? I don't trust it at all!"

But now their own journal and charts confirm such information and many a one has died and been buried as a consequence of their ignoring my advice. One might well say that the chart of the first expedition is to be trusted even less since it forgets the islands off Kamchatka opposite Oliutora[27] and the finest harbors at Avacha and before Avacha at the Uka and Oliutora rivers. Also, thirty miles from Kamchatka, according to their information, no land had been found, yet Bering's Island is only twenty miles straight to the east, and the mainland is forty miles distant.[28]

On September 5, it rained very hard in the morning. Several times in the afternoon, it seemed to clear up but always clouded over again. We could not remain anchored in this place any longer because the wind had now veered southwesterly. Accordingly, we weighed anchor about two o'clock in the afternoon and saw just then two Americans paddling in their boats toward shore, and we moved to such a place that once again we had shelter from the island toward the west. Around five o'clock, we reached a desirable place and dropped anchor again.

About half an hour later, we saw again nine Americans in their boats paddling in a line toward the ship with the same shouting and ceremonies as the first time. Yet only two approached our ship; again they gave us gifts with sticks of falcon feathers with iron-colored face paint.

On their heads, these people had hats made of tree bark, stained red and green, which resembled in shape the eyeshades people customarily put on the head: the crown was uncovered and the hats seemed to be invented only to shade the eyes from the sun.[29] Between this hat and the forehead, some had stuck colorful falcon feathers, others, reed grass,[30] in the same way as the Americans on the eastern side of Brazil have feather bundles.[31] And here again I found a clear indication that the Americans originated in Asia since the Kamchadals and Koriaks are accustomed to wear the same kinds of hats, of which I acquired several for the Kunstkammer.[32]

When these Americans understood from our many signals that we wanted one of their hats, they gave us two of them. On one was affixed a small carved image or sitting idol of bone which had a feather sticking

FIG. 21. Imperial Academy of Sciences, St. Petersburg: Library (*Bibliothek*) and Museum (*Kunstkammer*), to which Steller intended to send Aleut hats. (Courtesy of the Smithsonian Institution, photo no. 18225)

in its behind, which doubtless was to represent the tail. In exchange we presented them with a rusty iron kettle, five sewing needles, and a thread.

After they had considered the exchange and consulted each other, they headed for shore without further ceremony, lighted a big fire, and shouted loudly for a time. Then, because it soon became dark, we did not see them any more.

Here I observed again that these people deem it a curious ornament to pierce the face anywhere as we do the earlobe and to insert various stones and bones. One of these fellows had stuck diagonally through the septum of his nose a slate pencil two and a half inches long, exactly like those we use to write on slate tablets. Another had a piece of bone one inch long under the lower lip crosswise above the chin. Still another had the same kind of bone set in the forehead, and finally yet another a piece even in both sides of the nose.[33]

From these observations, it is again apparent how thoughtlessly I was contradicted when among other things I reported that I considered the Chukchi to be Americans or that Americans were staying among them, the reason being that I had learned from more than ten people that among the Chukchi there were to be found people who have set pieces of walrus teeth into their noses and cheeks. When I asked the Russians what these meant, I was told that each and every one on the mainland opposite made use of such ornaments, which I have now with my own eyes found to be the way I recorded it a year before in my *Historical Account of Cape Chukchi*.[34]

Finally, I noticed on all these persons that they have very little beard; most among them have none at all, in which characteristic they again resemble the inhabitants of Kamchatka.

But with all this there remains this question to discuss: Whether these Americans live on the mainland or on these islands. I think that these people do not live continuously on these islands, but stay only through the summer and spend the winter on the mainland.[35] The reason for this: they may be enticed to come here by the large number of birds and birds' eggs of which the Kamchadals are so very fond that, at extreme danger to life and limb, they gather them from the cliffs even though every year some of them break their necks over it. It is at any rate known about Kamchatka that of all foods whale and seal blubber is preferred as the most delectable. Now, since the seals are most numerous around these islands and also since the dead whales the sea throws out cannot make it to the mainland because the islands are in their way and thus are thrown out on the islands, it is quite believable that the people come here in the summer for this reason alone but in the winter go to the mainland. The less one can winter here for lack of wood for building and burning, the more one has reason to believe also that the island where we took on water connects with America landward in the north and that all the other islands are not far from it.

Even though on September 6 we had cloudy weather the entire day, because of winds southwest by south, which were very useful for our departure, we sailed around the eastern side between two islands and then into the sea.[36] The Americans on shore raised their voices once again in farewell, and we thought we got a glimpse of people and huts on the nearby low island[37] situated opposite to the east.

When we were a half-mile out to sea, we were especially surprised by the innumerable sea birds we caught sight of on the northern side of this island,[38] and I noted—besides the cormorants, auks, gulls, sea parrots, fulmar, and Greenland sea pigeons—an entirely black snipe with red bill and feet which continuously nodded its head like the redshank, as well as a very beautiful black pied diver never seen before,[39] together with other strange birds never seen before.

By the way, the wind was so favorable that toward two o'clock in the afternoon we were well out of sight of the mainland as well as of all the islands.

But the many whales we met with right at the beginning, of which one rose aloft upright out of the sea for over half its length, gave us indeed to understand that a storm was coming up.

6. Storms at Sea

On September 7, wind and weather were the same as on the previous day. Toward noon we were already more than twenty miles away from the last island. In the afternoon, the wind intensified, and the increased swelling of the waves forced us to take in sail. It stormed furiously all night so that we ran only under the mizzen. Given these conditions, the late fall season and the great distance from Avacha, the officers as well as the crew suddenly became discouraged. The unhealthy water already now daily reduced the number of ablebodied men, and many were heard to complain a lot about previously unheard-of adversities. Therefore, men already began to express doubts about reaching home and to raise questions about whether we should spend the winter in Japan or America, although there was really no inclination for either.

On September 8, it was cloudy all day, but the wind decreased and shifted from west by north before noon to west by south in the afternoon. Under both these winds, we therefore sailed gradually toward the south and by evening found ourselves on the Avacha parallel of 53 degrees. Overnight it turned altogether calm.

On September 9, toward morning, a light wind arose out of the east, with which we progressed until eight o'clock at one and a half to two knots, but it increased so that toward ten o'clock we continued at four knots or a mile an hour. In the morning it rained a little and at the same time it was overcast, but in the afternoon it turned very clear on the horizon, though without sunshine. According to our ship's reckoning,

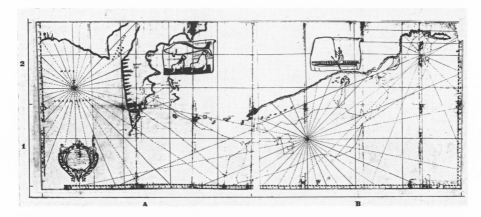

FIG. 22. Bering expedition chart, with Waxell's sketches of an Aleut and of a sea cow (top), fur seal (left), and sea lion (right). (Reprinted from Efimov, *Atlas of Geographical Discoveries*, no. 101)

we were at about twelve o'clock still 312 Dutch miles away from Avacha.

On September 10, it rained toward morning and was also overcast. However, about noon we had a little sun, and later the sky cleared up gradually on the horizon. The wind was at first south-southwest and thereafter southwest by south, and about noon we reckoned we were 298 miles from Avacha. It is remarkable that, despite lengthy and numerous experiences, some people could still not understand that this shifting of the wind was, again, caused by the proximity to land, that accordingly, without reflecting on the parallel, we should turn southerly since the land turned southerly, and at 54 degrees was doubtless to be expected. Moreover, such an observation was confirmed through seeing horned puffins, the gull called John of Ghent, and the gull called Wagel by the English,[1] flying constantly from north and west toward the south. Likewise, some seaweed came floating along, as is usual close to the land.

On September 11, the wind and weather were as on the previous day. We traveled twenty miles within 24 hours and reckoned about noon that we were yet 278 miles from Avacha. We saw signs of land today, as we did yesterday.

On September 12, the whole day was cloudy and gloomy, also, calm; the signs of birds and different floating objects were constant as before.

When we expected favorable wind about evening, we got a wind straight out of the west along with rain. At this time we got only two miles farther.

September 13 was a clear day. Toward morning a northwest-by-west wind turned up, and it continued until two o'clock in the afternoon. Then it died away. Besides, many whales were seen sporting about and augured no good.

On September 14, we had a very severe storm out of the northwest all day and night, and at noon we were obliged to drift. Our reckoning then was 258 miles[2] from Avacha.

On September 15, a pleasant day cheered us up. At noon we saw again the long-desired sun. Toward evening an unusual coolness raised our hopes for a north wind since we had been able, with the northwesterly wind from five o'clock in the morning, gradually to get back on our course, which also would have happened if we had been a few degrees farther south and twenty miles farther west in the channel[3] in which they had wrongly tried to convince themselves they were. But as it was, we were under and behind the land, which no one, however, would believe, even though toward evening an owl[4] that had come from the shore could be seen for a half-hour around our ship, as could many river gulls.[5] Toward evening several porpoises[6] were seen rushing about. They pursued their play for a quarter of an hour and gave us two thoughts: first, that we were near land and, second, that a storm was imminent, because these animals especially signal a change at sea and, as is known, are thereby impelled to such play.

On September 16, at midnight we got a southeast wind that continued until nine o'clock, but then suddenly shifted from south to west and from there to north, but from there it returned to the west, and until about three o'clock in the afternoon when it began to rain, the wind remained south-southwest. However, before noon we had sailed ahead so far with this wind that at twelve o'clock we reckoned we were yet 240 miles from Avacha. And this was our first play with the southeast wind, which we later encountered so often and became so familiar with that we actually knew its trick beforehand. In the afternoon, we saw a very great quantity of seaweed floating toward our ship from the north, the same large bunches as on August 2 and the following days along and between the American islands.

On September 17, we had violent and at the same time very change-able winds. However, the wind remained for the most part northwest by west. At noon we reckoned ourselves 234 miles from Avacha. This day we saw the birds constantly flying from the north to the west.

On September 18, we had showers, the wind southwest by west. At midday we were 229 miles from Avacha. At sunset I observed whole flocks of small snipes[7] and other land birds flying out of the north to the west.

On September 19, we enjoyed clear weather, yet it was rather cold. The wind blew northwest by west. At midday we were 226 miles away from Avacha, and at various times we saw sea beaver or otter.

On September 20, the winds and weather were as on the day before. During the night the wind died down completely.

On September 21, we enjoyed very pleasant weather and continuous sunshine; at the same time, the sea was calmer than we had observed it for two months. Toward evening there appeared for the second time the southeast wind, which, however, at one o'clock after midnight shifted to northwest by west.

On September 22, the weather was very pleasant, the wind northwest by north.

On September 23, it stormed all day and night, and we sailed north-erly with a southwest wind. This evening there died the second man on our ship, the grenadier Tretiakov.

On September 24, we had overcast weather most of the day. Toward evening we saw to our greatest terror and shock land lying in front of us at 51 degrees. The mainland and the high mountains covered with snow we saw at a distance of six to eight miles, but the numerous islands were only three to four miles before us.[8] We took bearings[9] from the land, but because we were too close and too far north and also sailing with a southwest wind straight for the land without being able to pass to the south of it, we quickly turned back into the sea toward the east. This would not have been necessary if we had taken the warnings by all the signs that we were close along the land, known for a long time and called to mind so abundantly, and if we had gone farther south. As it was, the unfortunate proposal of Master Khitrov to go still further north had, to our very ruin, almost been approved this morning, be-cause he imagined that the land extended directly to the west on the latitude of 56 degrees and also thought that we were already in the channel. It was most fortunate that we got to see the land while it was still day and before the storm hit, which occurred shortly thereafter, because otherwise we should surely have run on it during the night or else been driven by the southeast wind against our will without a chance of escape and been dashed to pieces on the shore.

In this confusion we heard by chance an odd thing: the officers began to say, according to the evidence of our reckoning, this is certainly the place where we lost Captain Chirikov. Back then, as we were for the second time sailing south, having just weathered a storm, we were told by the men that land had been sighted to the north, which, at the time, we did not believe and thus we lost the right way, as I have written. Without doubt, Captain Chirikov went ashore here. This circumstance I have already mentioned at the beginning of this descriptive account.[10]

On September 25, until noon, we let ourselves drift before an increasing and continuous storm with the lower sails, mizzen, and foresail (just as during the previous night) to get away toward the southeast from the land, in constant danger of losing spars and masts because of the very powerful wind. But in the afternoon we ran solely under the mizzen sail because we were already rather far from land and, because of the west wind, needed no longer fear being driven on the land.

On September 26, the west wind indeed subsided a bit, but the sea, set in far too great an agitation, continued to swell in the same direction, and for the third day we sailed back toward the east.[11]

On September 27, during the night, we again encountered a very violent storm with a southeast wind, but it veered to the west after an hour, continued with the greatest force, and we heard the wind charge periodically as if out of a channel with such terrible whistling, rage, and frenzy that we were every moment in danger of losing the mast or the rudder or even of receiving damage to the body of the ship itself from the power of the waves because the waves struck like shot out of a cannon, and we expected the final blow and death every instant. That veteran steersman Andreas Hesselberg could not remember, out of his fifty years of experience at sea, ever having endured a storm like this one.

On September 28, the storm continued with even greater violence, with mixed hail, lightning, and rain. For the fifth day, we continued to drift back to the southeast.

On September 29, it seemed throughout the day as if the storm would let up. But about ten o'clock at night, the wind, which had suddenly shifted to the southeast, heralded once more the most horrible storm, thereupon turned once more to the west, and continued as before.

On September 30, at five o'clock in the morning, we got a storm out of the southwest so redoubled in violence as we had met with neither before nor later. We could not possibly imagine that one could be greater or that we would be capable of enduring it. Every moment we expected the shattering of our ship, and no one could sit, lie down, or stand. No one could remain at his station, but we were drifting under God's terrible power wherever the enraged heavens wanted to take us. Half our men lay sick and weak, and the other half was healthy out of necessity but thoroughly crazed and maddened by the terrifying movements of the sea and ship.

There was much praying, to be sure, but the curses accumulated during ten years in Siberia would allow no granting of a prayer. From the ship, we had not a fathom of visibility because we lay buried continuously between the cruel waves. Moreover, we could neither cook nor had we anything cold to eat except half-burned biscuits, which were already in short supply. Such being the situation, neither courage nor counsel was to be found in anyone. All too late did they begin to regret that affairs had not been handled properly, that they had blundered in this or that. Let no one think that the dangers of this situation are exaggerated, but believe rather that even the cleverest pen would find itself incapable of describing our misery sufficiently.

On October 1, this terrible southwesterly storm continued with the same violence. And now, for the very first time, the officers began to think that if God would help with surviving the storm, they would seek a harbor in America, considering that it was late fall, the weather too severe and variable, that we had been driven back too far to the east, and that most of the men were sick and weak, because to go a few degrees farther south was too far out of the way for them. But I could not possibly believe them sincere in such thinking because everybody's possessions and servants[12] were in Kamchatka.

I saw, on September 24, two phenomena that I had never seen before in my life, namely, the *ignes lambentes*—Castor and Pollux—called by seamen St. Elmo's fire, and then the most terrifying rapid movement of clouds, which during the storm shot like arrows before our eyes.[13] It even happened that the clouds shot out of two directions toward each other with the same agility.

On October 2, the storm began to come to an end, but more than 24 hours were needed for the sea to calm down because of the too violent swells; the wind remained southwest and the air gloomy. Since September 24, we had been driven back toward the east more than fifty miles. We had 24 sick and two dead.

What I thought would happen did. Already they were talking again of Kamchatka, where they wished God would let us go this year—because we are so stubborn, no matter how much our private interests may thereby suffer.[14] But our joy was short-lived. Toward ten o'clock at night, we got a southeast wind once more with the usual symptoms and a violent storm. Because of it, people's minds again became as loose and unsteady as their teeth were from scurvy.[15]

On October 3, we drifted under the mizzen sail because of the very violent storm. Moreover, for the first time the air was very clear and extraordinarily cold.

On October 4, it began to be a little calmer, the air remained clear and very cold, although we had sunshine for several hours, and we used the lower sails. However, our joy was again short-lived, being all of a sudden interrupted by a southeast wind with rain and later by a violent storm out of the southwest. Yet we were as well accustomed to storms as we were to daily deaths.

On October 5, we sailed under the mizzen sail because of the all too violent storm. Moreover, the air was very cold and extraordinarily clear.[16]

On October 6, we likewise moved under the mizzen, for although the storm was somewhat diminished, the sea was nonetheless still very high. We saw the sun during most of the day, yet some storms bringing hail and snow occurred as well, and soon thereafter we saw rainbows twice. At the same time the air was very cold. Toward evening, we saw many small sharks[17] moving around our ship for the first time on this voyage. At night the wind subsided. This day our ship's brandy came to an end.

On October 7, the air was cold and clear. Toward morning around seven o'clock, we began to use the lower sails again, but with poor success because of the very high swelling sea. The wind was southwest by west.

On October 8, during the day the wind as well as the weather was like the previous day's. At three o'clock in the afternoon, however, the nasty southeast wind suddenly picked up with terrific force. Two hours later, with a west wind, we again encountered a very severe storm with mixed rain and hail. It seemed then as if they would finally resolve to go to America since during this storm we were sailing even with the lower sails to the northeast.

On October 9, the wind and storm became yet more violent. We were driven all day to the northeast, yet we had sunshine all day and a very clear night.

On October 10, the storm continued with the same violence. Lieutenant Waxell was intent on persuading the Captain-Commander— who, because of having rested too much,[18] was laid up with a very severe case of scurvy again—that he should agree that we should approach the American continent to spend the winter there since the impossibility of reaching Kamchatka[19] was obvious. Also, within a few days we would no longer be capable of managing sails and ship because of the many sick, and to all appearances each and every one would perish in the sea with all belongings. But the Captain-Commander, who had been deceived so many times, now trusted the one as little as the other, and included his total opinion in the order to make a vow and to collect money, to give one half to the Russians for the expedition church in Avacha, but the other half to the Lutherans for the church in Viborg.[20]

On October 11, we got very beautiful clear weather and sunshine, the wind west by northwest, but we sailed southwest. Toward night the wind died completely, and at one o'clock it became as calm as on September 21. But after midnight a strong south wind started up. With it we sped so fast to the west that we traveled one and three-fourths miles within a single hour.

On October 12, we sailed with this wind, west by north. But toward noon the wind turned southwesterly, and about six o'clock in the evening we had, once again, a violent storm with snow, rain, and hail. We also saw a rainbow.

On October 13, the storm died down. Because of contrary west winds, we tacked westerly between south and north. Before noon we often saw the sun, but in the afternoon it began alternately to rain and hail in sheets.[21] Toward evening we saw a rainbow again.

On October 14, the sea became completely calm. At the same time, the air was clear, the sun shone, but it was rather cold. Again this day there was talk about the American mainland. But since our officers talk constantly about whatever comes into their heads, I am not going to believe their talk until they consider beforehand what they want to say, especially since up to this point they have not had any thoughts, since they only think, do, and talk about what they see and as far as they see with their eyes.

On October 15, we had sunshine all day, moderate northwest winds, and a calm sea.

On October 16, the weather was very pleasant and warm, the sea very calm. Toward evening, at six o'clock, God sent a strong south wind with which we sailed away first at three, then at four knots. In the night the wind veered easterly so that we continued on at five, six, and six and a half knots. As soon as it became daylight, the wind blew northeast and became so strong that we dared to proceed only with the lower sails.

On October 17, it rained all day. We had now for the first time for 24 hours been sailing with a steady northeast wind, although it was too strong. After we had traveled 24 miles within twenty hours, the wind became so strong that we were forced to drift from four o'clock in the evening. At night it stormed rather hard, but began to calm down in the morning.

On October 18, it was by turns overcast yet very cold, the sea rather quiet, the wind northwest by north. We sailed all day more than two and two and a half knots, southwest by west. Now we had 32 sick. But the sick as well as men ablebodied only out of necessity were extremely depressed over the variable winds.

On October 19, the winds, course, and weather were as on the day before. This day grenadier Kiselev died.

On October 20, the wind, course, and weather were the same as before, yet it stormed during the night. This day, the *sluzhiv* Kharitonov died.

On October 21, the winds, course, and weather were all the same. But toward evening, we had a storm, and the soldier Luka Zaviakov died.

On October 22, we had clear weather, sunshine, heavy frost, a westerly wind, and we adjusted the course north by east directly toward the mainland, which all of a sudden had been firmly decided because Lieutenant Waxell had been told that only fifteen barrels of water were left, of which two had become defective and mostly drained out when crewmen had tried belatedly to fix the hoops on them. Before the voyage, wooden hoops on the water barrels were to be replaced with iron ones since the wooden hoops decay in a ship on a long trip. But in their hurry to get under way, the officers had declared them good enough without foreseeing the present circumstances.[22]

On October 23, the wind shifted, and with the wind the zeal of the officers to go to America. So before noon we sailed to the north with a southeasterly wind and in the afternoon and night with an east wind, so that, despite bad weather and hail falling in sheets, we traveled 31 miles within 24 hours, and thus we sailed away from the American shoreline with thirteen water barrels, either to reach Kamchatka or to run aground at the first opportunity at the first and best island. This alternative was discussed openly so as to dampen the spirits of ordinary seamen and the sick still more.

On October 24, the wind and weather were the same as the day before. But toward evening the wind became northerly. With it we came so far that in Waxell's judgment[23] we were 134 miles from Avacha and in second mate Iushin's, 122 miles, and we were gradually nearing the 53d parallel since they did not wish to find any more land in the way. The decision was made to remain steady at 52 degrees so that in the event of an extreme shortage of water, we could use all the winds along the land of Kamchatka. If the wind became northerly, we could sail to the first and second Kurile islands and anchor there. But if it became southerly, we could more readily sail into Avacha harbor. As for east winds, they were favorable for anything.

This plan, which was brought up by Lieutenant Waxell, was indeed the most reasonable thing in case we wanted to reach Avacha and not let something else deter us. The future, however, will show how steady they were in this plan and for what reason (of which, however, not a one seemed ready at hand even as a pretense), and on whose instigation, five days later they criminally deviated from it. This was the reason for our staying out all winter and for the ruin of many men and the ship—nay, even of all—had God not preserved us by an evident miracle, wherein the officers have as little part as their own understanding and conscious-ness convinced them to have. Moreover, danger and death suddenly got the upper hand on our ship to such an extent that not only were the sick dying but also men claiming to be healthy, who, on being relieved at their posts, dropped dead from exhaustion, for which the small portion of water, the lack of biscuit and brandy, the cold, dampness, exposure, vermin, fear, and terror were not the least causes.

On October 25, we had very clear weather and sunshine, but even so it hailed at various times in the afternoon. We were surprised in the morning to discover a large tall island[24] at 51 degrees to the north of us, which on the outward voyage we had had 40 miles to the east of us.[25] At midday we were at 50°35' N.

On October 26, the sea was very calm, the air cloudy and frosty, and at various times we had snow and hail intermittently. Toward noon we reckoned we were still 108 miles from Avacha.

On October 27, we got a south-southwest wind toward one o'clock in the night and sailed northwest with it night and day to reach the agreed-on latitude of 52 degrees; at midday we reckoned we were still 90 miles from Avacha. In the afternoon the wind became so severe that it changed to a storm. But since now we had become bolder and had come to know our ship and masts better, we nevertheless kept the top-sails up all day.

We could now observe very clearly that we were within the channel because the waves were not as high even when a storm had arisen and because the winds were no more subject to such quick changes. I also observed that the storms were not as severe as in September with the same strong winds. The reason for this is that the air, being heavier and colder, causes a greater pressure on the water.

Therefore I concluded that this phenomenon—namely, that waves driven by winds of the same force reach up the shore twice as high in fall and winter as they usually do in spring and summer—is caused by the pressure from the center toward the periphery[26] because of the re-sistance of the shore. Furthermore, the air is purified in autumn through frequent hail and snow squalls, and these, in falling down, subdue by their weight the swelling of the waves. This same activity also explains the fact that now the air is clear and bright, whereas, by contrast, in spring and summer there is nothing but fog and gloomy air, since the west, southwest, and south winds, which mostly blow continually in spring and summer, fill the air with nothing but moisture that even by the occasional north wind is only driven here and there but not entirely blown away. On the other hand, the moisture is condensed in various forms by this wind's coldness and is precipitated out of the air as hail or snow. Therefore, too, the air becomes clearer after each squall and subsequently remains calm for a while, until new moisture has collected in the same place.

On October 28, we were astonished again in the morning by a novelty: when day broke, we saw a great change in the water, from which we could distinctly conclude that we must be near land. When the lead[27] was let down, we found ourselves at a depth of fourteen fathoms. Shortly afterwards the air cleared up, and we saw an island lying before us and in our way at a distance of one mile, which lay northeast and southwest in relation to the land of America, not very high, but low land whose shore was flat and sandy.[28]

It is apparent that we perceived God's gracious help for the second time since we would have been done for if we had come here a few hours earlier in the gloomy night or if God had not even now pulled up the fog. We could very well conclude that besides this island yet others had been and were still lying here and there along our route, which we sailed by in the night without realizing it, which had indeed been manifested by seaweed continually floating toward us from shore and also by the fact that during these days a diver, called *starik*,[29] came flying aboard ship at nighttime. It passes the night in cliffs and, like an owl, flies during the day against everything it sees indistinctly close by. That is why they are caught alive by hand in large numbers around Avacha. A person supplied with a coat simply sits down close to one; they are accustomed to assemble under the coat as if it were a prepared nest.

Here we were fortunate that Master Khitrov's disastrous plan was not accepted. He wanted to stand at anchor here in the open sea, set out the boat, and haul water from shore, notwithstanding that we all together consisted of ten weak men still able to give a hand who would not have been able to retrieve an anchor from the bottom. Just as, in the storm following three hours later, we would have found our common grave here in the waves.

On October 29, we continued our course with the same wind. It rained at times throughout the day.

In the morning hours on October 30, at a latitude of 50 degrees and several minutes, we sighted once more two adjacent islands separated from one another by a narrow channel, and these were taken to be the first two Kuriles,[30] primarily according to statements given and features cited by the Kamchatkan inhabitants. But because no one would dare to affirm it with certainty, our officers cast it thoughtlessly to the four winds and also would not listen to those who thought they saw the mainland beyond, although the matter could also be concluded from four other signs: (1) the many sea otters that appeared around our ship, which during our voyage we had never encountered so frequently and are so abundant around the Kurile Islands; (2) that we suddenly got a west wind as a sign that we were along land; (3) the observed latitude, which is the same as that of the first Kurile island; (4) the thick fog in the west over the land, whereas in the east it was clear.

If we now compare the position of Lopatka and the first two islands with the course of five days straight north from there and the distance covered, also comparing it with that distance that we traversed on a west-by-south course to Bering's Island, as well as with the distance of Bering's Island twenty miles opposite from the mouth of the Kamchatka River, one can see without any doubt that we had been at the first two Kurile islands, although the officers to this hour wish neither to know nor to believe it. Just as they will forever owe an answer[31] to the question why they went up north to 56 degrees and consequently revoked their own resolve not to go needlessly above 52 degrees, therefore also having laid the basis for our staying out and the destruction of the ship.

Consequently, against all reason, we sailed north because, as Master Khitrov said to Lieutenant Waxell, the reckoning of longitude would not hold good since they still calculated more than 60 miles to Avacha. And they therefore would rather gamble with our well-being than give the impression of having erred in this, even though as soon as an error is concealed and not indicated, the whole chart as well as the reckoning becomes incorrect and uncertain. On such a long trip, with so many storms and currents and so much tacking, a mistake of 34 miles would not at all be interpreted amiss, since too precise an accuracy would arouse in intelligent people either the impression of a miracle or the suspicion of humbuggery; especially since it is known that the method used to determine the longitude, lacking a better one, was indeed the best but subject to a lot of inaccuracies.

But it appears from many circumstances that there was concealed behind the decision a very secret reason for personal intentions: they wanted to go north to be able to pretend an urgent necessity for sailing into the mouth of the Kamchatka River and not to Avacha. These intentions could fairly clearly be deduced in part from the faulty communication with the Captain-Commander as well as the mutual jealousy between Lieutenant Waxell and Master Khitrov. And therefore our subsequent ruin is to be imputed more to artificial than to natural winds!

On October 31, November 1, 2, and 3, nothing noteworthy occurred, except that our sick were suddenly dying off very quickly and numerously and we could hardly manage the ship any more or make alterations in the sails. We sailed, however, to the north, up to 51, 52, 53, 54, 55, to 56 degrees—utterly betrayed by two people.[32]

On November 4, in the middle of the night, we sailed west by south with serviceable winds.

On the morning of November 5, sail was ordered to be shortened to avoid running aground. Everyone stood on deck and looked around for the land because the matter was announced with very mathematical certainty.

To the astonishment of us all, it came to pass that at nine o'clock land was sighted.[33]

7. Running Aground on Bering Island

*H*ow great and extraordinary was the joy of everyone over this sight is indescribable. The half-dead crawled out to see it. From our hearts we thanked God for his favor. The very sick Captain-Commander was himself not a little cheered, and everyone spoke about how he intended to take care of his health and to take a rest after suffering such terrible hardships. Cups of brandy, here and there secretly concealed, were produced to sustain the pleasure. We heard trumpeted forth with the voice of a herald the coolly spoken words, "If there had been a thousand navigators, they could not have hit it within a hair's breadth like this in their reckoning. We are not even half a mile off."

Sketches of Avacha were taken in hand. The land was found to agree completely with the sketches: Isopa, Cape Shipunski, the mouth of the harbor, and the lighthouse[1] were pointed out. Although they could have known according to the reckoning that we were at the very least at 55 degrees and regardless of the fact that Avacha was still two degrees farther south, the course was set toward the north because they saw a cape they called Shipunski.

When we had sailed around the imagined Isopa, which was the outermost point of the first island, and were in the inlet between the first and second island, whose channel we could not yet see to regard them as islands, it happened that the noon sun prompted an observation, according to which we were between 55 and 56 degrees, north latitude; consequently, we began to doubt, not unreasonably, that this was the region around Avacha. They endeavored to go back around the southeast end of the first island, which we had considered to be Isopa, but in vain, though they tried, tacking, until evening. Toward evening we turned to the north to get away from the land because we expected a storm, which indeed turned up in the night.

Since the sails remained standing on the mast and topmast as they had stood during the day, not bound up, and could not be taken in by the weak remnant of men in the rising storm in the middle of the night, the shrouds of the mainmast were torn to pieces by the mighty force of the wind and the sails so that in the morning, after the restless and stormy night had changed into a most pleasant day and weather, we did not dare to carry as much sail as we could and needed to carry.

Therefore, on November 6, Master Khitrov, having previously brought the Lieutenant to his point of view and persuaded the subordinate officers and ordinary seamen, proposed that the Captain-Commander, in consideration of the late time, the bad weather, the ruined shrouds, the useless mast, the distance to Avacha, and the small number of sick and feeble sailors and soldiers, should hold a council in which it would be resolved to go ashore in a bay before us in the west where a harbor was conjectured to be at a distance of six miles as determined by the naked eye. And this was then also brought about in the following way: the Captain-Commander insisted that we should attempt to reach the port since we had already borne and hazarded so much and even now had still six barrels of water and could use the foremast and proceed with the lower sail. Both officers argued against his opinion and insisted on going ashore in the bay, having won over the subordinate officers and crew to this plan, who consented to it and were willing to put their signatures to the decision if, as unknowledgeable individuals, they could be assured positively that this land was Kamchatka. If it was not, they would be willing to risk the utmost and work to their last hour.

Nevertheless, some people, by smooth as well as harsh words, were made to sign against their will because—Master Khitrov professing that if this were not Kamchatka, he would let his head be chopped off—the matter now depended on a very few.

Then the Captain-Commander ordered the adjutant, at that time reduced in rank to sailor, presently Lieutenant Ovtsin,[2] to express his opinion. But when he concurred in the Captain-Commander's opinion, the two officers answered: "Out! Shut up, you dog, you son of a bitch!"[3] So he had to leave the council.

At last, according to rank, my turn came also. But reflecting on Ovtsin's example, I answered: "I have not been consulted about anything from the start, and my advice will not be taken if it is not just as you want it. Besides, the gentlemen themselves say I am no seaman, so I would rather say nothing."

Then I was asked if I would not at least, as a credible person (which I was now for the first time considered), add a written statement attesting to the sickness and miserable condition of the crew, which in good conscience I agreed to do.

And thus it was decided to enter the bay and land there, but from there to send for posthorses for the transport of the crew to Nishnei.[4] Although the site contradicted the opinion that this could be Kamchatka because the mainland of Kamchatka lies northeast-southwest from Cape Chukchi to Lopatka, whereas Bering's Island lies northwest-southeast, still hope remained that it could be one of the Kamchatkan capes, most of which lie in the aforesaid direction. Although the land seemed too large for a cape and none on Kamchatka is known to surpass Shipunski, which is 15 miles long, this island could at least be estimated at 25 miles by eyesight,[5] and, besides, other points of land extended from it way out to sea so that by all rights it could be considered rather a land apart than a cape. Although it could and should be decided from all this that it neither was nor could be the land of Kamchatka or a cape, and, besides, no one on our ship professed to know it, the false notion from the first expedition reassured everyone that no island could be found this close to Kamchatka at this latitude, where exploration had been undertaken at sea for fifty miles to the east.

Therefore we sailed into the bay straight to shore without further concern about anything.

When toward four o'clock in the evening we got so close to land that we were but a mile away yet for three hours no officer had appeared on deck (as customary in all dangerous circumstances) and they all were gently and sweetly asleep, I went to the Captain-Commander and asked that he might please order that at least one of the officers be at his watch to look for a spot where we could drop anchor because it appeared that they intended to drift ashore without further precaution. Whereupon both were called on deck but did not show any greater care than to order holding straight for the shore.

When later, toward sunset, we had gotten within two versts of shore, they began to lower the lead[6] and advanced a verst closer, where finally at nine fathoms they dropped anchor. By now it was nighttime but very bright from the moonlight, when after the lapse of a half-hour such a heavy surf came up at this place that the ship was tossed back and forth like a ball, on the point of hitting bottom, and the anchor rope broke so that we could think of nothing but the ship's being smashed to pieces on the bottom. The confusion became still greater because of the constant breaking of the waves, the cries and lamentations, so that we knew neither who should give orders nor who was being ordered. All they did, terrified and gripped by fear of death, was to shout that the anchor should be cut and a new one thrown into the surf.

When they had lost two anchors in half a quarter-hour, the present Lieutenant Ovtsin with the then-boatswain came at last and forbade the casting of any more anchors because it was to no avail as long as we were tossed hither and yon between the waves on the reef, but they advised rather to let the ship float. When we were across[7] the reefs and surf, the aforesaid men who kept their wits and could make reasonable decisions let the last anchor drop, and we were situated between the surf and the shore as in a calm lake, suddenly calm and free of all fear of being stranded.

How strange were the positions held and how wise the speeches made during this time can be concluded from the fact that some, while in obvious danger to their lives, could not keep from laughing. One asked, "Is the water very salty?" as if death were sweeter in sweet water. Another cried out to encourage the men: "Oh, we are all done for! O God, our ship! A disaster has befallen our ship!" And God now revealed the resolute hearts that had been bursting with courage before!

The biggest speechmaker and adviser in all things kept himself hidden until others, with God's help, had found counsel. Then he, too, started to encourage the men that they should not be afraid. But he was pale as a corpse in his resoluteness.[8]

In this confusion, once again a bit of folly occurred. Although we had carried with us for some days several dead soldiers and the dead trumpeter to bury them ashore, they were now flung without ceremony head over heels into the sea since some superstitious persons, at the start of the terror, considered the dead as the cause of the rising sea.

All through the night, it was very pleasant and bright.

On November 7, we again had a very pleasant bright day and north-west winds.

This morning I packed up as much of my baggage as I could get together, and because now I clearly saw that our ship could not hold beyond the first severe storm, when it must be driven either into the sea or on shore and broken into pieces, I went ashore first, together with Plenisner, my cossack,[9] and several sick men.

We were not yet on the beach when something struck us as strange, namely, some sea otters came from shore toward us into the sea, which some of us at first from a distance took for bears, others for wolverines, but afterwards got to know only too well.

As soon as I was ashore, Plenisner went hunting with a shotgun, but I reconnoitered the natural environment,[10] and, when I had made various observations, returned toward evening to the sick, where we also found the Lieutenant very weak and faint. We treated ourselves to tea, whereby I said to the Lieutenant, "God knows if this is Kamchatka."

But he answered me: "What else would it be? We will soon send for posthorses. But we will let the ship be brought by cossacks to the mouth of the Kamchatka River. We can always raise the anchors. The first priority is that we save the men."

During this time Plenisner came, related what he had observed, and brought a half-dozen ptarmigans,[11] which he sent to the Captain-Commander with the Lieutenant to invigorate him through this fresh food. I, however, sent him some nasturtium plants and brooklime[12] for a salad.

Meanwhile, two cossacks and a cannoneer came who had killed two sea otters and two seals, news that appeared quite extraordinary to us, and we reproached them for having taken the pelts and not bringing the meat in for our refreshment. Whereupon they fetched a seal because it appeared to them better to eat than the sea otter.

When it was evening, I cooked a few ptarmigan as a soup and ate it with Plenisner, young Waxell, and my cossack. During this time, Plenisner made a hut of driftwood and an old sail. Under it we slept over-night together with the sick.

On November 8, we enjoyed pleasant weather once more.

This morning Plenisner and I made an agreement that he should shoot birds while I was to look for other things that would be usable as food, but toward noon we should meet one another at this place.

At first I went with my cossack to the east along the beach, gathered various natural specimens, and chased a sea otter, whereas my cossack shot eight blue foxes[13] whose numbers and fatness and also the fact that they were not at all shy surprised me extraordinarily. And since I saw at the same time on the beach many manatees,[14] which I had never seen before—nor could I even know what kind of an animal it was since half of it was constantly under water—and since my cossack, to the question whether this was not the *plevun* or *makoai*[15] of the Kamchadals (about which I had gathered only verbal information), answered that this animal existed nowhere on Kamchatka, and since at the same time I did not notice the slightest tree or shrub, I came to doubt that this could possibly be Kamchatka, but was perhaps an island, in which opinion the sea clouds over in the south confirmed me still more, that this land was not wide and accordingly was an island everywhere surrounded by water.

Toward noon I came to our hut. After I had eaten there with Plenisner, we both decided to go with our cossack to the west along the beach and look around for woods or timber. But we did not find the least bit. On the other hand, we saw several sea otters and killed some blue foxes and ptarmigans, and on our way home we sat down by a small stream, treated ourselves to tea, and thanked God from the heart that we had sufficient water and firm ground again, whereby we reflected on everything—on what strange things had happened to us, and on the unjust proceedings of various men.

Today an attempt was made by bringing out the anchors, large and small, as many as we had, to make the ship as secure as possible, and the ship did not come ashore.

In the evening as we sat around a campfire, having eaten our meal, a blue fox came and before our very eyes took away two ptarmigans—the first instance of so many future tricks and thefts.

Through the following words, I encouraged my sick and feeble cossack and thereby made a start of our future comradeship, since he regarded me as the cause of his misfortune and reproached me for my curiosity, which had brought me in this misery: "Cheer up!" I said. "God will help. Even if this is not our country, we still have hope of getting there. You will not die of hunger. If you cannot work and wait on me, I will wait on you. I know your honest heart and what you have done for me. Everything I have is yours also. Just ask and I will share with you half of all I have until God helps."

But he said: "Good enough. I will serve your majesty with pleasure. But you have brought me into this misery. Who forced you to go with these people? Could you not have enjoyed the good life on the Bolshaia River?"

I laughed heartily at his candor and said: "Thank God, we are both alive. If I have dragged you into this misery, then you have also, with God's help, a faithful friend and benefactor in me. My intentions were good, Thoma. So let yours be good also. After all, you do not know what could have happened to you at home."

Meanwhile, I let this conversation serve to concern myself about how we could shelter ourselves against winter by building a hut, if this country should not be Kamchatka but an island. In the evening, therefore, I began to discuss with Plenisner that we should build a hut in any case, and, no matter how circumstances might turn out, we would stand by each other in word and deed as good friends. Even though he did not want to agree with my opinion that this was an island, he pretended to, in order not to depress me, and consented to my proposal to build a hut.

On November 9, the wind was easterly, the weather rather tolerable.

In the morning we went out to scout for a site and to gather wood, and we surveyed the spot where we later built and the whole command spent the winter and put up their dwellings. However, we spent altogether too much time killing foxes, of which Plenisner and I killed 60 in a day, partly slaying them with an ax, partly stabbing them with a Iakut *palma*.[16]

Toward evening we went back to our old hut, where we encountered more sick who had been brought ashore.

On November 10, the wind was easterly, the weather clear before noon, overcast in the afternoon, and in the night the wind blew a lot of snow around.

We carried all our baggage a verst away to the site that we had selected the day before for building a dwelling. During this time, a number of sick were brought ashore from the ship, among them also the Captain-Commander, who spent this evening and night under a tent. Together with others I was with him, and I was amazed at his composure and strange contentment.

He asked what I thought of this land.

I replied, "It does not look like Kamchatka to me." I explained that the abundance and tame self-possession of the animals alone clearly indicated that it must be a sparsely inhabited or entirely uninhabited land. Nonetheless, it could not be far from Kamchatka, since the land plants I had observed here were precisely the same in number, species, and size as in Kamchatka, whereas, on the other hand, the most peculiar plants discovered in America were not to be found here in similar locales. Besides, I had found a poplar window shutter with cross moldings brought some years ago at high tide and washed over with sand at the place where we later built our huts. I showed it and at the same time drew attention to the fact that it was certainly Russian workmanship and undoubtedly from the *ambars* erected at the mouth of the Kamchatka River, and it might well be that this was Cape Kronotski, which, by all sensible reasons and experience—though reliable information was wanting—was the most likely place. But still I did not refrain from expressing the doubts I had about it because of another experience. I showed a piece of a fox trap I had found the first day on the beach, in which, instead of iron teeth, there were *zubki*,[17] or teeth, of a shell[18] that authors call Entale.[19] I mentioned not having any information that this shell was found on Kamchatka, and I had not seen any either. Rather, it was to be supposed that it had drifted here from America and that this invention had been attached for lack of iron, since through trade in Kamchatka iron teeth and pins could be found in abundance among all Kamchadals, and I had not received any word of such an invention in spite of all my inquiries. At the same time I also disclosed my view with regard to the unknown sea animal, the manatee, and the character of the sea clouds opposite in the south.

Whereupon he replied, "The ship probably cannot be saved. May God spare us our longboat!"

Toward evening, after we had eaten with the Captain-Commander the ptarmigans that Plenisner had shot during the day, the assistant surgeon Betge and I came to an agreement: that if he liked, he could stay with us, for which he thanked me. And thus our company was four men strong.

So we walked to our new homesite, sat by a campfire, and over a cup of tea discussed how we would put our plan into effect. To that end, we erected a small hut, which I covered with my two overcoats and an old blanket. We covered the cracks on the sides with dead foxes that we had killed that day and had lying about in heaps. Then we went to bed.

But Betge went to the Captain-Commander.

About midnight a violent wind arose that brought a lot of snow with it, blew off our roof, and chased Plenisner, my cossack, and me from our beds.

We ran all along the seashore in the night, gathered driftwood together, brought it to a pit like a grave dug for two people, and decided to spend the night here. We put crosspieces of wood over the top, covered the roof with our clothes, coats, and blankets, made a fire to keep us warm, and went to sleep. God be thanked, we spent the night very well in this way.

The next day, November 11, I went to the sea and hauled up a seal, whose fat I cooked with peas and consumed with my three comrades, who during this time fabricated two shovels and started to enlarge our "grave."

In the afternoon, the Captain-Commander was carried to us on poles and had a tent of sailcloth put up on the spot that we at first picked out for our dwelling, and we treated him, as well as the other officers who came to our "grave," to tea.

Toward evening both officers went back to the ship, and Master Khitrov proposed to the Lieutenant to spend the winter aboard ship in the open sea since they would have there more warmth and comfort than ashore, where, lacking wood, they would have to endure the winter under a tent. And this proposal was accepted as very reasonable, although three days later the Master came ashore of his own volition and could not be made to go back aboard ship even under orders when he was supposed to beach the ship.

At any rate, we enlarged our dwelling in the earth by digging, and we strenuously gathered wood everywhere on the beach for its roof. Every evening we put up a light roof, and we acquired the fifth man, assistant constable Roselius, for our company. Several of the rank and file who still had some strength left also began to dig out a four-cornered "grave" in the frozen sand, and they covered it the next day with double sails to keep the sick under it.

On November 12, we worked busily on our house and saw also that others, following our example, dug out a third dwelling for themselves in the same way, which later got its name from its initiator, the boatswain Aleksei Ivanov.

That day many sick were brought from the ship, among them some who, like the cannoneer, died as soon as they came into the air, others in the boat on the crossing over like the soldier Savin Stepanov, others once on shore like the sailor Sylvester.[20]

This afternoon for the first time with Plenisner and Betge, I went hunting or, as we afterwards called it in Siberian, on the *promysel*. We clubbed four sea otters, of which we hid half in the river which afterwards received the name Sea Otter Creek;[21] the field on which they were killed became Sea Otter Field.[22] The meat, together with the pelts and entrails, we carried home.

We got home at night, made various tasty dishes from the liver, kidney, heart, and meat, and dined on them with thanks and prayers that God might not deprive us of this food in the future and thereby force us to feed on the stinking carcasses of the hated foxes, which, for this reason, we did not intend to kill off but wanted only to frighten.

But already we considered the precious otter pelts as a useless burden that had lost their value, and because we did not have time to dry and prepare them, they were thrown down from one day to the next until they finally spoiled entirely, together with many other skins, and were chewed up by the foxes. On the other hand, we began to value some things more highly that formerly we had had little or no regard for, such as axes, knives, awls, needles, thread, shoelaces, shoes, shirts, stockings, poles, rope, and the like, which many a one would formerly not have deigned to pick up.

We realized that our character, knowledge, and other superior traits would in the future neither entitle us to respect and preference before others, nor be sufficient to maintain our lives. Therefore, before shame and necessity forced us, we ourselves resolved to work according to the strength we still had left and to do what we could, so as not to be laughed at later or to wait first for an order.

Thus we five Germans[23] also entered into a community of goods among ourselves concerning the victuals we still had left and with it one household management that in the end we might not fall short. Of the others—three cossacks and the late Captain-Commander's two servants who later joined us—although not treating them as before, we nevertheless demanded that they obey when we decided something together since, after all, they got all the household goods and other necessities from us.

Meanwhile, we began to call each and all by their patronymic and first names to win over the men so that if something unfortunate should occur in the future, we could count more on their loyalty and be a jump ahead. And we soon saw that Peter Maximovich was more obliging than Petrusha[24] had been earlier.

Besides, although we came to an agreement among ourselves this evening about how we would arrange our housekeeping in the future in case this or that misfortune occurred, since the hope of getting to Asia, so far as we were concerned, was not altogether abandoned, we discussed the unfortunate circumstances in which we all had been placed in such a short time that, setting aside the routine work belonging to everyone, we were now bound to work in a way we were not used to just to maintain a difficult life. Nonetheless, we admonished each other not to lose heart and, with the greatest possible cheerfulness and earnestness, to do everything necessary for our own happiness as well as for the welfare of others and by our efforts to support in all sincerity the strength and initiative of all the rest.

This day I took over to the Captain-Commander a young sea otter, still nursing on its mother, and recommended it to him as persuasively as possible, that he might order it to be prepared for him for lack of fresh food.

But he declared a very great aversion for it and wondered at my taste,[25] which was adapted to the circumstances of time and place, and he preferred to refresh himself as long as possible with ptarmigan, of which he got more from our company than he could eat.

On November 13, we continued our building project[26] and divided into three parties. The first went to work to bring the sick and provisions from the ship; others dragged home large logs four versts from Wood Creek.[27] I and a sick cannoneer remained at home. I took over the cooking, while he constructed a sled with which to haul wood and other necessities.[28]

And everywhere we looked on nothing but depressing and terrifying sights.

Even before they could be buried, the dead were mutilated by foxes that sniffed at and even dared to attack the sick—still alive and help-less—who were lying on the beach everywhere without cover under the open sky. One screamed because he was cold, another from hunger and thirst, as the mouths of many were in such a wretched state from scurvy that they could not eat anything on account of the great pain because the gums were swollen up like a sponge, brown-black and grown high over the teeth and covering them.

The foxes, which now turned up among us in countless numbers, became accustomed to the sight of men and, contrary to habit and na-ture, ever tamer, more wicked, and so malicious that they dragged apart all the baggage, ate the leather sacks, scattered the provisions, stole and dragged away from one his boots, from another his socks and trousers, gloves, coats, all of which yet lay under the open sky and for lack of ablebodied men could not be protected. They even dragged off iron and other implements that were of no use to them. There was nothing they did not sniff at and steal from, and it seemed that these evil animals would chastise us more and more in the future, as actually happened. For this punishment perhaps the popular Kamchatkan fox skins may be responsible, and thus, like the Philistines,[29] we were to be punished, in turn, by foxes.

It also seemed that, the more we slew and the oftener we tortured them most cruelly before the eyes of others, letting them run off half-skinned, without eyes, without tails, and with feet half-roasted, the more malicious the others became and the more determined, so that they even penetrated our dwellings and dragged away everything they could get to, even iron and all kinds of gear. At the same time, they made us laugh in our greatest misery by their crafty and comical monkey tricks.

Having taken on the position of cook, I took up yet a second func-tion, to visit the Captain-Commander now and then, and to give him a hand in one thing or another since he could now have little service from his two servants, who were sometimes not present when he asked for a drink of water.

Moreover, because we were the first who had set up housekeeping, we were able to come to the assistance of some of the weak and sick and to bring them a warm soup, and we continued in this way until they were somewhat recovered and were able to care for themselves.

This day the barracks[30] was finished, and during the afternoon we carried in a lot of the sick. But because of the narrowness of the space, they were lying about everywhere on the ground, covered with rags and clothes. Nobody could nurse the others, and there was nothing but wailing and complaining whereby they many times called God's judgment down for revenge on the originators of their misfortune, and this sight was so pitiful and sad since one pitied the other, but no one could render suitable assistance to the other, so that even the most courageous should have lost heart.

On November 15, all the sick were finally brought ashore. We took one of them, named Boris Sand, to take care of in our dwelling. God brought him back to health within three months.

Master Khitrov begged us fervently, for God's sake, to take him into our partnership and to assign him a corner because he could not possibly lie among the ordinary seamen who day as well as night reproached him for all kinds of past affairs, accused him of all kinds of mistreatment, and let out all kinds of threats. He said he could not stand it any longer, and he would consequently have to die under the open sky. But because our dwelling was already crammed full and no one was allowed to take action on anything without the foreknowledge of the others, we were all opposed because we were all offended by him, and we refused him all hope, because he was healthy and lazy, and he alone had plunged us into this misfortune.

During the following days, our misery and the work became ever greater. All the sick were finally brought ashore, Lieutenant Waxell last of all. He was in such terrible shape from scurvy that we all gave up hope for his life. But we did not fail to rush to his and the others' assistance with household and medical help as best we could, forgetting all his previous behavior. We were now all the more interested in his recovery, being fearful that after his death, when the command would fall to Master Khitrov, by some dreaded calamity our deliverance from this place could be delayed for a very long time or not happen at all because of universal hatred and mistrust.

In spite of the Lieutenant's urgent request, we could not take him into our hut, but we promised to see to it that a special one would be built for him and several of the sick. We had our men do it, and in the meantime he had to bear being with the others in the barracks.

On this day, through three men[31] who had been sent out, we also received the sad news (which depressed the common ranks even more and made them more difficult) that in the west they had not found any signs that this was Kamchatka—rather that human beings had never been here.

Besides, we were in daily fear that by the constant storms the ship might sail suddenly into the sea and with it all our provisions and hope of deliverance would be lost since, because of the high waves within three or four days later, we could not get to the ship any more with the boat—and because too many difficulties were encountered with Master Khitrov, who already some time ago had been ordered to beach the ship. Also, ten or twelve men, who up to now had worked beyond their capacity without relief and to the end of this month had often been obliged to go into the cold sea up to their armpits, were so exhausted that we anyway saw our impending doom to be close at hand.[32]

Generally, want, lack of clothing, cold and dampness, weakness, sickness, impatience, and despair were daily guests.

Even a little rest was enjoyed with the secret condition that we should be strengthened by it for the even harder and more incessant work that could be foreseen far into the future. But when, toward the end of November,[33] the packet boat was put on the beach by a storm better than human industry could perhaps have accomplished it, people started to relax.[34]

8. Death of Bering

I now consider it unnecessary to set down here everything as it happened to us from one day to the next in the order in which it is found in my diary, since from here on, except for the weather, which I will treat separately, and except for our daily efforts, seldom did anything special happen. Nevertheless, I shall not omit extraordinary happenings in the proper place, noting the time.

Our hopes being raised in view of the food supplies, limited though they were, and the tedious labor of going to the ship suddenly having become unnecessary, people began, after a few days, to refrain from any work, to relax, and to carry out only the necessary housework, which was, even so, still too heavy.

For the second time, three men[1] were dispatched who were to turn eastward and go inland to explore the country thoroughly, because hopes were still kept up—though with little encouragement[2]—that it could be Kamchatka and that a mistake in latitude had perhaps been made, that this was the region around the Oliutora, a view corroborated by the fact that foxes are equally numerous there and are also perhaps descended from Kamchatkan foxes. Others still wanted to take it for Cape Kronotski, and although the lack of any basis for this view could be seen everywhere, it was as if they wanted to deceive themselves in order to live more happily with this hope sustained.

The following persons died ashore: right at the start[3] the old and experienced steersman Andreas Hesselberg, who had served at sea over fifty years and who had, at the age of 70 years, performed his service in such a way as befits a faithful servant. He had to suffer the misfortune, however, that although he had left behind in the fleet so many decent men who knew his merits and who had partly profited from him, he now was treated as a silly child and idiot by men who had reached half his age or one-third his skilled experience and who also had recently learned a part of what they knew from him. He saw himself despised in such a way that one could not but wonder at his fate with special sympathy—how such long, faithful service and good conduct could be followed by such a miserable and despicable end. It came about only because the Captain-Commander and others thought so little of his remonstrations, when from a foolish fancy and arrogance they looked down on everyone who did not agree with them in order to do alone whatever they wanted, with the consequences that occurred later.

Besides him, there died two grenadiers, one cannoneer, the Master's servant, and one sailor.

On December 8, Captain-Commander Bering died, from whom this island later got its name, and a day later the Master's mate, Khotiaintsov, who was his former adjutant. Finally, on January 8, the last man of our crew to die perished; namely, the ensign Lagunov, the thirtieth in number.[4]

Inasmuch as the lamentable end of Captain-Commander Bering has made different impressions on different people, I cannot but stop here a while and mention some prior circumstances.

The late Captain-Commander Vitus Bering was by birth a Dane, by faith a righteous and godly Christian, by his conduct a well-mannered, friendly, quiet man, and for that reason always popular with the entire command, both high and low. After two voyages to the Indies, in 1704 he entered Russian service as a lieutenant with the fleet, in which for 38 years until his end in 1741 he remained with the greatest possible faithfulness, having earned his promotions up to the rank of captain-commander. He was employed for the realization of various plans, of which the two expeditions to Kamchatka are the most important.

There are different sources available for judgment on how he conducted himself on this most recent, great, and—because of all our many sufferings—very difficult expedition. Nevertheless, impartial minds cannot judge otherwise than that he always strove to the best of his strength and ability to carry out, in the best way, whatever he was or-

FIG. 23. The cross on Bering's grave, erected in 1880 by N. Grebnitskii, then Russian governor of the Commander Islands. The inscription reads, "In Memory of Bering, December 19 [N.S.], 1741." (Courtesy of the American-Scandinavian Foundation; reprinted from Stejneger, "Witus Jonassen Bering," 306)

dered, although he himself admitted and often lamented that his strength for enduring such a burden was often inadequate; that the expedition was made much larger and more lengthy than he had projected; and also that, at his age, he wished for nothing better than that the entire enterprise might be taken from him and entrusted to a young, energetic, and determined man of the Russian nation who in many cases could proceed more courageously and auspiciously than an old man and foreigner.

Although it is known that this departed man was not born to make quick decisions and conduct swift enterprises, yet the question remains if, considering his faithfulness, patience, and cautious deliberation, another with more fire and heat would not have delayed more a work with such innumerable dissensions and encumbrances or, by overly dictatorial actions, entirely destroyed these regions of the country, when this prudent man, free from all private interest, could not, with such a large command and various inclinations of those he commanded, prevent these things. When he was busy putting out a fire in one place, it was breaking out in another. What could be imputed to the departed consists in this—through too lenient a command, thereby granting impermissible liberty, he caused half as much damage as the other party would have through too sharp, heated, and often ill-thought-out actions. Examples of both are available.

Thus I observed that he had too great an esteem for the officers under his command and also had too great expectations given their understanding, insight, and experience. They allowed themselves to be misled thereby, not into making the same judgments about him, but into intolerable arrogance and license—nay, a total contempt for him as well as for other persons and endeavors. They showed only too clearly that they were much too small-minded to deserve great esteem; knowing their own capabilities only too well, they considered his esteem to be the result of fear and lack of an ability to judge.[5]

Thus it happened that when he promoted one mate, they were totally convinced that it happened according to natural and international law, and their unenlightened minds promenaded about in all parts of worldly knowledge like a magnetic needle at the pole. Thus it could not fail to happen that their actions were as far off the projected goal as were the motives of their enterprises from reason itself.

But, for all this, the reward he finally got as thanks was that, when in the swampy areas around Okhotsk and on Kamchatka, he wanted to help out and help up each and every one, whoever had fallen into a morass, they leaned so hard on him that he himself had to go under. Since he took to his grave everyone's receipted bill, he thereby unjustly received the funeral text that he died like a rich man and was buried like the ungodly. The interpretation of that will be familiar to those who know that he took with him on the voyage a man whose most serious crimes he sought in every way to vindicate on Kamchatka and, after a successful voyage brought completely to an end, to free him of all guilt by sending him off to St. Petersburg. It was this man who later contradicted him in everything, became the author of our misfortune, and after Bering's death his greatest accuser.[6]

When, moreover, the late Captain-Commander frequently, out of gratitude to God, used to mention with praise how, from his youth, good fortune had always come to him and still two months earlier he had been in fortunate circumstances, the much more astonishing, indeed, did his most miserable, pitiful end appear to us and some others.

He would undoubtedly still be alive if we had reached Kamchatka and he could have had the benefit of a warm room and fresh food. As it was, he died more from hunger, cold,[7] thirst, vermin,[8] and grief than from a disease. At last, because of the cold the fluid that had for a long time shown up in a swelling of the feet and had originated in a prematurely checked tertian fever, and because of the atonic constriction of the joints,[9] which was caused by the cold, the internal and external parts of the fluid moved into the abdomen. At the same time, a *fistula ani* manifested itself and, on breaking open, showed a dark discharge[10] as a sign of an internal gangrene.[11] This was followed shortly by mortification of the tissues[12] and by death itself on December 8, two hours before daybreak.[13]

As painful as it was to behold his parting from the world, his composure and earnest preparation for death and his blissful end itself, which took place while he still had full command of reason and speech, are worthy of admiration.

Although he well knew that he had discovered an unknown land for his burial, he nevertheless did not want to discourage the others still more by making it known at the wrong time; yet it was obvious that he was now concerned only for the well-being of his command without worry for his life. He wished nothing more than our deliverance from this land and, from the bottom of his heart, his own complete deliverance from this misery. He might well not have found a better place to prepare himself for eternity than this deathbed under the open sky.

We buried his corpse the next day close to our dwelling with rites like those of our church.[14] Here he lies between his adjutant,[15] a commissary, and grenadiers. At our departure, we placed a wooden cross to mark his burial site,[16] which, according to the custom of the Russians in Siberia, is at the same time a sign of a new land made subject to the Russian Empire.

9. A Long Winter

After the death of the late Captain-Commander, we had already made sufficient progress, praise God, that the whole command could seek refuge against the onslaught of winter in five underground dwellings.[1] They all stood side by side on the site we had originally selected for housing and were named as follows: the barracks, the Lieutenant's yurt, my dwelling, Aleksei Ivanov's, and Luka Alekseev's[2] yurt. Before each dwelling stood several barrels, in which, for lack of *ambars*, we could keep our meat supply from the foxes, and racks on which we hung up clothing, laundry, and all sorts of things.

Now that the dying had come to an end, the men had little by little recuperated, and on holy Christmas Day many were well again thanks chiefly to the excellent water, the meat of various sea animals, and the relaxation, our whole endeavor was to maintain ourselves through the winter and regain our vigor in order to take on the labor for our deliverance the more heartily in spring. Our efforts to achieve this end were divided into three chief tasks[3] of which the first, for lack of sufficient provisions, was to kill sea animals so that the meat might be our real nourishment. Bread, on the other hand, would be eaten only as a treat.

From the middle of November until the beginning of May, every man received per month 30 pounds of flour and several pounds of barley groats, the latter of which lasted only two months. In May and June, each received only 20 pounds of flour. In July and August, even this amount ceased, and we had to be content with meat alone because, with everyone's consent, we reserved 25 puds of flour for our trip to Kamchatka. Nevertheless, by our careful and frugal management, it happened that, from the beginning to the end, we were no day totally without bread, and each yurt still was able to prepare for the trip so much biscuit that we all took along half the amount to the port, and of the 25 puds of flour, only 5 puds were consumed during the trip.

There was a particular calamity concerning the flour. After lying for two or three years firmly pressed into leather sacks, it had gotten thoroughly soaked when the ship ran aground. Lying in salt water for a long time, it became a tincture of all kinds of materials contained in the ship—gunpowder and other trash—and had to be consumed without much anatomical speculation. At first, until we got used to it, it caused such gas that our stomachs swelled like drums. Since we had no oven, we were neither able to bake bread, nor wanted to because of the housekeeping. Instead, every day we fried fresh Siberian *kolaches*, or cakes, in seal or whale oil and finally in manatee fat. One by one they were counted out to each man at mealtimes. Only after a lapse of twelve months did we once again get to eat bread, when shortly before our departure we erected two ovens to prepare food for the trip.

I and a few others who had supplied their own provisions added them jointly to the store of provisions and received thereafter the same shares as the others.

As far as our principal nourishment, namely, the meat of sea animals, was concerned, we were furnished enough of it, yet not without astonishing effort and labor, which we could have avoided if we had had any kind of order among us and had not been living in a state of nature,[4] through envy and jealousy making the animals wary by constant hunting day and night and from the beginning driving them away from the vicinity. In hunting these animals, one tried to deceive the other and in every way to get the advantage over the other, especially the nearer spring came and the hope increased of being able to transport the pelts to Kamchatka with great profit.

Moreover, when the sickness had scarcely been cured, a new, worse epidemic broke out. I mean the dissolute gambling with cards; for entire days and nights, nothing went on in the dwellings but card playing, first for money, now held in low esteem, and, when this was gambled away, the fine sea otters had to give up their precious pelts. In the morning at roll call no other talk was heard than: "so-and-so has won a hundred rubles or more," "so-and-so has gambled away so much." Anyone who had altogether ruined himself tried to recover through the poor sea otters, which were needlessly and thoughtlessly killed merely for their pelts, the meat being thrown away. When this was not enough, some began to steal and stole pelts from the others, whereby hate, quarrels, and strife were spread in all the dwellings.

Although I frequently remonstrated with the officers about how unjust this was and that they should forbid it, I could achieve nothing primarily because the officers themselves were addicts.[5] When a disgust appeared among the men, the officers whetted their appetites with novelties to accomplish thereby a twofold purpose: (1) to get the money and pelts of the men; (2) to persuade the men through this mean familiarity[6] to forget the old general hate and former bitterness.

Meanwhile, the gambling addiction prevailed to such an extent that no one bore our deliverance much in mind any more. The construction of the new ship proceeded sleepily. On the ship, many necessary materials and objects were ruined, being left in the water—such as compasses and the general journal itself—over which I had made so many remonstrances and received so many curious answers that we perhaps would not have gotten ready in this year if several upright petty officers had not with all their might insisted on doing away with the gambling entirely, which after it occurred in June, suddenly brought about an entirely different appearance to the matter.[7]

In November and December, we killed sea otters at Sea Otter Field and Goat Creek from three to four versts from our dwellings; in January at Whale Creek,[8] from six to eight versts; in February at the Cliffs[9] and the Great Cliff,[10] from twenty to thirty versts. In March and April and the following months, when the sea otters were altogether driven away from the north side around our dwellings, we went overland to the south side and carried back the otters twelve, twenty, thirty, to forty versts.

Our *promysel*, or hunt, of these animals occurred in the following way: in all seasons of the year—yet more so in winter than in summer—these animals go from the sea to the land to sleep, rest, and engage in all sorts of play with each other. At low tide, they lie on the rocks and dried-out sandbanks, at high tide ashore on grass or snow, a quarter, half, even a whole verst from the shore but mostly close to the shore.

Since on this uninhabited island they have never seen nor been made wary by human beings, they feel entirely secure, engage in their Venus game on land, and bear their young there—different from the way it is on Kamchatka and the Kurile Islands, where they go ashore either never or very rarely.

During moonlit evenings and nights we usually went two, three, or four persons together, provided with long and sturdy birch poles. We traveled quietly along the beach against the wind as much as possible, looking around diligently everywhere. When we saw one lying or sleeping, one person very quietly went up to it, even crawling close to it. The others, meanwhile, cut off its path to the sea. As soon as it had been stalked so that it could be reached with a few leaps, a man jumped up suddenly and beat it to death with quick, repeated blows over its head. But if it escaped before it could be reached, the others together chased it still farther inland from the sea, closing in on it steadily while running, until however nimbly and skillfully it could run, this animal would at last, exhausted, fall into our hands and be killed. But if, as frequently happened, we met with a whole herd together, each man selected one especially close to him, and thus the affair came off still better.

In the beginning, we needed little diligence, cunning, and agility since the whole shore was full of them and they lay in the greatest security. But after that, they were so wise to us[11] that we saw them go ashore warily and with the greatest care; they first looked around and turned their noses in all directions in order to ascertain by smell what was hidden from their eyes. Even when they had looked around long enough and wanted to rest, sometimes they jumped up as in a fright, looked around them again, or went back to the sea. Wherever a herd lay, they posted watchers everywhere.

The malicious foxes which intentionally roused them from sleep and made them watchful also hindered us. On their account, we always had to seek new places and go hunting ever farther away and to prefer dark to bright nights and unpleasant to calm weather in order to spy on the otters.

But despite the problems, from November 6, 1741, to August 17, 1742, we killed more than 700 of the animals,[12] consumed them, and took their pelts along to Kamchatka as proof.

145

But because we killed them needlessly only on account of their pelts—yes, frequently letting pelt and meat lie if they were not black enough—it came to such a point that we lost hope of being able to build a ship. For in the spring, when provisions had been consumed and the labor begun, these animals had already been driven completely from the north side for fifty versts on both sides of our dwellings.

We regaled ourselves with seals. They, however, were too cunning to venture farther inland, and it was great luck when we could sneak up on a seal.

The sea otter, which the Russians[13] at first mistakenly regarded as a beaver and therefore called Kamchatka *bobr*, is a genuine otter and differs only from the river otter in this—it lives in the sea and is almost half again as large,[14] and in beauty of the nap it is more like the beaver than the otter.

It is a genuine American sea animal, existing in Asia more as a guest and newcomer,[15] which lives in the Beaver Sea from 56 to 50 degrees, where America, opposite, is closest and both continents are separated only by a channel of forty to fifty miles, which, moreover, is filled with a lot of islands, making the arrival of this animal possible in the aforesaid region of Kamchatka, since it otherwise would not be able to go over a wide sea. According to information collected from the Chukchi nation, I was certain that this animal is found in America opposite of Kamchatka from 58 to 66 degrees,[16] since the Russians around Anadyrsk had received some pelts through trade. But the reason that this animal is not to be met with above 56 degrees on the Kamchatkan shore is that since Kamchatka from there draws farther north but America farther east, the sea between has a greater width than these animals, for the reasons touched on above, can overcome. Consequently, there are fewer or no islands at all in the space in between, which is also believable according to the nature of the thing, since the islands are to be considered as remnants of the mainland torn away only by certain occurrences. From 56 to 50 degrees, we met with the sea otter on the islands in sight of the American mainland[17] and at 60 degrees close to the continent at Cape St. Elias itself, 500 miles east of Kamchatka. This sea otter without a doubt is the very same animal that the Brazilians on the eastern side[18] of America call *ilya* and *carigueibeiu*,[19] according to the testimony of Markgraf and of Ray;[20] consequently, this sea animal is found if not on all yet in most places on the western as well as the eastern side of America. Accordingly, my former supposition is now a settled fact—the sea otters, which during winter and spring come with the drift ice in great numbers on the Kamchatkan coast, are carried here not only from the American continent itself but also frequently from the islands in the channel that the ice must pass. I have seen with my own eyes how much these animals like to lie on the ice, and how with the mild winters they were carried, asleep and awake, on few thin ice floes with the rising tide onto our island and with the ebbing tide away into the sea.

This animal is usually five feet long, and at the breastbone where it is thickest it is three feet in circumference. The largest weigh, with entrails, 70 to 80 pounds.

As far as shape is concerned, it is like an otter[21] in all respects with the sole exception of the hind feet, which are flat and agree in structure with the flippers of the seals. The entrails are likewise formed as in the otter.

The skin, which lies loose on the flesh as in dogs and shakes everywhere while the animal is running, is so far superior in length, beauty, blackness, and gloss of hair to the river otters' pelts that these can scarcely be compared with it. The best pelts are sold in Kamchatka for 20 rubles, in Iakutsk for 30, in Irkutsk for 40, and at the Chinese border, in exchange for their wares, for from 80 to 100 rubles.

The meat is rather good to eat and tasty, but the females are much tenderer and tastier, and they are against the course of nature most fat and delicious shortly before, during, and after giving birth. The nursing otters, which because of their poor pelts are called *medvedki*,[22] or young bears, can be compared at all times with a nursing lamb because of their tenderness, both roasted and boiled.

The male has a bony penis like the seal and all other sea animals. The female has two breasts next to the genitals. They have intercourse in the human way. In life, it is an extraordinarily beautiful and pleasant animal, as well as amusing and comical in its habits; at the same time it is a very cajoling and amorous one. When one sees them running, the gloss of their hair excels the blackest velvet. They lie together as families; the male is with its female, the half-grown offspring called *koshloki*,[23] and the nursing young. The male caresses its female by stroking, for which he uses the front feet like a dog, and lies on her, but she teasingly often pushes him away from her. Not even the most loving human mother engages in the same kind of playing with her children, and they love their children in such a way that they expose themselves to the obvious danger of death. When the young are taken from them, they cry aloud like a little child and grieve in such a way, as we discovered several times, that within ten to fourteen days they dry up like a skeleton, become sick and weak, and do not want to leave the land. When fleeing,[24] they take their nursing young in the mouth, but the grown ones they drive ahead of them. If they are lucky enough to escape, they begin, as soon as they are in the sea, to ridicule their pursuers so that one cannot look on without particular amusement.

They stand in the sea upright like humans and hop up with the waves, hold the front foot over the eyes and look at one as though the sun were bothering them. They lie on their backs and scratch their noses with their front feet, they throw their children in the water and catch them again. When a sea otter is attacked and cannot see an escape route anywhere, he blows and hisses like an infuriated cat. When he receives a blow, he gets ready to die in this fashion: he lies on his side, pulls his hind feet after him, and covers his eyes with his front feet; and when he is dead, he lies like a dead person since he crosses his front feet on his chest.

His food consists of sea crabs, conches, small fish, a little seaweed, also meat.

I would not hesitate, if we did not shrink from the slight expense, to take a few such animals to Russia and tame them—nor do I have the least doubt that they would propagate themselves in a pond or river, since they care little for seawater, and I have seen that they remain for several days amusing themselves in lakes and rivers.

Moreover, this animal deserves the greatest respect from us all, because for more than six months it served us almost solely as our food and at the same time as medicine for the sick.[25]

Whoever desires more detailed information about this animal can find it in my *Description of Sea Animals*.[26]

Our second chief effort consisted in carrying wood. It likewise was considered one of our greatest and most difficult tasks since except for low willow shrubs there was not a single tree to be found on the whole island, whereas the wood thrown up infrequently by the sea lay under the snow from one arshin up to one fathom deep. What was found close around us had been promptly gathered in the beginning for building and burning. Already in December we hauled wood from four versts away, in January and February from six to ten versts, in March from fifteen to sixteen versts.

But in April when the snow settled and left the beach, this labor was suddenly dispensed with, not only because we found enough wood close by but also because when we started to dismantle the ship, we got as many shavings and as much wood unsuited for the new ship as we ever needed for heating our yurts and for cooking our meals, giving us no little relief. The sea animals as well as the wood, however, were carried home on our backs by means of a wooden crossbar fastened on the chest with ropes. Our lightest load was 60, more often than not 70 to 80 pounds, besides axes, kettles, and shoemaker's and tailor's tools, which we had to haul with us everywhere in case a rip and split were to occur in our clothes and shoes.

We had along only summer clothes and shoes for three months, but because we daily tore so much with the heavy labor, even the holiday clothes, overcoats, and coats had to be made into work clothes, the suitcases[27] into boots, and the leather provision sacks into soles. Since nobody wanted to work for money, each man always had to be as best he could shoemaker, tailor, glover, butcher, carpenter, cook, and attendant on foot. Some in a short time developed such skills that in the future they would be able to earn their bread amply in all these trades.

The third task was housekeeping, which consisted in constant cooking so that meals would be ready all the time, no matter at what hour hungry workers might come home. We had made the following arrangement in our yurt, which afterwards was accepted and retained as a standing rule by all the others: since there were five of us Germans, three commoners, or Kamchatka cossack sons, besides the Captain-Commander's two servants (over whom, according to his testament, I had been appointed guardian), that is to say, altogether ten persons, one of us and one of the commoners (or according to our discretion two of each category), at all times went on the *promysel*, while the rest[28] went for wood. One German and one Russian were cooks, in which job we Germans yet had this advantage that we neither were allowed to light the fire, nor to go for water, nor even to open or close the flue. And they also washed and put away the cooking and table utensils after meals, for which they got from us kettles, dishes, plates, spoons, tablecloths, and other utensils, but we had the title[29] of "head chefs," and they "assistant chefs." They also had to obey us in all other things and be at our disposal so that everything might proceed properly, and consequently every day each one knew his work and responsibility without being reminded of it. This arrangement also made all work tolerable, maintained joy and affection among us, and kept food and drink in abundance and better prepared than in all other dwellings. Yet at any time when we deliberated over anything, each person was allowed to express his opinion, and the best advice was taken without regard to person.

In such a state of mind we celebrated Sundays and holidays, the sacred festival of Christmas no differently from what we would have done had we been where we belonged. On public and great political holidays, we entertained, invited the officers, and enjoyed, with help of tea instead of other beverages, with many cheerful speeches and good wishes, the same pleasures in the shade as in other places where everything is in abundance.

On December 26, the scouts[30] sent out a second time returned with the news that we were on an island which they had gone around to the east. Yet they had found so many distinctive marks on the beach, such as Kamchatkan rudders, bottoms of fish barrels, and other signs, that we could not but surmise that Kamchatka was only a slight distance from here.

On January 29, the first sea lion was killed by our yurt. Its meat was found to be of such extraordinary flavor and quality that we wished nothing more than that the animal might more frequently come into our hands. The fat resembles beef marrow, and the meat almost resembles veal.

On February 1, by a violent northwest storm and a very high tide, our packet boat was carried so far up the beach that we had good hopes[31] of being able to launch it at high tide—provided only that we could raise the anchors again in the spring—since it did not seem to be badly damaged, because the hull still held the water it had taken in. But this misapprehension was due to the fact that it had been filled inside pretty much with sand, which did not let the water run out. Nevertheless, it was apparent that in the future dismantling of the ship we would be spared much effort since it had been pushed so far onto land.

On February 25, the recent mild weather induced us to make arrangements for the third dispatching of a party to explore the country to the west, and to this end the assistant navigator Iushin, together with four men, was sent off. But within six days they got only up to the point of land extending northward sixty versts from here, and, after turning the whole exploration into an otter hunt, they returned on March 8 with a poor report, later found untrue. Because they had given as the reason for their return that they had not been able to continue further on account of the steep cliffs reaching into the sea, a new council was held on March 10, in which it was decided to order the boatswain's mate, Aleksei Ivanov, who was proposed unanimously by all, to go by way of the Wood[32] Creek overland to the south and to go along the beach until he reached either the end of the island or the mainland itself, if indeed it was attached to the mainland—for some were still of the opinion that this was Cape Kronotski.

On March 15 they set out on their journey, but on March 19 they unexpectedly returned with the same report that they could go no further in the south because of steep cliffs extending into the sea. But they had missed the right way, as I discovered later on my own trip. Meanwhile, they did bring with them a curious report in two parts: (1) that they had found chips and fragments of the sloop[33] constructed in Avacha the previous winter, and the carpenter and soldier Akulev found here pieces that he had cut off in Avacha; (2) they also described to us an animal they had seen on land for the first time in their lives, which, according to their statement, we took for a *kot*, or fur seal, and which later became only too well known.

On March 22, this same boatswain with his previous traveling companions set out again on the journey, provided with the same instructions as for the first, with this added order that he go on the north side as far as the point extending to the north, and from there continue his way overland toward the south. If he found an obstruction in the south, he should go north again or along the mountains until he either reached the mainland or the end of the island. In the latter event, they should all turn back promptly to delay the construction of a new ship no further. But if they came to the mainland and Kamchatka, half of them should go on to Avacha with the reports, and the other half should turn back to bring us news. Together with three others from our yurt, I accompanied them. At Wood Creek, we went overland for the first time, and on the same day we caused a severe defeat among the sea otters which were together in a herd and feeling so very secure that we killed ten and could have killed a hundred if we had not been concerned more for the meat and our general welfare than for the pelts.

The snow had settled in spring, enabling us to go south overland, where the sea otters and seals were not yet scared away and were found in the greatest numbers; we were much encouraged by this discovery, and we frequented this new locale diligently, even though the way was very far and extremely fatiguing because of the mountains. But three times such accidents occurred on this route that almost a third of us were nearly lost.

On April 1, constable Roselius, assistant surgeon Betge, guard marine Sint, and a cossack left our dwelling as usual for a *promysel*. Toward evening such a violent storm came out of the northwest that no one could stay on his feet or see a step ahead. Moreover, the snow fell a fathom deep during the night, and we did not recall having experienced a more violent storm since our arrival on this island. Our comrades, about whom we at home were in the greatest anxiety, almost perished one and all; after they lay the entire night under the deep snow, they could scarcely work themselves out and get to the beach. The guard marine, however, had been separated from them and lost without any news, and perhaps none of them would have come back if the storm had not ended toward daybreak. The next day we worked for several hours before we were able to dig ourselves out of our dwelling; at the very time the entrance had luckily been cleared, three of our men arrived, senseless and speechless, and so stiff from the cold that, like immovable machines, they could hardly move their feet. The assistant surgeon, totally blind, unable to see, walked along behind the others.

We undressed them immediately, covered them with bedding, and with tea water and other remedies we brought them, thank God, to the point that we were anxious only about the guard marine, who was, however, found by the men after an hour wandering about the beach in a daze, in an even more miserable condition, and brought to us. We could not help but think that he would lose hands and feet since he had been lying in a creek the whole night and was hard as a stone and his clothes had frozen to his body, but God restored him without any injury whatsoever. It took the assistant surgeon eight days to regain his sight.

Although this experience scared us badly, the rest of us intended to tackle the matter more wisely and, if it became absolutely necessary, to bide our time for better weather. And, therefore, on April 5, because we were out of meat, I, Plenisner, my cossack, and the late Captain-Commander's servant went on a *promysel* to the south in the most pleasant weather and sunshine. Having killed as many otters as we could carry right after our arrival near the sea, we were sitting around a campfire at a cliff, intending to spend the night, when unexpectedly we encountered some dangerous bad luck. Toward midnight we got such a violent northwest storm with so much snow that we were unable to seek refuge. The cossack was already covered with snow so high that he lay buried without being able to move. I sat in the snow and sought to warm myself and drive away death's bitterness by constantly smoking tobacco. The other two were running to and fro incessantly as true *hemerodromi*,[34] even though because of the wind they could barely keep on their feet.

When day dawned, hardly being distinguishable from the gloomiest night, my other comrades would permit me no rest under the snow, and I finally got up so that we could together seek a cave and stone crevice. After much wandering about, without having found a retreat, we returned, half dead, full of despair. Since my urging would not make him get up, we dug my cossack forcefully out of the snow and agreed to split into two parties and, because of the continuous storm, to make another attempt to save our lives. In this the cossack was more successful than we. After half an hour's search, he came on a very wide, roomy cave in a rock, which undoubtedly had resulted from a great earthquake.[35]

Having received this news, we went there in the greatest hope, loaded with wood and meat, and here found ourselves in a dwelling protected against all winds and snow. It had been formed by nature so wonderfully that we realized right away how useful this find prompted by necessity would be for us in the future. Besides finding shelter and enough room for ourselves, we got with it an *ambar* in which we could keep our provisions from the thievish and malicious foxes. We also found a naturally made fireplace so that we could heat this cave like a room and cook comfortably without being in the least annoyed by the smoke, which drifted up and above us out a narrow crevice.

Here we revived right away, thanked God, and spent three days because we had to go on new *promysels* and rest up, since the foxes had eaten our provisions during the storm. We returned home on the fourth day with rich booty and good news, when our comrades already were worried whether we would ever reappear.

Later the cave as well as the bay were named after me since it was discovered by my party.[36]

Several days before us, the assistant navigator Iushin with our only ship's carpenter,[37] who had undertaken to build a ship alone and on whom, therefore, all our hope of deliverance rested, went on a *promysel* with three other persons. When they likewise were obliged to seek a crevice, finding one near the sea, it happened that, because of high water, they were kept there as in a prison for seven days without food and wood and did not return until the ninth day when we already believed them either drowned or crushed to death by an avalanche.[38]

When we came home on April 8, we received the joyful news that these persons, so essential to us, had turned up again; also, that the boatswain had returned on April 6 with the news that we were really on an island and that they thought they had seen high mountains in the northeast. And I thought according to the latitude that it could be none other than the American mainland,[39] considering that this is an island of which nothing is known on Kamchatka.

When we now saw no way left to get from here to Kamchatka (also because of the absence of woods) other than by dismantling the old packet boat and building a small ship from it, on April 9 we decided on this course of action in a council. At the same time, the following arrangement was made, which was to last from the date on which the dismantling began until construction of the new ship was completed: (1) Those twelve men who could work with an ax should remain at all times and without stopping at this work. (2) All the others, excepting only the two officers and me, should *promysel* and work in such a way that when one party came home from the *promysel*, they were to rest a day, but at the same time do the housework, prepare meals for the others, and then repair their clothes and shoes, but on the third and subsequent days they should work on the ship until their turn came again to go on the *pro-*

mysel. (3) All meat was to be brought to a common place and every morning each cook from each yurt was to be given his share by a petty officer so that the carpenters who were living in different yurts would not suffer any want.

After each and every one had signed this agreement, we began the following day to take care of the most important preliminaries. We removed materials from the ship and brought them together in one place on the beach. Whetstones were also cut and set in a trough; tools were cleaned of rust and sharpened; a forge erected; crowbars, iron clubs, and large hammers forged; wood gathered, and charcoal made. This last job was much too laborious and very much delayed the work itself.

Although we foresaw very great difficulties in view of the sea animals' having been frightened away and because of the long *promysels*, since the closest hunting grounds were eighteen to twenty versts away from here, nevertheless, all of a sudden the good Lord greatly raised our spirits through the following events. On April 18, the men from the barracks killed a fur seal that weighed, with fat and meat, at least twenty puds. On April 19, these same men killed another of the same size, and it became apparent that the whole command could be fed for a whole week with two or at most three animals.

Since, moreover, I knew, from information obtained when I was still on Kamchatka, that these animals move each spring in herds of countless numbers up past the Kurile Islands and the Kamchatkan coast toward the east and return from there back to the south in September, the females for the most part being all found to be pregnant, I concluded from this that these islands beyond all doubt are the place where these animals stay in summer in order to give birth and that, therefore, these first were at least only forerunners of more to come. In this thinking we did not find ourselves deceived later on.

And afterwards, together with the assistant surgeon, I also killed one, which was followed later by innumerable herds, which within a few days filled up the whole beach to such an extent that we could not pass by them without danger to life and limb—nay, in some places since they covered all the ground, they forced us to scale the mountains and to continue our way up there.

Yet shortly after, there arose two difficulties in this unexpected and amazing abundance of God's blessing. The first consisted in this, that these animals were found only on the southern side of the island, opposite Kamchatka; consequently, they had to be dragged at least eighteen versts from the nearest locality to our dwellings. Second, the meat of these animals smells like fresh white hellebore.[40] It became offensive and in many men caused violent vomiting as well as diarrhea.

We discovered nonetheless that another, smaller kind of fur seal, grayer in color and arriving in even larger numbers, had much tenderer and better-tasting meat and could be eaten without any odor and disagreeableness. Also, directly opposite our dwellings, a closer route to the south was later discovered which amounted to scarcely half the distance of the earlier one. Thus it was decided to keep two people there continuously, taking turns in killing them. They always had so much meat on hand that the parties sent out daily could immediately put it on their backs and make the round trip in a single day.

During this time we were further encouraged in that on April 20, a day before we started to dismantle the packet boat, a large whale, fifteen fathoms long and quite fresh, was beached at Goat Field[41] five versts west of our dwellings. From it we collected so much blubber and oil in two days that on our departure from the island we left behind several barrels full.

Shortly afterwards, the sea lions, called *sivuch*[42] on Kamchatka, also appeared frequently, and although no one dared to kill this fierce animal, we cut up one that, wounded on Kamchatka with a *nosok*, or harpoon, had escaped and was beached near us, dead and still fresh.

During the whole of May and half of June, we lived on the meat of young and female fur seals.

On May 5, the beginning of our ship and future deliverance was made by the installation of the sternpost and stem on the keel. Afterwards Lieutenant Waxell invited each and all to his dwelling, and in the absence of other beverages entertained us with Mongolian *saturan*, or tea soup, with flour roasted in butter. On this occasion we were quite merry despite much wishing and longing.

Aside from its delight, the pleasant weather of spring let us enjoy many advantages. After the snow had thawed, we found so much wood lying here and there on the beach that we were much encouraged in view of the charcoal required by the forge. With the approach of spring, we also got many edible and tasty plants and roots;[43] eating these provided variety as well as medicine for our emaciated bodies. Foremost among these were the Kamchatkan sweet grass; the bulbs of the sarana lily, which is available in far greater quantity and size than in Kamchatka; a kind of plant whose leaves are like celery in taste and shape, and whose root is similar to parsnip in taste; and the roots of wild celery. Besides those, we ate the leaves of the oysterleaf, the shoots of fireweed, the roots of bistort. Instead of black tea, we made infusions of the leaves of ling-onberry, and instead of green tea, of the leaves of a wintergreen and later a figwort. For salad we had scurvy grass, brooklime, and bitter cress.

10. Sea Cow

On May 11 and the days following, not only did the snow begin to thaw mightily, but the continuous rains with winds originating in the southeast also caused such high water that the creeks overflowed, and we could scarcely hold out in our subterranean homes, which became filled with water from one to two feet high. This caused us, after the rain stopped, to leave our winter homes and to build summer ones above ground. Nevertheless, the winter ones were still visited after the water had soaked into the ground.

However, the building of the ship was halted by the rain for several days. Afterwards it continued with even greater enthusiasm when, much to our surprise, we discovered that the ship could be readily dismantled, an outcome we had not at first anticipated because the ship was new and very solidly built, and we did not have the tools for pulling it apart. Work on the new ship also increased daily so that, along with hope, everybody's zeal for work increased tremendously.

When, toward the end of May, the planking had all been finished and set on the keel, we began no longer to doubt at all the possibility of our being able to travel from here to Kamchatka in August; and we were intent only on how to eliminate the troublesome transport of meat and have the food at home by the capture of sea cows which were daily present before our very eyes in great numbers on the shore. That way the work would go even faster, considering that already the men lacked vigor, and their shoes and clothes were badly tattered from traversing the very difficult route cross-country to the south and over the mountains.

FIG. 24. Steller's sea cow, a composite skeleton 30 feet long collected by Leonhard Stejneger on Bering Island in 1882, now in the U.S. Museum of Natural History. (Courtesy of the Smithsonian Institution, photo no. 85-5541)

Therefore, on May 21, we made the first attempt, with a large manufactured iron hook to which was fastened a strong and long rope, to cut into this huge, powerful sea animal and to pull it ashore, but in vain because the hide of this animal was too tough and hard. We also did not fail to make several experiments and change the hook. But these attempts turned out even worse, and it happened that these animals escaped into the sea with the hooks and ropes.

Finally, the most extreme necessity forced us to think of the most expedient means,[1] since the men for the reasons given above were no longer capable of continuing the former hunt. For this purpose, toward the end of June, the yawl, which in the fall had been badly wrecked on the rocks by the waves, was repaired. A harpooner and five other persons for rowing and steering took their places in it. They had a very long rope lying in it in proper order, in exactly the manner as in Greenland whaling, one end of which was fastened to the harpoon, with the other held on shore in the hands of the other forty men.

They rowed very quietly toward the animals, herds of which were foraging for food along the coast in the greatest security. As soon as the harpooner had struck one of them, the men on shore started to pull it to the beach while those in the yawl rowed toward it and by their agitation exhausted it even more. As soon as it had been somewhat enfeebled, the men in the yawl thrust large knives and bayonets in all parts of its body until, quite weak through the large quantities of blood gushing high like a fountain from its wounds, it was pulled ashore at high tide and made fast.

As soon as the tide had receded and it was stranded on the dry beach, we cut off meat and fat everywhere in large pieces, which with great pleasure we carried to our dwellings. A part we stored in barrels. Another part, especially the fat, we hung up on racks. And at long last, we found ourselves suddenly spared all trouble about food and capable of continuing the construction of the new ship by doubling the workers.

This sea animal, which was first seen by the Spaniards in America and with many intermingled inaccuracies first described by the Spanish physician Hernandez and after him by Carolus Clusius[2] and others, they called manatee. The English call it either the sea cow, like the Dutch, or, like Dampier, *Mannetes*, from the Spanish language. This sea animal is found on both the eastern and the western side of America and has been observed by Dampier (and this is very strange) with fur seals and sea lions in the southern hemisphere as well as by me and others in the northern.[3]

The largest of these animals are four to five fathoms long and three and a half fathoms thick around the region of the navel where they are the thickest. Down to the navel it is comparable to a land animal; from there to the tail, to a fish.

The head of the skeleton is not in the least distinguishable from the head of a horse, but when it is still covered with skin and flesh, it somewhat resembles the buffalo's head, especially as concerns the lips.

In place of teeth, it has in its mouth two broad bones, one of which is affixed above to the palate, the other on the inside of the lower jaw. Both are furnished with many crooked furrows and raised ridges with which it crunches seaweed as its customary food.

The lips are furnished with many strong bristles, of which those on the lower jaw are so thick that they resemble the feather quills of chickens and clearly show by their interior hollowness the actual nature of hairs generally, which are likewise hollow.

The eyes of this animal, without eyelids, are no larger than sheep's eyes.

The ears are so small and concealed that they can hardly be found and recognized among the many grooves and wrinkles of the hide until and before the hide is cut off, when the ear duct because of its polished blackness catches one's eye; yet it is hardly spacious enough to accommodate a pea. Of the outer ear, not the slightest traces are to be found.

The head is joined to the rest of the body by a short and indistinguishable neck.

Below, on the chest, there are two strange things to be seen. First, the feet, consisting of two joints, have outermost ends rather like a horse's hoof. Underneath, these are furnished with many short and densely set bristles like a scrub brush, and I am not prepared to say whether to call them hands or feet, for the reason that, besides the birds, there is no single two-footed animal. With these forefeet, it swims ahead, beats the seaweed off the rocks on the bottom, and when, lying on its back, it gets ready for the Venus game, one embraces the other with these as if with arms.

The second curiosity is found under these forefeet, namely, the breasts, provided with black, wrinkled, two-inch-long teats, at whose outermost ends innumerable milk ducts open. Brushed against rather hard, they give off a great quantity of milk, which in taste, fat content, and sweetness excels the milk of land animals, but is otherwise not different.

Also, the back of this animal is formed almost like that of an ox. The middlemost backbone sticks up raised. Next to it on both sides is a flat hollow the length of the back. The sides are round lengthwise.

The belly is plump and very expanded, and at all times so completely stuffed that at the slightest wound the entrails at once protrude with much hissing. Proportionately, it is like the belly of a frog.

From the genitals, the body suddenly diminishes very markedly in its circumference. The tail itself becomes thinner and thinner toward the flipper, but immediately before the flipper it is still on the average two feet wide. By the way, excepting the tail flipper, this animal has no fin, neither on the back nor on the sides, wherein it is again different from the whale and other sea animals. The tail flipper is parallel with the sides of the animal, as with the whale and the porpoise.

The male organ is like an ox's as concerns length and position; but in its shape and nature like a horse's, nearly a fathom long and with a sheath fastened under the navel. The female genitals are directly above the anus, nearly oblong, square, and at the upper part, provided with a strong, sinewy clitoris one and a half inches long.

Like cattle on land, these animals live in herds together in the sea, males and females usually going with one another, pushing the off-spring before them all around the shore. These animals are busy with nothing but their food. The back and half the belly are constantly seen outside the water, and they munch along just like land animals with a slow, steady movement forward. With their feet they scrape the seaweed from the rocks, and they masticate incessantly. Yet the structure of the stomach taught me that they do not ruminate, as I at first supposed. During eating they move the head and neck like an ox; when a few minutes have elapsed, they heave the head out of the water and draw fresh air by clearing their throats like horses. When the tide recedes, they go from the shore into the sea, but with the rising tide they go back again to the beach, often so close that we could reach and hit them with poles from the beach.

They are not in the least afraid of human beings, nor do they seem to hear too faintly, as Hernandez asserts contrary to experience.[4]

I could not observe indications of an admirable intellect, as Hernandez declares, but they have indeed an extraordinary love for one another, which extends so far that when one of them was cut into, all the others were intent on rescuing it and keeping it from being pulled ashore by closing a circle around it. Others tried to overturn the yawl. Some placed themselves on the rope or tried to draw the harpoon out of its body, in which indeed they were successful several times. We also observed that a male two days in a row came to its dead female on the shore and inquired about its condition.

Nevertheless, they remained constantly in one spot, no matter how many of them were wounded or killed.

They play the Venus game in June with lots of lengthy diversionary tactics. The female flees—slowly—ahead of the male with constant detours, and the male pursues her incessantly. But when the female tires of this mock flight and the vain enticements, she lies on her back, and the male completes intercourse in the human way.

When they want to rest on the water, they lie on their backs in a quiet spot near a cove and let themselves float slowly here and there in that position.

These animals are found at all times of the year everywhere around this island in vast numbers such that the entire coast of Kamchatka could continually supply itself plentifully from them with both fat and meat.

The hide of this animal has a dual nature. The outer hide is black or blackish brown, an inch thick, and with a consistency almost like cork, around the head full of grooves, wrinkles, and holes. It consists of nothing but perpendicular strands that lie hard upon one another as in a crosscut Spanish reed or cane. The individual bulbs of the strands are round at the bottom, and therefore the upper layer can be easily separated from the true hide, but in the hide itself lie the cavities of the bulbs, giving it the look of the surface of a thimble. It is my opinion that the outer hide is thus a composition of many hairs in a continuous body of crusts, and I found these crusts just this way in the whale.

The inner hide is somewhat thicker than an oxhide, very strong and white in color. Underneath this, a layer of fat surrounds the entire body of the animal. It is a lobe of fat four fingers thick. Then the flesh follows.

The weight of this animal, with hide, flesh, meat, bones, and entrails, I estimate at 200 puds or 80 short hundredweight.[5]

The fat of this animal is not oily or flabby but rather hard and glandular, snow-white, and, when it has been lying several days in the sun, as pleasantly yellow as the best Dutch butter. The boiled fat itself excels in sweetness and taste the best beef fat, is in color and fluidity like fresh olive oil, in taste like sweet almond oil, and of exceptionally good smell and nourishment. We drank it by the cupful without feeling the slightest nausea. In addition, it has the virtue of acting as a very gentle laxative and diuretic when taken somewhat frequently; therefore, I consider it a very good remedy for chronic constipation as well as gallstones and urine blockage.

The tail consists of nothing but fat, and it is much more agreeable than that in other parts of the body. The fat of the calves quite resembles the meat of young pigs, but the meat itself resembles the meat of young calves, and it swells up so that it doubles its volume[6] and is boiled entirely within a half-hour.

The meat of the old animals is indistinguishable from beef and differs from the meat of all land and sea animals in the remarkable characteristic that even in the hottest summer months it keeps in the open air without becoming rancid for two whole weeks and even longer, despite its being so defiled by blowflies that it is covered with worms everywhere. I attribute the reason to the diet of plants and to the salt-

163

peter usually mixed in them, from which the meat itself also gets a much redder color than the meat of land and carnivorous sea animals.

It was evident that all who ate it felt that they increased notably in vigor and health.[7] This was noticeable especially in some sailors who had relapses and had been unable to recuperate up until now. With this, all doubts were now ended about what kind of provisions we should go to sea with; and by means of sea animals it pleased God to strengthen us human beings who had suffered shipwreck through the sea.

As concerns the inner structure of these wonderful creatures, I refer curious readers to my detailed description of this animal,[8] but here note only briefly (1) that the heart is divided into two parts and thus, contrary to the usual heart, is double, and that the pericardium does not surround it directly, but forms a special cavity; (2) that the lungs, enclosed in a firm, sinewy membrane, are situated at the back, as in birds; therefore, it can hold out longer under water without breathing; (3) that it has no gall bladder, but only a wide gall duct, like horses; (4) that the stomach has a similarity with the stomach of a horse, just like the entrails; (5) that the kidneys, like those of calves and bears, are composed of very many small kidneys, each of which has its distinct ureter, pelvis, little arteries, and papillae, and that they are two and a half feet long and weigh thirty pounds.

From the head of this animal, the Spaniards customarily take out a bone, hard as stone, and sell it to the druggists and apothecaries under the false name of a stone, calling it *lapis manati*. I sought it in vain in so many animals that I therefore have the idea that it is a product of the climate or that this is a distinct species of the animal, especially since the inquisitive Mr. Dampier mentions two species near the island of St. Ferdinand.[9]

Moreover, I was not a little astonished that despite asking scrupulously about all animals on Kamchatka, I heard nothing about this one before my return from the voyage, whereas on my return I received information that this animal is known from around Cape Kronotski to Avacha Bay and is sometimes thrown ashore dead. Lacking a special name, they have given it the name "kelp-eater."[10]

11. Returning to Kamchatka

Since now all difficulties about the dismantled ship and food were over and since also for a change we sometimes caught in our half-rotted fish-nets so many fish that we were supplied for eight days from a single haul, we made progress with the help of many hands, with redoubled courage, and with the constant exertion and friendly encouragement of Lieutenant Waxell so that toward mid-July, insofar as its hull was concerned, the ship stood ready on the stocks. The rest of the time up to August 13 was spent in making rigging, spars, and masts, in blacksmithing, in the tedious burning of tar from old ropes, and in erecting a platform for launching the ship, costing all the more trouble because we were poorly supplied with wood and other materials. The wood for the platform was everywhere hauled in from distant parts of the coast; fastening down the platform was effected by putting the cannons on it.

Others built a storehouse in which to keep the materials we left behind. Still others were busy with construction of an oven and preparation of biscuit for the trip. Some prepared the barrels (which had to be made fast for the voyage) with iron hoops and ropes because such work had earlier been left undone in Okhotsk. Some reconnoitered the bottom of the sea. There was not a one wanting to be idle, nor supposed to be, the closer and dearer to each was the hope of deliverance from this island to his homeland. Although the hope of acquiring more otter pelts made some wish to spend yet another winter, they finally out of shame would not consider it.

On August 8, everything was in order and ready for the voyage. In the afternoon, we all said a prayer in which we begged God for a successful launching of the ship (which was dedicated to the holy apostle Peter and named after him), and having finished our prayer, in the name of God we began the launching.

But to our great consternation, it happened that the ship stood still and by its weight pressed down on the platform, which had been inadvertently built too low. Nevertheless, we worked with all our strength and, by using winches, raised it up so far that the mistake could be remedied by means of a few thick planks pushed in on the sides between the ship and the platform, and thereupon the ship was successfully launched. But by that time the high tide had subsided, and the final launch into the sea remained suspended until the next day when, at flood tide, the ship was successfully let into the sea.

Subsequently we worked night and day.[1] On August 11, the mast was set in place and secured with shrouds. Next, water and provisions and everyone's baggage were loaded in.

Everyone had to declare in writing beforehand how much weight he wished to take along. Whatever exceeded the allowed weight was left behind.[2]

While the vessel was being loaded, the carpenters were still making a small boat that could be placed on deck so that we could use it in an emergency.

Our ship's provisions consisted of 25 puds of rye flour; five barrels of salted manatee meat; two puds of peas; and one barrel of salted beef, which had been spared even in our often-urgent need on the return voyage from America. In addition, each man was given four pounds of butter. Most who had managed economically had retained so much from their small provision that, on departure, they were able to bake a half-pud of biscuit from it and take it along. Those, however, who had earlier lived too well made themselves biscuit of dried manatee meat.

On August 13, one and all, with much inner turmoil, left their dwellings for the last time and went on board the ship. It was either going to take us to the frontiers of Asia and our beloved fatherland or, after so much toil, hope, and longing, would pass judgment on our miserable pilgrimage according to the will of the Highest. When we all had boarded the ship, we realized for the first time how crowded the space was and how difficult the voyage would be for that reason. We lay one on top of the other and crawled over one another. The Lieutenant, Master Khitrov, I, and the Lieutenant's son had in the narrow cabin ultimately the best space. The other 42 men were lying in the hold, which was packed so full with water barrels, provisions, and baggage that the crew could scarcely lie between all that and the deck. At all times three men shared two places because the entire crew was divided into three watches. But because the space was still too crowded, we began to throw into the sea the pillows, bedding, and clothing that had been brought along from the shore.

The new ship was 36 feet at the keel and 42 feet from stem to stern.[3]

In the meantime, we saw the foxes on the beach inspect our dwellings with the greatest glee and occupy them as theirs; it seemed to amaze them that no one hindered them as usual. Besides, they found so many remnants of fat and meat come to them as their share in one fell swoop, to which diversion we left them on our part from the bottom of our hearts.

On the morning of August 14, we besought God in a special prayer for his blessed help and support for a successful voyage. Then we weighed anchor.[4] Because the west wind helped us to pass by the southeastern point of the island, we elected—although the mouth of the Kamchatka River was twice as close and our ship scarcely in condition to endure an autumn storm—nevertheless the straight course to Avacha Bay. We advanced with a slight wind to such an extent that toward noon we were in the channel between Bering's Island and the island lying parallel five miles[5] opposite to the east, and toward evening we reached the southeast end of our island.

This afternoon we spent in high spirits since in bright and pleasant weather we passed by the island on which we knew all the mountains and valleys, whose paths we had climbed so many times with great effort to scout for our food and for other reasons and on which we had bestowed names from various circumstances and events. Thereby God's grace and mercy became manifested to all, the more brightly considering how miserably we had arrived there on November 6, had miraculously nourished ourselves on this barren island, and with amazing labor had become ever more healthy, hardened, and strengthened; and the more we gazed at the island on our farewell, the clearer appeared to us, as in a mirror, God's wonderful and loving guidance.

Late in the evening we had come so far, thank God, that we were opposite the outermost point of the island.

On Sunday, August 15, the wind was gentle before noon, and we still had the southern side of the island in sight. Toward nightfall the wind increased, and after we cut and let drift in the sea the ship's large yawl, which up to now had served us so well but now had become a hindrance to our ship, we also completely lost sight of the island, and with wind and weather being very favorable, we began now to continue the straight course to Avacha west by south.

But toward midnight we were suddenly struck by the utmost terror because our ship was all at once filling with water through an unknown leak, which incident seemed all the more dangerous since everybody was familiar with the soundness of the new ship, and since the wind was strong, space cramped, and thus everyone was in everyone else's way. Also, because the ship was so tightly loaded, it was extremely difficult to discover the cause of the leak. Moreover, the pumps, when their use was most necessary, were plugged by numerous chips left in the hold since someone had forgotten to put kettles under them.[6] In these circumstances, the sails were immediately taken in. Some cleared the baggage out of the way and looked for the leak. Others unceasingly poured out water with the kettles. Some threw into the sea the iron cannonballs and grapeshot brought along from the shore. And so it most fortunately happened that, when the ship was lightened and the leak in the ship plugged—the leak had been meanwhile discovered by our carpenter just where he had supposed it was and turned out to be above the waterline—we saw ourselves rescued from even this danger and from our sinking. But since through this accident we had been so fortuitously warned, we did not neglect to correct the oversight and to put kettles in under the pumps[7] in the hold. It was also observed that this leak had occurred when the ship, after the platform broke, had been raised up with winches whose upper part had been attached under the waterline, and the boards had the more easily been moved out of alignment since, to speed up construction, they had been fastened only with iron nails without a single wooden peg.

On August 16, we continued the course we had started. On Tuesday, August 17, we suddenly caught sight of the mainland of Kamchatka; we came out of the sea opposite Cape Kronotski and found ourselves hardly a mile from shore since we caught sight of it during dark, foggy weather. Nevertheless, we stuck to the plan to sail for the harbor, from which we were still approximately thirty miles distant. However, since there was either a complete calm or contrary wind the whole time along the Kamchatkan shore, we spent another nine days tacking until, finally, on August 26, after using the oars 24 hours without a break, we arrived in the night at the entrance to the bay, and on the evening of August 27 anchored in the long-sought harbor itself.

As great as was the joy of each and all over our deliverance and safe arrival, yet the contrary[8] and unexpected news that we received from a Kamchadal at the entrance put us in a far greater agitation and a complete forgetfulness of ourselves. Everyone had considered us dead or otherwise come to grief; our property left behind had fallen into other hands and had mostly been carried off. Therefore, joy and sorrow often changed in a few moments, according to the nature of the news about general and special happenings. We were all so accustomed to misery and wretched living that, instead of other enterprises, we considered that the previous circumstances would always continue and thought we were dreaming the present ones.

The next day, after we had heartily thanked Almighty God in a common prayer for his gracious protection, our miraculous preservation, and our happy return to Asia and at the same time to each one's fatherland,[9] the naval officers[10] decided to go on to Okhotsk this autumn. I bade them farewell and prepared to hike the thirty miles to the Bolshaia River and to reach my own longed-for people. I arrived there safely on September 5 and joined in celebrating the high festival of the name-day of Her Majesty, our most gracious Empress.

After some weeks had passed, we received the news that, because of strong contrary winds, the ship destined for Okhotsk had returned to the harbor to pass the winter. But at Bolshaia River the news of our reaching port had not been transmitted to the galliot *Okhotsk* because of the negligence of the commander there, even though the galliot did not sail out of the river mouth to Okhotsk until the third day after receipt of the news in the *ostrog*. Because of these two incidents, we had to bear being counted among the dead eight months longer than necessary.

APPENDIX

Physical Description of Bering Island

The events of our voyage from June 5, 1741, until our arrival on Kamchatka have been related; what remains is to give a brief report of Bering Island itself and of what in nature is found there—its admirable creatures revealed to us there in astonishing numbers. From a full description of this island, the character of all the others that lie in the Canal de Pico[1] in large numbers is also revealed, which news is also of common interest. I therefore divide the following essay in two parts: the first contains the character of the land and its peculiarities and the second everything that is on it.[2]

This island—which got the name of Bering's Island from the late Captain-Commander, head of the expedition, of whose death and burial we have written—lies off the coast of Kamchatka from the northwest to the southeast at a latitude of 55 to 56 degrees. The northwest point lies due east or east by south at a distance of about 20 Dutch miles directly opposite the mouth of the Kamchatka River or Cape Kamchatka; the southeast part, however, is 60 miles away from Avacha Bay and the port of St. Peter and St. Paul within it. The island itself is 23.5 Dutch miles or 165 versts long and of differing width. The southeastern point is only 3 to 4 versts wide along 2 miles of length toward the west to the place that we called Impassable Cliffs;[3] 5 versts from there to Sea Lion Bay; 6 versts from Sea Otter Cliffs,[4] near Whale Creek; again 5 versts across from Aleksei Ivanov's stone, where to the south is a very large bay; 7 versts across from our dwellings; 8 versts at Wood Creek. From there the width of the island increases more and more until finally the greatest

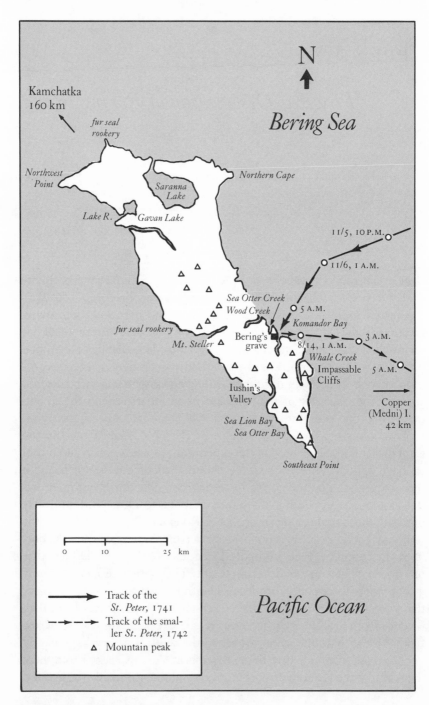

FIG. 25. Bering Island, 1741–42.

width amounts to 23 versts or 3.25 miles opposite Northern Cape,[5] or the cape extending toward the north, which is 115 versts distant from the southeast point. From there the island again draws away to the northwest and decreases gradually in its width so that it is 5 versts wide at a distance of 135 miles from the southeast point, 3 versts at 150 versts, and up to 165 versts (making up the entire length of the island) it gradually decreases in width to a single verst. The width of this island therefore is entirely out of proportion to its length, and I do not recall ever having read or heard that such islands exist in other parts of the world, although the islands we saw near America and in the channel have everywhere such a proportion.

This island is a succession of barren cliffs and mountains joined one to the other. Separated from each other by numerous valleys running south and north, they stand aloft from the sea like a single rock. The question about how this island originated, whether it is not a remnant from the mainland that formerly connected Asia and America together by land, I leave to others more skillful to decide.[6] At least the following give no slight basis and occasion for future speculations: (1) the broken coast of Kamchatka as well as America, (2) the many rocky promontories extending from five to ten miles into the sea, (3) the numerous islands in the channel, and (4) the position and hence resultant form of the islands and the slight width of the channel itself.

Because of the altitude of this island, in clear weather it can be seen from at least ten to twelve miles out at sea, and consequently it is very possible that, on a voyage from Kamchatka to this island, Kamchatka as well as this island can be seen clearly, although it is impossible to see either the island from Kamchatka or Kamchatka from the island. The inhabitants of Kamchatka have for a long time surmised that a land must exist in the east across from the mouth of the Kamchatka River, because a steady fog was observed there, however much all other places on the horizon cleared up now and then.

The highest mountains on this island are not over 1,000 fathoms high,[7] covered with common yellowish clay half a foot deep, under which to a depth of two to three feet a layer of poor, yellowish, crumbling rocks has its beginning and continues uniformly to bedrock, as I have observed on the steep cliffs along the shore. Generally, the mountains in those parts that face the sea toward the north and south are, in their coherence, solid and undivided, whereas those that open inland east and west through valleys are fissured and disintegrated by considerable moisture, which through freezing breaks up the rock. The mountains everywhere keep a similar northeast to southwest direction.

The valleys, together with the mouths of creeks and springs, all open up everywhere north and south to the sea, and run from their source in the southeast along the land toward the northwest end, and from the northwest toward the southeast end,[8] as I observed everywhere on trips around the island and noted day by day in my journal. Inland, flat, even places are nowhere encountered but only high mountains and narrow valleys. But because the valleys are filled mostly with streams, it is necessary to take the route over the lowest mountains when wanting to go to the southern side of the island, which was even more toilsome for us since we were often heavily loaded with animals and meat while having to clear the way over them. Level places must therefore be sought only along the coast and where the mountains draw inland from the seashore one-half or at most one verst in a semicircle, and such places are encountered wherever streams occur. And this constant relationship can be observed: wherever a mountain extends south or north toward the sea in the form of a point, the shore behind it is level and broad. The steeper the mountain's point toward north or south, the smaller the level land behind it. But the more gradually the point falls away, the larger the level land behind it. This also occurs when the mountains extend from southeast to northwest along the island: the larger the level spot and the lower the mountains, the larger are the streams; the steeper the mountains along the shore, the smaller but the more numerous are the streams.

Where the shore and mountains, steep on the inland side, solid in their coherence, fall away vertically, lakes are always to be found from one verst to a half from shore. These lakes empty into the sea through streams. The reason is that the moisture from snow, rain, and evaporation discharges itself forcefully all at once in such steep places, but the springs issue forth at the foot of the mountains. As a result, the earth becomes soft and porous and from time to time is loosened by the water and is washed away until finally, when the upper stratum is dispersed,[9] the other—namely, the crushed rock and gravel—remains behind; this then makes up the bottom of the shores and rivers. But the origin of lakes in large, level plains, which commonly have a muddy, mucky bottom, is to be explained otherwise; that is, because the mountains are steep and do not gradually extend downward into the land, a greater space remains at the foot of the mountains for water, which allows it a place to stay and thus furnishes the place for a lake. Otherwise, where the mountains gradually fall to level land, a valley comes into existence, and in its central and lowest part a stream.

The mountains consist of a plain gray rock. But where they run parallel to the shore, the point extending into the sea is usually changed into a clear grayish and solid sandstone that is good for grinding. This circumstance seemed very remarkable to me because it almost appeared as if the rock that has an entirely different structure had the contact of the seawater to thank for this form.

In many places the shore is so narrow that at high tide a person can pass by only with great difficulty. In some places a person can pass by only at low tide. But in two places it is utterly impossible, of which one is not far from the southern, the other not far from the northwestern point, and these came about by chance from earthquakes, the great running of the sea, the washing out of the bottom by the waves, and the annual breaking up of the mountains by freezing water. Of this one sees evident signs partly in large heaps of stones, partly in pillars and rocks standing detached in the sea and torn away from the shore. These are often encountered in such places. The southern side of the island is much more rent along the shore, rockier, and provided with more cliffs than the northern. On the northern side, one can walk everywhere along the coast except at Impassable Cliffs[10] and behind the northward extended point of land, which is very steep and replete with cliffs and fallen rocks on the shore.

At various places I encountered wondrously strange views that at first glance were more like the ruins of large cities and edifices than a chance display of nature, as in the case of the cave[11] that I named—the mountains appear to be a rampart and the ledges on them the bastions and bulwarks of genuine fortifications. Behind the cave, many separate cliffs are scattered here and there along the coast; some of these convincingly resemble pillars; and others, walls of old large buildings; others, vaults and arches, through whose opening one can walk as if they had been purposefully made.

I also noticed these differences: if on the northern side a bay indents the shore, as is the case near our dwellings, the land lying directly opposite in the south extends into the sea at an angle. When the area of the shore in the north is wide and sandy, then its opposite in the south is the narrower, rockier, and more broken. Where, on the other hand, the shore on the north side is not passable, that on the south side is the broader, flatter, and sandier.

Various caves and fissures that originated at various times from earthquakes are encountered in various places, of which the cave named after me and Iushin's Crater[12] are the largest and best-known.

On the highest mountains and their uppermost peaks, I have observed that a heart or kernel, as it were, projects from their center and terminates in a barren, conical, upright rock, which, though it does not differ substantially from the entire rock mass, is, in any event, much more fragile, purer, and therefore has a definite shape. In 1739, I encountered such peaks of alabaster on the mountains along Lake Baikal and on Olkhon Island within it. Others, which resemble malachites, are green and somewhat transparent and like the stalactites I received from Anadyrsk with the report that there, too, they shoot up out of the summits of the mountains, and that where they have broken off, they are said to grow out again. These seem to be effects of the internal movement and especially the pressure of those mountains toward the center, and thus these points seem to be a kind of stone crystal or of materials that have been pressed from the center up—matter, formerly movable but afterwards hardened, that constitutes the purest, inner nature of the stone.

Whenever the land suddenly changes direction and draws abruptly to another area, I always noticed that the shore ahead of it for one or two versts becomes very rocky and that the mountains, inland to the shore, run very steep and are divided at the outermost points in many separate rocks and pillars. By the way, Bourguet observed in the Pyrenees that the upper surfaces of mountains, through their many ridges running in a certain direction, give the appearance that they owe their origin to the waves of the sea, which they resemble.[13] I have noticed the same thing not only on the mountains of this island but everywhere in all of Siberia and Kamchatka. What he observed about the shape of valleys and the points and bays lying opposite them, I also find very true in this part of the world, as well as the conclusion from this that such change arose gradually through severe floods, earthquakes, and other occurrences.

As for the seashore, it is so remarkably formed that it can be said without any question that we were preserved on this land by a miracle of God and saved from total ruin. Although this island is 23 Dutch miles long, there is nevertheless on the north side not a single place that in any way could be good for a harbor, even for a small ship. For two to three versts, in some places four to five, the shore is beset with nothing but rough crags and rocks so that a person can walk out toward retreating water at ebb tide with dry feet for as many versts, which later at high tide are under water again. With the falling tide the waves rise so high and fall with such crashing on these rocks that often afterward we could not look out at them from the shore without fright. From all the pounding of the waves on the rocks, the sea becomes so frothy that it looks like milk. During our stay we came to know only a single narrow passage on this side that was clear of rocks, so that one could anchor there in calm seas, and this is that part of the coast about eighty fathoms wide into which God wisely and lovingly led us, who were blindly running under full sail to the shore, full of vexation and despair to our destruction, just as He later led us out again through this very portal.[14] At this place is also the largest bay situated on the north side.

From all circumstances, it can be seen that this island in former times was much larger and wider than it is nowadays, and these rocks lying in the sea are the debris and first boundaries of its extent, which is evident for five reasons. First, the rocks in the sea in their position line up in the same direction as the mountains on shore. Second, the streams flowing from the valleys have an open channel through the rocks as well. Third, the seams that are of black, green, and alabaster on rocks in the sea can be followed in an unsevered line to the shore and to the foot of the mountains, certain proof that the shore in olden times went that far and was an uninterrupted line. Fourth, it is an established rule that where a mountain slopes gradually to the shore, or the shore is low and sandy anyway, the sea, too, gets gradually deeper and deeper away from the shore, but where the shore is steep and sharply sloping, at that place the sea is suddenly rather deep, hard under the shore, and often, in a distance of twenty fathoms, sixty to eighty fathoms deep; but the sea under the steep cliffs on this island is no deeper than in other places, because its bottom is filled with fallen rocks. Fifth, we saw clearly for ourselves in a short time how much rock was washed off the mountains at Iushin's Valley in winter and fell off by itself in spring, burst open by the frost. It also happened that on June 18, I continued westward under a cliff along the sea, but found on my return after several days that, in this brief time, the whole rock face had plunged into the sea, and the whole area acquired another aspect.

The south side of the island is formed very differently from the northern, and although the shore is much more rocky and broken up, there are nevertheless two places along it where one could sail close to the shore, and with small or flat boats, such as skerry boats, enter the mouths of rivers (or rather, of the lakes that open into the sea through a short canal) and stop as if in a harbor. The first place is seven Dutch miles from the southeast point in a large bay,[15] which, quite uniquely, can be noticed from afar at sea because of the stone pillars found at the southeast end; we called the place Iushin's Valley after its discoverer, the navigator Iushin.

The other place is 115 versts from the southeast point and 50 from the northwest point and yet more recognizable because the shore turns from north to west at just this spot.[16] In the bend itself is the mouth of a small river, which is the largest of all on this island and at high tide is six to seven feet deep at its mouth. This river leads into the largest lake[17] on this island and becomes ever deeper from the sea to the lake, so that without much trouble one can reach the lake one and a half versts away from the sea through the river and remain there safely since the lake is surrounded on all sides by steep cliffs like walls that protect against all winds. I have called this river Lake River,[18] and the place itself is otherwise further recognizable in this way—opposite its mouth to the south lies an island[19] that is one mile in circumference and only one mile away from the river's mouth. From here westward for five versts, the shore is sandy, even, and flat, and the sea is free of rocks, because I saw no surf or waves playing on them, even though I stayed there for three days of observation.

From the highest mountains of this island, one sees in bright and clear weather the following lands: on the southern side two islands, of which one is about a mile in circumference, oblong in shape, and at a distance from the shore of Bering Island of one mile in the south and fifty versts or seven miles at the northwest point.[20] The other island[21] consists of two high split rocks in the sea, in circumference about two to three versts, and two miles away from Bering's Island. It lies to the southwest directly opposite the northwest point itself.

From the northwest point, one sees mountains in the northeast, very high and covered with snow,[22] at a distance of about fifteen to twenty miles, and I consider these to be a promontory of the American continent itself rather than an island (1) because the mountains at a distance seem too high to be the mountains of an island; (2) because at a like distance on the mountains near our dwellings on the north side directly opposite in the east we often observed very clearly exactly the same kinds of high, white mountains and judged from the height and sweep that this must be the American continent. At various times there was another island to be seen as well between Bering Island and the supposed mainland of America. From the southeast point I saw in the southeast, in very bright and clear weather, another island (although very indistinctly).[23] Even in the clearest weather I observed a continual fog to the west and southwest over Kamchatka, by which I at all times clearly determined its nearness.

On the north side, there lies another island, about twelve to fifteen miles long, likewise northwest-southeast like Bering's Island, thus parallel with it.[24] The channel or the sea between the two is in the northwest approximately only three miles wide, and opposite the southeastern cape of Bering's Island it is five miles wide, and this island extends beyond Bering Island still very far into the sea and ever more easterly. The mountains on that island are lower than those on Bering's Island, and at both ends a large number of high and separate rock chimneys and pointed pillars stand in the sea. It was this island that we first caught sight of and considered to be Kamchatka, because it appeared in the west and the channel in between was so hidden from our view by the land that we looked at it and considered it to be one with Bering's Island; in the foggy and dark autumn weather, we could not detect the deception until we had already been shipwrecked on Bering Island a long time. For if we had noticed this channel at the time before we landed, we could no doubt have concluded that this was not the mainland of Kamchatka because no island was known at this latitude so close to its coast, and therefore we would have just continued the voyage through this channel to Kamchatka, as we did in 1742 on our homeward voyage with the new ship.

As for the weather, it differs very little from that on Kamchatka, except that the storm winds are much more violent and perceptible because the land lies in the sea without direct protection and is at the same time very narrow and unwooded. Besides, the wind so doubles its force when it sweeps through the deep and narrow valleys that a person can keep on his feet only with great difficulty. Also, it causes a terrible whistling and noises that are even more terrifying since the sea on the cliffs of the shore already fills the air with its crashing. We had the most violent storm winds in February and April with southeast and northwest winds. With east winds we had mild and clear weather; with northerly, cold and clear.

The highest tides we received on February 1 with northwest winds. The suddenly melting snow and the heavy rain toward mid-May caused the other flooding.

Earthquakes occurred three times. Among these, the one that occurred on February 7 about one o'clock in the afternoon accompanied by a west wind was the most violent and lasted six full minutes. I was underground at the time and, with others, heard several minutes beforehand a sound and a strong subterranean wind moving from south to north with a violent hissing and roaring, and it became ever stronger the closer it came to us. The roaring had already stopped when the shaking began. It was so violent and perceptible that the posts in our dwelling moved and everything started to crack.

I immediately ran out of the dwelling toward the sea to observe what was going on in nature. Although the movement continued, I could nevertheless not perceive the slightest extraordinary movement in the sea. The air, by the way, was bright and clear and the weather pleasant.

The earthquake on July 1 occurred toward evening, about five o'-clock, in very bright and pleasant weather; the wind was easterly.

We had not the slightest reason to complain about great cold, and accordingly it did not happen in the two years 1740 and 1741[25] that ice gathered in the sea that could drift here from the mainland.[26] I often wished to confirm by it even more my opinion that the drift ice on Kamchatka came from American rivers and that the sea otters got on it when it passed the islands in the channel and was there awhile driven about by the winds.

On our arrival on November 6, we did not yet encounter any snow ashore, except on the high mountains, whereas in the middle of October, not only on Kamchatka but also four degrees farther south at Lopatka and Avacha, the snow has already fallen one arshin deep. But it also stays longer and does not melt in level places before the middle of May, on the mountains before the middle of June, and on the highest mountains and northern spots, ever.

The snow falls in the same amount as on Kamchatka and lies on level ground one and one-half fathoms deep. The narrow valleys between the mountains are often drifted shut with snow from top to bottom because of violent storm winds. It often happens that an entire mountain, especially in spring, suddenly rids itself of snow. We were therefore in not a little danger since we had to go under such mountains after our food. It is also well known in Kamchatka how many men on sable and mouflon hunts are lost every year in avalanches.[27]

From the middle of May until the middle of June, we had mostly cloudy weather and rain. The best weather was from then to the middle of July. Although it was the time of considerable heat, it was still so cool toward evening and during the night that a warm fur coat was quite tolerable.

The entire time of our stay on this island we never heard thunder. I once observed the aurora borealis.

The greatest changes on this island result from earthquakes and high tides, and clear indications of vast inundations are evidenced by driftwood, whalebone, and entire sea cow skeletons washed up far inland and between the shore and the mountains. And from the age of the wood, I concluded very clearly that, at the flooding that befell the Kamchatkan coast and the Kurile Islands in 1738, the water on this island was also at a height of more than thirty fathoms. Not only entire trees that I encountered on mountains at such a height but also the sandspits and new hills deposited on the seashore close by, from which large trees stuck out still undecayed, testified to this flooding. Concerning the new hills which arose from the flooding, I thought it remarkable that, in their form, position, number of peaks and valleys, they conformed completely with the high mountains at whose feet they had recently been created. I therefore concluded that the high mountains themselves owe their form, position, and divisions to the wondrous forming power of the waves, and that the origin of the larger may reasonably be explained through the chance formation of the smaller.

As for plants, animals, and minerals on this island, undoubtedly the splendid and salutary water is the most noteworthy among the minerals.

Although this island has such a slight width in consideration of its length, and although no stream flows more than five or six versts from its source, yet it is surprising that they are so numerous (there are over sixty of them) and that there are as many valleys as streams on this island. Among them are several so large, especially those that flow out of lakes, that at the mouth they are eight, ten, to twelve fathoms wide, and at high tide two to three, but some few four to five feet deep. Most streams have no depth at their mouths for these three reasons: (1) Although the land slopes down to the sea, it becomes suddenly elevated immediately before the seashore; the streams flow very swiftly and at the obstacle on the shore divide themselves into many arms and consequently become too weak to form a channel on the shore; (2) for simply this reason all these streams frequently change their mouths; (3) the mouths themselves at the sea constantly become stopped up with sand. Therefore May is the most convenient month in which to look for a harbor. For when in July and August the snow is completely melted, most of the streams become so small that at the mouth they have hardly a depth of one foot. (However, the Lake River is an exception.) For this very reason, these streams rise so much when it rains continuously for two or three days that they overflow their banks.

Among the streams are very many that crash down from high cliffs and mountains with great noise, amusing the curious onlooker. I noticed one stream falling down in steps over a cliff that has been washed out like a wide staircase just as if this had been done diligently by artifice. The water itself, in lakes as well as in streams, is, because of the stony bottom and the swift movement, uncommonly cold, pure, and light; hence, it is very salutary, and we all felt its effect on our sick and exhausted bodies with immense benefit and delight.

Reference Matter

Notes to Translation

Complete authors' names, titles, and publication data can be found in the Bibliography, pp. 229–38. The following abbreviations are used in the notes.

A   *The American Expedition*, by Sven Waxell
B   *Beschreibung von dem Lande Kamtschatka*, by Steller
BV   *Bering's Voyages*, by Frank A. Golder
D   *De bestiis marinis*, by Steller
F   *Flora of Alaska*, by Eric Hultén
G   *Georg Wilhelm Steller*, by Leonhard Stejneger
MS   Steller's Manuscript Journal
R   *Reise von Kamtschatka nach Amerika*, ed. Peter Simon Pallas
RS   "Report to the Imperial Governing Senate," by Steller
S   "Second voyage de Kamtschatka à Amérique," trans. Jean B. Scherer
T   *Topographische und physikalische Beschreibung der Beringsinsel*, ed. Peter Simon Pallas

Page numbers in these sources are cited in the form A5 (p. 5 of *The American Expedition*) or BV2: 10 (p. 10, vol. 2, of *Bering's Voyages*).

TITLE PAGE

1. MS title page: "Subjecta des 3. fachen Natur Reiches" (Subjects of the threefold natural kingdom).

PREFACE

1. Steller's major scientific findings on Kamchatka, Bering Island, and elsewhere in Siberia.

2. Stejneger interprets "die Alten" (R5) as "the old mapmakers" (BV2: 10), noting that Mercator and others used Promontorium Tabin on their maps as early as the late sixteenth century. Such an interpretation is too specific; Steller's reference is simply to old or ancient writers.

3. Cape Chukchi (East Cape or Cape Dezhnev) is situated at 66° N.

4. Cape Lopatka, at the southernmost tip of the Kamchatka Peninsula.

5. Steller uses the German or Dutch mile, which is 4.61 English statute miles. Even so, he very much underestimates the distance from Cape Lopatka to the nearest point of the American mainland (the tip of the Alaska Peninsula), which is about 365 German miles or nearly 1,700 English miles.

6. This cape extends northward into the Arctic Ocean about 90 miles northwest of East Cape, or Cape Dezhnev. Bering did not know a cape by this name. Steller, as well as Müller, located it near the southeast end of today's Chukotsk Peninsula. Both err in failing to give Bering credit for having sailed in 1728 directly north into the Arctic Ocean to 67°18' N. See Müller, *Bering's Voyages* 71; Lauridsen 39–49; and Fisher 101:*n*41.

7. Mikhail Gvozdev, in 1732 (not 1735, as in MS1), discovered Big and Little Diomede islands, King Island, and the American continent (near the present-day village of Wales on the Seward Peninsula); however, he did not land on the continent.

8. Martin Spangberg, like Bering, was a Dane and second in command to Bering during the 1728 voyage to the Arctic Ocean. He later made two voyages to Japan. Spangberg is variously spelled Spanberg and Spangenberg.

9. Aleksei Chirikov, captain of the *St. Paul*, on the voyage to America.

10. Also known as Petropavlovsk, established by Bering's orders in 1740 within Avacha Bay on the southeast coast of Kamchatka. It has become the principal city of Kamchatka (1983 population, 237,000).

11. I.e., from Bolsheretsk to Avacha Bay, about 140 miles over a mountain pass.

12. Steller reported to the Senate that Bering told him in the winter of 1741 at Petropavlovsk that he (Steller) was needed on the voyage because "if he, the Captain-Commander, should land, then there would be nobody under his command who could explore and identify the nature of the soil, the minerals . . . the animals, birds, fish, plants, and such . . . nobody [who] could observe and compose a lengthy historical description and include not only that which is curious but also that which is useful [and that] none of the officers, even if someone were able to, had enough time to observe the nature, height, customs, habits, and dwellings for a long period of time of any people who were found and [there were none] who could compose a historical description

of those peoples from which one could see what land and what nation this is, how they differ, and how they resemble the others, particularly the American peoples" (RS270).

13. These included, at Steller's headquarters at Bolsheretsk, 1740–41, Stepan P. Krasheninnikov, Aleksei Gorlanov, Johann Christian Berckhan, Aleksei Danilov, Peter Antonov, and Osip Argunov. Steller took a seventh assistant, Thoma Lepekhin, with him on the voyage with Bering.

14. In his report to the Senate, dated Nov. 16, 1742, Steller says that on Mar. 31, 1741, he sent a petition to inform the Senate of his sea voyage with Bering, enclosing it with his report about his trip from Iakutsk to Kamchatka via Okhotsk (RS270). The Empress was informed of Steller's appointment in Bering's report of Apr. 18, 1741. Bering wrote: "Steller . . . is now here, and he has stated in writing that he has the necessary skill in searching for and assaying metals and minerals. . . . Steller stated that besides this he would, in accordance with his responsibility, make various observations on the voyage concerning the natural history, peoples, conditions of land, etc. If any ores should be found, adjunct Steller will assay them" (Fisher 128).

15. In view of his *De bestiis marinis* (Of marine beasts), mostly written in the spring of 1742 on Bering Island, Steller seems unduly modest. However, his statement reflects disappointment that he could not study America and the "Americans" much more fully.

16. Today's Kayak, Nagai, and Bird islands.

17. Steller declared that on Mar. 20, 1741, when he arrived at Petropavlovsk, "I was altogether not received as it would have been suitable according to my character, but was treated like a common soldier and as his underling by Bering and the others, and was not called on for any advice as to the planning of the sea voyage" (Pekarskii 595).

18. Not so nowadays. There is no probability of an ice edge south of 56° N on July 1. See LaBelle and Wise 34.

19. Steller, of course, is mistaken.

20. On July 1, up to the point where Bering turned around in 1728 at 67°18′ N, there would today be only a 25 percent chance of encountering an ice edge. See LaBelle and Wise 32.

21. In 1739, Müller supplied Steller with a manuscript copy of his "Geographie und Verfassung von Kamtschatka" (compiled from written and oral sources at Iakutsk in 1737); this work states: "If . . . the Dutch discovered a small island to the east [of the Kurile Islands], to which they gave the name Staten Island, and from there farther to the east saw a large land that they named Company Land and believed that it was connected to the continent of

North America, then no explanation can be given about the matter from . . . narratives of the Japanese and inhabitants of Jeso" (B52).

22. A Spanish navigator whose voyage from China to Spanish America may be as fictitious as the land named for him. According to Waxell, the decision to go southeast toward the "so-called Juan de Gama's land" was made on the basis of a map brought to a sea council on May 4, 1741, by the professor of astronomy Louis de la Croyère, whose famous mapmaker half-brother, Joseph Delisle, had drawn it for Bering. Waxell notes, with bitterness, that "certain false and unfounded information had been used" (A100–101). Being outside the naval command, Steller was excluded from this sea council.

23. Sofron Khitrov, Bering's fleet master.

24. Bering's headquarters from 1737. Located on the northwest shore of the Sea of Okhotsk opposite the Kamchatka Peninsula, it was founded in 1646 but achieved importance only with the conquest of Kamchatka and the beginning of shipbuilding there in 1714.

25. I.e., at Bolsheretsk, a stockaded post, or *ostrog*, on the Bolshaia River near the southwest coast of the Kamchatka Peninsula. It was founded in 1702 and became the port of entry from Okhotsk and one of the three major posts on Kamchatka (the other two being the upper and lower post on the Kamchatka River) until superseded by Petropavlovsk.

26. Indigenous tribes, some nomadic and noted for their use of reindeer, living on the Kamchatka Peninsula north of the Kamchadals (Itelmens) and south of the Chukchis. Waxell identified the rebellious natives as Kamchadals, not Koriaks (A98–99).

27. The Tigil River is about 500 to 600 versts (about 350 miles) north of Bolsheretsk *ostrog*.

28. "The entire project" refers to the expedition as a whole, and the "two separate voyages" refers to the decision to make two voyages to America during two successive sailing seasons instead of wintering in America as Bering had earlier intended. The Pallas text provides a very different meaning. The manuscript journal reads: "Solcher gestalt sahe sich so wohl der Hl. Capitain Commendeur als die übrigen Herren officir genöthiget zu Ausführung des ganzen projects 2. besondere Reise zu bestimmen" (MS5). The Pallas text reads: "Durch diese Umstände sahe sich denn der Capitain-Commandeur sowohl, als die übrigen Offiziere genöthigt, um nicht Mangel zu leiden, zwei besondre Reisen zu Ausführung des Projects zu bestimmen" (R13–14), translated by Stejneger, "Owing to these circumstances the Captain Commander as well as the other officers, in order not to incur a shortage, found themselves compelled to organize two separate voyages for the accomplish-

ment of this task" (BV2: 20); namely, to attempt transport of provisions from Okhotsk to Avacha two separate times.

29. Peter Kolesov, Kamchatka commander, 1739–43.

CHAPTER 1

1. Among the essential items were three quadrants, one chronometer, one compass, one spyglass, eleven books of navigation, one bundle of charts, two bundles of calculations, and seven maps. See Bancroft 90: *n*14.

2. I.e., Thoma Lepekhin.

3. Laurentz Waxell was only 11 years of age; his father, Sven, was 40 years.

4. A total of 78 left on the voyage; the list of 45 survivors in BV1: 235 omits Laurentz Waxell; 32 died (BV1: 281–82). For a complete roster, see G253–55.

5. *Fucus gardneri*, common in the North Pacific.

6. "Sterna turneri" (MS6).

7. August 24 is incorrectly given in MS7.

8. MS7: "vieles unnöthige" (literally, "much that was unnecessary") is Steller's editorial comment.

9. One of the best known of these Nuremberg mapmakers was Johann Baptist Homan, who, on the orders of Peter the Great, received sketch maps of Russian explorations and was consequently able to publish, by 1722, a map of northeast Asia showing Kamchatka. See Urness 121–24. However, it was Joseph Nicolas Delisle, Academy geographer, who in 1731 included Company Land on a manuscript map he made for Bering's use (map in Müller, *Bering's Voyages* 35). See Preface, note 22.

10. I.e., in the Atlantic.

11. Canton is at 23° N, and the Maldive Islands are, of course, in the Indian Ocean. Steller's examples are geographic rather than "human" errors; he seems inconsistent here.

12. June 18 is incorrectly given in MS8.

13. July 18 is given in MS8 and RS271. However, Steller claims that he sighted land on July 15 and others the next day (see below).

14. MS8 incorrectly gives 49°.

15. The Latin means "expressions of exclamation and amazement."

16. MS8: "sie sind in Gottes Rathstube gewesen" is another embedded sarcastic editorial comment. Pallas made the remark negative by adding "nicht": "Sie sind nicht in Gottes Rathstube gewesen!" (R19), translated, "You have not been in God's council chamber!" in BV2: 26.

17. A phrase omitted by Pallas. See Introduction.

18. Doubtless an allusion to the *Franckeschen Stiftungen*. See Introduction.

19. Pallas's text is brief: "Auch der Capitain Spangberg kann hiervon einen klaren Beweis abgeben, da er sich gegen die von der Academie der Wissenschaften Abgeordnete gleichergestalt aufgeführet" (R20), translated "Even Captain Spanberg's attitude gives a clear proof of this, as he conducted himself towards the representatives of the Academy of Sciences in a similar manner" in BV2: 27. What the manuscript journal says is: "Davon auch der Capitain Spangberg ein klahres Beyspiel seyn kann, der sich gegen die von der Academie der wissenschaften Abgeordnete dergestalt aufgeführet, dass man wohl sagen kan, er wisse dass er Capitain seye, habe aber doch den geringsten Matrosen Streich noch nicht vergessen" (MS9).

20. Isabella A. Abbott, G. W. Wilder Professor of Botany, University of Hawaii at Manoa, has identified Steller's pre-Linnaean botanical terms for seaweed found in BV2: 27–28, *n*51, as follows: *Quercus marina glandifera Bauhini* as *Fucus gardneri*; *Alga dentata Raji* as *Odonthalia floccosa*; *Fuci membranacei calyciformes* as *Constantinea rosa-marina*; *Fucus clavae effigie* as *Nereocystis luetkeana*; and *Fucus lapathi sanguinei foliis Tourn.* as *Delesseria decipiens*. The absence of supporting specimens (as from the Bering expedition) is, says Abbott, "one of the banes of the life of taxonomists" (letter to Frost, Nov. 7, 1986).

21. MS9: "*Urticas marinas rubras* und *albas.*" See BV2: 28, *n*52.

22. Today's Sea of Okhotsk.

23. This grass is *Calamagrostis canadensis Langsdorffi* (F103).

24. Kenyon (p. 66) concludes that the longest escape dive a sea otter (*Enhydra lutris*) can make is "probably less than 6 minutes."

25. MS11: "*Ilra.*" Georg Markgraf's *Ilya* is possibly a spotted-necked otter (*Hydrictis maculicollis*). See below, Chapter 9, note 20.

26. The sea otter is a North Pacific species whose habitat extends in an arc from Lower California to Kamchatka, and, contrary to Steller's belief, from Kamchatka to Japan. See Chanin 142.

27. Steller could not know that the distance between Attu Island and the Commander Islands is more than twice 20 German miles (250 English miles).

28. Mount St. Elias is indeed higher than any Siberian peak, and its range, so close to the sea, is an especially stunning sight on a clear day.

29. Friedrich Plenisner, Steller's friend.

30. The comment "gehen viele mit grosen Winden schwanger" (MS13) reveals Bering's penchant for sarcasm.

CHAPTER 2

1. Kayak Island, consisting of a single mountain range that reaches its highest point, 1,620 feet, at a pyramid-shaped peak at its south end.

2. MS13: "Am Sonntage den 18."

3. It is possible that in the early eighteenth century part of the Bering River flowed into the open sea through the channel between Kayak Island and the mainland. Today, with the land much elevated, Okalee Spit blocks most of the channel, and, according to Andrew Smallwood, a Cordova fisherman who frequents the area, strong three-knot ocean currents sweep in an arc from Cape Suckling to Kayak Island's northeast coast, and submerged reefs across the channel make navigation extremely hazardous.

4. MS14: "den 19. Monntags." Steller repeats this error immediately below.

5. Steller's suggestion that the ship seek anchorage here reflects his eagerness to begin exploration with access to the mainland. Khitrov could not see until the next day that the north end of the island was a V-shaped bay (see Khitrov's sketch map below). In 1790, Martin Sauer learned from an old Eskimo "that at the north extremity of Kay's [Kayak] island, there was a bay sheltered from the wind; that the entrance at low water was as deep as his double paddle (which is about seven feet); and that there are runs of fresh water into it, but no great rivers" (Sauer 195). In 1778, Captain Cook chose to land on the northeast side of the island, even though the bay within the north end must have been visible to him. Today, there is no bay at all because the land rose some 10 feet during the great earthquake of 1964; however, geologists Gil Mull and George Plafker report gradual submergence over many years before 1964 (Mull and Plafker 143–44). In any case, historical evidence would suggest that Kayak Island was some 20–30 feet lower than it is today.

6. Khitrov, in his journal, speaks of "a submerged reef of rocks . . . seen in low water" (BV1: 99). The ship did not proceed into the large inner bay (Controller Bay) north of the strait between Kayak and Wingham islands (Kayak Entrance) but anchored off Cape St. Peter south of Wingham Island in the outer "bay" formed by the two islands. See Khitrov's sketch map.

7. The *St. Peter* anchored at 6:00 A.M. in 22 fathoms about 1 mile from Kayak Island and 3.5 miles from Wingham Island (ship's log, BV1: 96).

8. The German *Vorgebürge* is a literal translation of the Latin *promontorium*. The reference to the "cut-off head" is attributable to the synonym for *Vorgebirge*, or *Kap*, which derives from the Latin *caput*, or "head."

9. The MS omits a phrase in R29: "oder endlich den graden Weg nach Hause suchen sollte" (or finally seek the straight way home), which also ap-

pears in S49: "ou enfin s'il ne voudroit pas mieux prendre la route la plus courte pour retourner chez nous" (or finally if it would not be better to take the shortest way home).

10. Pallas offers these further comments in a footnote, "Es ist unbegreiflich, dass an keine ernstliche Untersuchung und Besitznehmung des entdeckten Landes hat gedacht werden wollen; und fast sollte man muthmassen dass die ertheilte allgemeine Instruction unzulänglich gewesen seyn müsse, oder dass in so entfernten Gegenden alle Subordination und Furcht verschwunden" (R29), a statement translated, "It is incomprehensible that there was no thought of real exploration and taking possession of the land discovered; one might almost conjecture that the general instructions issued must have been insufficient, or that in so distant parts all subordination and discipline had vanished" (BV2: 37). Lev S. Berg, Soviet authority on the Bering expeditions, wrote: "Steller's reproaches are completely justified here. Bering's indifference to scientific work . . . is . . . unforgivable because the aim of the expedition was to examine the new land; that is, to investigate it in all aspects and to establish ties with the inhabitants" (Berg, *Discovery of Kamchatka*, 211). Whereas Pallas and Berg side with Steller, Stejneger generally favors the Captain-Commander: "Bering's first thought was for the safety of his ship and his men. . . . So he resolved that the first thing to do was to search for a sheltered harbor. The next was to obtain fresh drinking water. Everything else was secondary" (G264). Bering's instructions are most fully interpreted in Fisher 120–32 *passim*.

11. I.e., to the "High Governing Senate" (Steller's report of Nov. 16, 1742, quoted in Pekarskii, 596).

12. MS15: "sezte ich allen respect auf die Seite und betete ein besonderes Gebeth."

13. Steller says of his altercation with Bering, in his report to the Senate, dated Nov. 16, 1742: "But when I saw that I was treated so irregularly and I was left neglected and despised, and could achieve nothing with sweet words, I used sharp words with him, Captain-Commander Bering, saying that I would speak truly and publicly testify to the High Governing Senate, protesting against him in terms he deserved. But since such brave pride has become customary with many people in distant lands, I achieved nothing except that with great indignation and harmful words I was lowered from the ship. Without any help, with one servant under my command, he exposed me to grave misfortune and death, he who led the scolding of me in front of the others. But since through harsh actions and through fear he could do nothing, he changed everything to friendship and ordered the trumpet to be blown as I was

taken to the shore together with people seeking water, thinking that I could not distinguish this and would take dishonor as a sign of honor, and thus my proposals would longer remain objects of derision" (RS271).

14. Mining was developed, and mineralogists trained, in this city founded in 1721 by Peter the Great and named for his wife, Catherine I. Steller evidently knew that in the Senate's instructions to Bering, dated Mar. 16, 1733, "it was stipulated that two or three assayers were to be sent from the metallurgical works at Ekaterinburg . . . to eastern Siberia, in addition to another assayer named Simon Gardebol', who had been sent to Kamchatka in 1727 with Captain Dmitrii I. Pavlutskii" (Fisher 128). Fisher uses a Russian spelling for the German surname "Hartepol."

15. "Mit diesen wurde ich abgefertiget wässerige observationes zu machen, so wie andere während Zeit windige" (MS16) is in Pallas's text "Mit einem andern Theil wurde ich nach dem Wasser abgefertigt, um wässrige Beobachtungen zu machen, da andre dagegen nach windigen aus waren" (R31); translated "With another party I was sent off after water, to make watery observations, while others were out on a windy expedition" (BV2:41). Clearly, "diesen" refers to water barrels, but the referent of "andere" is less clear. It appears to refer to the officers talking and monitoring the wind on deck aboard the anchored ship rather than to Khitrov's party moving toward the shelter of the inner bay.

16. About 10:20 A.M. The same yawl left the ship at 10:00 A.M. and returned at 11:00 A.M. with the first load of fresh water and the news of a fire site, "human tracks, and a fox on the run" (BV1:96). Stejneger, during a brief evening visit to Kayak Island in 1922, placed the landing at the mouth of a stream (Watering Place Creek) on the southwest coast of the island (BV2:41, *n*73); and John F. Thilenius, on the basis of evidence then available to him, placed it at the mouth of a stream (Pyramid Creek) within the bight formed by Cape St. Peter and the northwest shore (Thilenius 62). More recent evidence—namely, the discovery of bark stripping on huge trees behind Cape St. Peter (see note 33 below) and variants in S57–58 and S63 (see notes 32 and 47 below)—point to the mouth of an unnamed stream south of what is today's Cape St. Peter. This site is now the obvious choice: It was only a mile ESE from the anchorage of the *St. Peter* or less than half the distance to either of the other two sites proposed; of the three possibilities, it is the only site to which the yawl could go, fill a half-dozen or so barrels with fresh water, and return to the ship, all in about a single hour.

17. This infinitive phrase is omitted in the Pallas text (R31).

18. De Laguna has determined that the people on Kayak and Wingham

islands in the eighteenth century were a branch of the Chugach Eskimo of Prince William Sound. She states, "The Chugach were apparently intruders into Controller Bay and its islands, but when they first began to occupy it, and whether they ever established more than seasonal hunting camps, we do not know" (De Laguna, *Under Mount Saint Elias*, 18). However, Chugach legends suggest that they were not "intruders" but a people from the north who "sailed away into the sea" in a *baidarka*. "First they saw Kayak, then Kochak [Middleton Island]. They landed on these islands, lived there long enough to have children, left them, and sailed farther" (Johnson 1), eventually peopling the entire south-central Alaska coast from Kodiak to Yakutat. On Kayak Island, they apparently settled in the vicinity of Cape St. Peter, whose reefs provided a ready source of food and whose inland spruce provided bark and timbers for *barabaras*, or subterranean dwellings. The relationship between the Chugach and "the shadowy tribe of Cilquarmiut"—which, according to Osahito Miyaoka (73–75), was a Bering Sea Eskimo remnant possibly living winters on the south end of Kayak Island and summers fishing along the coast nearly to Icy Bay (see Dall, *Alaska*, 401; and idem, *Contributions*, 21)—is uncertain. Were they an isolated band of the Chugach or a distinctly different people? In any event, by the time of Bering's arrival, the Chugach Eskimo shared the Controller Bay area with two other peoples. Michael E. Krauss, an authority on Eyak Indian language and culture, believes that during this same period, "a center of Eyak settlement was on the mainland of Controller Bay" (quoted in De Laguna, *Under Mount Saint Elias*, 19). At the same time the Tlingit were beginning to converge on the area from Icy Bay. Had Bering wintered in Controller Bay, Steller evidently could have studied both Eskimos and Indians.

19. Probably near the southwest side of today's Cape St. Peter.

20. In his report to the Senate, dated Nov. 16, 1742, Steller says that here "not long before my arrival Americans had eaten, and, perhaps when they saw me with my servant, had run away and left a sign of their flight, a wooden hammer made in the Kamchadal manner, an arrow, and many other items" (RS271).

21. A detailed description of such "Kamchatkan ways" is not, however, included in Steller's *Beschreibung*.

22. The bones were possibly a mountain goat's (Birket-Smith and De Laguna 346).

23. I.e., on Kamchatka, where in 1743 Steller wrote the journal of his voyage with Bering, using his travel diaries. The Jacob's mussel is a scallop (*Pecten caurinus*) and the blue mussel, *Mytilus californianus*. See BV2: 44, *n*77.

24. MS17: "Slatka trava."

25. Cow parsnip or wild celery (*Heracleum lanatum*); the plant tastes like licorice (F707). Steller discussed its use on Kamchatka (see B84–87).

26. Curiously, Steller does not say that American practice conforms with Kamchadal custom but vice versa, a reversal indicative of the haste with which he wrote.

27. Nomadic Koriaks who follow the reindeer.

28. Steller is the first scientist to propose Asian roots for Eskaleuts by comparing cultural affinities and adaptations. Today this theory is further supported by evidence of similar blood types and physiological characteristics.

29. On Kayak Island, on May 20, 1987, John F. C. Johnson, Chugach Eskimo ethnohistorian, spotted a lichen, *Alectoria sarmentosa*, that his ancestors used as tinder. However, John F. Thilenius, who has done pioneering botanizing on the island, doubts that Steller would have failed to recognize a lichen; it is much more likely, he writes (letter to Frost, July 24, 1987), that Steller collected, as a sample of tinder, a dried seaweed, of which there are various species found today on the shore.

30. This path probably existed in the vicinity of the mouth of today's Pyramid Creek.

31. A long knife with a wooden handle.

32. Both the MS and Pallas's text omit a phrase and two clauses after "Wir sahen" (We saw) translated in S57–58 after "Nous vîmes" as follows: "dans cette forêt qui est immense et qui pourroit fournir du bois pour la construction de vaisseaux pendant des Siècles" (in this forest, which is immense and which could furnish wood for the construction of ships for centuries). An editor (Scherer?) has drawn a line through "de vaisseaux" and substituted "navale." This information about trees suitable for shipbuilding contradicts Waxell's observation, "On the island there is plenty of small timber . . . which are [*sic*] not fit for building and not even for repairing a ship, for we looked for material for topyards but did not find it" (BVI: 272). Waxell, of course, remained aboard ship; and Khitrov, in looking over Kayak Island "for a piece of timber for the topsail yards" (BVI: 99), did not apparently land on the island.

33. Old bark-stripped trees are found today several hundred feet inland from the north shore of Cape St. Peter; reported by a National Park Service, Alaska Region, team (Susan D. Morton, John F. C. Johnson, and John L. Mattson) visiting the site in May 1986.

34. Birket-Smith and De Laguna consider this subterranean structure to be definitely Eskimo, not Eyak (pp. 347–48). However, they say that none

of its contents "gives us any clue as to the inhabitants of Kayak Island" (ibid. 347). However, Martin Sauer, a member of the Billings expedition, met an old Eskimo in Prince William Sound in 1790 who "remembered, that when he was a boy, a ship had been close into the bay on the west side of the island, and had sent a boat ashore; but on its approaching land the natives all ran away. When the ship sailed, they returned to their hut, and found in their subterraneous store-room, some glass beads, leaves (tobacco), an iron kettle" (Sauer, 193–94).

35. *Oncorhynchus nerka*, or red salmon; see BV2: 48, *n*88.

36. MS18: "Krana riba," or red fish.

37. An old Russian trading center, founded in 1181 as Khlynov, whose name was changed to Vyatka in 1780 and later to Kirov. It is located on the Vyatka River west of the Urals.

38. I.e., 6 additional versts.

39. Steller was stopped by the sight of sea water around today's Seacave Rock. He scaled the unnamed 430-foot hill south of the rock.

40. I.e., on the other side.

41. MS19: "auf eine Werste"; R36: "auf einige Werste" (some versts away); S61: "à la distance d'un mille" (at a distance of a mile).

42. MS19: "lustigen" (comical) appears to be an error for "luftigen." The knoll was probably on a low, narrow, wooded cape extending toward Wingham Island, the first stage in the development of today's Campsite Spit. Its breeziness, on a day of topgallant and topsail winds, would have been indicated by the smoke rising above the trees.

43. Steller describes these events somewhat differently in his report of Nov. 16, 1742, to the Senate: "Even though I could not see the people themselves on a hill covered with woods, I know that they were there because I saw a fire there. And though I tried by all means to approach them, I had to desist, and because of a cliff that was quite steep and reached into the sea, it was impossible to walk there" (RS271).

44. See Introduction.

45. MS19: "ich sollte mich nur geschwinde nach dem Fahrzeuge paken."

46. MS20 and R37: "nach Westen"; S63: "vers le sud" (toward the south). Steller could have walked in either direction from the landing site.

47. The clause in parentheses is not in the Pallas text; it is, however, translated in S63.

48. At 4:00 P.M. Bering ordered Nils Jansen, the boatswain (guided by Lepekhin?), to take "16.5 arshins [46 feet] of green material, 2 knives, Chinese tobacco, and pipes" (ship's log, BV1: 97). Waxell reports that these

items were "a piece of green krashenne or sleek-leather, two iron kettles, two knives, twenty large glass beads, two iron tobacco-pipes and a pound of leaf tobacco" (A106).

49. Doubtless the officers were amusing themselves at Steller's expense. Steller was obviously unaware that two knives were left in the underground dwelling he found.

50. On Sept. 9, 1741, Chirikov met Aleuts from Adak, who, he reported, were overjoyed to receive a knife and gladly carried fresh water in bladders by skinboat from shore to ship in return for additional knives (BVI: 304–5).

51. Khitrov returned to the ship at 9:00 P.M. (BVI: 97), Steller at 8:00 P.M.

52. Khitrov does not speak of a harbor in his report. He says that, in going between what is now Wingham and Kayak islands, "the depth of the channel was 25, 22, 18, 10, 7, 6, 4, and 3.5 fathoms, where it is possible to anchor" (BVI: 99).

53. After "a reconnaissance round the curve of the islands" (A105), Khitrov probably landed on the northeast end of Wingham Island (the end farthest from Kayak). In his journal, he says: "We came across . . . a hut which was made of hewn boards; the floor was also made of these boards. In place of an oven there was in one corner of the hut a fireplace" (BVI: 99).

54. Khitrov reports: "Near the hut was found a wooden basket in which were shell fish, which showed that the inhabitants here used them for food. We did not see any people, but it was quite evident that they had been here shortly before our arrival" (BVI: 99).

55. Birket-Smith and De Laguna write that neither Eyak nor Eskimo "claim to have made rattles of baked clay" (p. 349).

56. Steller underestimates the length of the island, which is nearly 5 German or 21 English miles. He is probably quite accurate in figuring its width to be about 2.3 miles (one-half German mile). Today, the width is less than 2 miles (except at Cape St. Peter and Campsite Spit) because of continuous erosion of nearly the entire western shore by sea currents. Landslides, which Stejneger reported in 1922, still occur today.

57. Today the north end of Kayak Island is about one mile from Okalee Spit, which extends from the mainland. The spit did not exist in 1741 (see Khitrov's sketch map above).

58. Steller's harsh judgment, reflecting his frustration of the moment, contrasts sharply with his earlier admiration of Bering's caution (see above).

59. R39: "zehn Stunden" (ten hours) is the time Steller spent on Kayak

Island. However, observations were made both from the ship and on land. The *St. Peter* was anchored for 25 hours, of which nearly 20 were daylight hours.

60. Khitrov's sketch map.

61. I.e., from Cape Lopatka to the mouth of the Kamchatka River.

62. MS23: "Am 26. Julii."

63. Salmonberry, or *Rubus spectabilis*. This berry is still large and abundant today, especially in the vicinity of Cape St. Peter.

64. The "familiar berries" are as follows: *Chamaecerasus* (*Lonicera involucrata?*) is bitter and purplish black, found chiefly in southeast Alaska; "rothe und schwarze Heidelbeeren" (MS23), literally, "red and black blueberries," are most likely lingonberries (*Vaccinium vitis-idaea*) and blueberries (*V. ovalifolium, V. alaskensis*), all found in south-central Alaska; "scurvy berries" are cloudberries (*Rubus chamaemorus*), a juicy, sweet, yellow berry found in peat bogs throughout Alaska; and *Empetrum* (*E. nigrum*) are crowberries, juicy, seedy, and black, also found in bogs but limited to south-coastal Alaska.

65. MS23: "Subjecta regni vegetabilis" (objects of the vegetable kingdom).

66. "Catalogus plantarum intra sex horas in parti Americae septemtrionalis iuxta promontorium Eliae observatarum anno 1741 die 21 [*sic*] Iulii sub gradu latitudinis 59" (see Introduction).

67. MS24: "Seehunde" is here very likely harbor seals, *Phoca richardii*.

68. Instead of "Hayen, Canes charcharias" (MS24) the Pallas text has "grosse und kleine Haien" (R42), or large and small sharks. However, Steller is probably identifying a species of North Pacific shark known as the great white or man-eater shark (*Carcharodon*) of the family Lamnidae. It reaches a length of 40 feet and feeds on both fish and sea mammals. See B147.

69. As both Pallas (R43) and Stejneger (G270–71) noted, the author in question is the English naturalist and artist Mark Catesby, F.R.S. The first volume of his two-volume *Natural History of Carolina, Florida and the Bahama Islands* was published in London in 1731 "at the Expence of the Author." The painting of the bluejay, filling an entire 12 by 16–inch page, faces 1: 15, where it is described in large type both in English and French. In "A List of the Encouragers of This Work" appears the name of Steller's mentor at the Academy of Sciences in St. Petersburg, "John Amman, M.D., Prof. Bot. Petrop." No doubt Amman introduced Steller to Catesby's work.

CHAPTER 3

1. MS25: "bey den Booten," the first of several instances in which a copyist has confused "Boot" (boat) and "Lot" (plumb-line).

2. Chirikov Island, so named in 1794 by George Vancouver (see BV1: 111, *n*53). This island, known since 1888 for its wild cattle, is not, however, wooded. Steller used "wooded" in the sense that a few scraggly trees (like alders) are present (see Chapter 4).

3. Sculpins, identified as *Hemilepidotus hemilepidotus* and *Megalocottus platycephalus* in BV2: 62, *n*130.

4. Mt. Chiginagak and neighboring peaks (see BV1: 335). NNW½W is halfway between NW by N and NNW at 331°52′30″.

5. MS26 "gestrandet" and S84 "nous echouée" contrast with R46 "gestanden." Since, according to the ship's log (BV1: 111), the *St. Peter* did not actually run aground off Chirikov Island, it can be assumed that "almost" was inadvertently omitted in the manuscript.

6. Semidi Islands (see BV1: 335–36). These islands also are "wooded" only in the sense indicated in note 2 above.

7. Both Steller (MS26) and Pallas (R47) make a distinction between "See-Bähren" ("sea bears," or fur seals) and "See-Hunde" ("sea dogs," or seals generally).

8. MS26: "See-Schweine Phocaenen." The porpoise belongs to the genus *Phocaena*.

9. Krasheninnikov obviously makes use of this description in writing a somewhat abbreviated version of the sea ape (see Krasheninnikov 160).

10. As Stejneger notes, *gallis* (roosters) in "wie bey den gallis" (MS26) is probably an error for *galeis* (sharks). Pallas, however, writes "wie bey Hahnen" (R47), translated "as in the case of roosters" (BV2: 64).

11. The name of the correspondent is Ioan Kentmannus (Johann Kentmann?). See Gesner 1:153, and note 12 below.

12. Gesner used the name "sea ape," not "Danish sea ape." However, he reported receiving the picture of the sea mammal from Denmark: "Simia marina quaedam, cuius iconem qualem a Ioan. Kentmanno accepi, hic exhibeo. Is Simiae marinae nomine e Dania sibi allatam scribit" (Gesner, *Icones*, 1: 153). Steller, writing in Kamchatka in 1743, probably had not seen the picture and description of Gesner's sea ape since 1738.

13. What did Steller see? Conrad Gesner (1516–65) published uncritically "everything known, speculated, imagined, or reported about all known animals" (Boorstin 427), and Kentmannus's sketch of the sea ape, published in *Icones animalium*, does not inspire confidence in its reality. Steller, however, must be taken seriously. He observed at close range his *simia marina* ("it could have been touched with a pole") and "for more than two hours." If he had obtained a specimen, would he have discovered this mammal to be nothing more than a bachelor fur seal, as Stejneger concludes it was "in all probability" (see

G278–81)? Yet on August 4–9, Steller had constantly observed sea otters, fur seals, and sea lions. Moreover, on Bering Island, in the spring of 1742, he studied and described in detail the behavior and anatomies of all three sea mammals. Could he, then, composing his journal in 1743, have been so mistaken? On the other hand, the absence of a specimen makes his description "imperfect," and Thomas Pennant's comment is apropos: "On animals of this species the fable of the Sirens might very well be founded" (Pennant 1: 211).

CHAPTER 4

1. That Bering was now ignoring Steller, even as ship's physician, is suggested by Bering's direct consultation with the assistant surgeon. Khitrov notes in his journal, "The assistant surgeon, Betge, has submitted a report in which he says that there are five men on the sick list, totally unfit for duty and that, of the others, sixteen are badly affected with scurvy and if we continue at sea until the late autumn these men too will be unfit for service" (BVI: 120).

2. Steller's hypothesis that the chain of islands would continue to sweep further southward is, again, a remarkable instance of his potential usefulness to the Bering expedition.

3. Here Steller was mistaken, for although the American continent was, indeed, still to the north, there was, on August 18, no land immediately south of the ship.

4. I.e., on the Atlantic side.

5. If this reply was made jokingly, Steller seemed unaware of the fact. He was, however, correct about Juan de Gama Land's being considered a part of the northwest coast of America (see BV2: 70–72, *n*148, and the photograph of the manuscript map prepared by Joseph N. Delisle, facing BV2: 70).

6. Vries Strait, so named after Maerten Gerritsen Vries, the Dutch captain who passed between Company Land (Urup) and Staten Island (Iturup and Kunashiri considered as one island) in the Kurile Islands. Steller evidently considered this strait, which he also calls "the channel," to be the first open water between America and Kamchatka.

7. The North Pacific codfish, *Gadus macrocephalus* (BV2: 75, *n*155).

8. Possibly a fulmar in a dark-plumage phase or a shearwater.

9. The outer Shumagins, including Nagai, Near, Turner, Bird, and Chernabura. Other islands, possibly visible, would be Simeonof and the Twins.

10. Nagai Island.

11. Near Island.

12. Turner Island.

13. Steller understood, of course, that he was not to share in the discovery of America's inhabitants.

14. A pond close to the sea, a mile and a half northwest of the ship's anchorage (see Khitrov's sketch map), on the east side of Nagai. This pond, which Frost visited as a consultant in history for the U.S. Fish & Wildlife Service in May 1985, is a quarter mile in both length and width and separated from the sea by only 50 to 200 yards.

15. The pond is, indeed, slightly salty even today. Given the driftwood on the shore of the pond, it is obvious that it is occasionally flooded by salt water during high tides or ocean storms.

16. Such water feeds into the west side of the pond farthest from the ocean.

17. I.e., as ship's physician.

18. Waxell, as officer in charge with Bering himself becoming ill with scurvy and keeping to his cabin, took responsibility for this decision. In his journal, which he later revised, he wrote: "The mate, Andreas Hesselberg, was at once sent to one of the largest islands to fetch water; he returned, speedily bringing two samples of water which we did not find particularly good, for they had a faint flavour of salt water. However, we had no time to lose and so we thought that such water was always better than nothing, for we could at any rate use it for cooking. Doing that, we would have to continue using the supply we already had for drinking water, and this, if need be, and being very sparing with it, we ought to be able to make see us through" (A108–9).

19. This is a lake, still unnamed today, extending a mile and a quarter across the width of Nagai Island. Although it is a half-mile farther from the place at which the *St. Peter* anchored, its eastern shore is actually a bit closer to the sea than "the preferred salty puddle."

20. In addition to the five islands previously visible, all to the north and the east, Steller was now aware of the three islands on the west side of Nagai: John, Unga, and Popof. These last two are large islands that may have appeared as a single island; Big and Little Koniuji islands and Simeonof to the northeast may also have appeared to be one island. The thirty-odd islands in the Shumagin group lie in an area roughly fifty miles square, but most of these would not have been visible to Steller.

21. Steller's guess is half the actual length: Nagai Island is 30 miles long. In some central areas it is 9 miles wide, or three times the width of 4 versts estimated by Steller. However, most of the southern part of the island, seen by Steller, is quite narrow, approximately 2 miles, or 3 versts, from east to west.

22. A variety of red fox, *Vulpes fulva*. Foxes no longer exist on Nagai.

23. This animal is probably the Arctic ground squirrel, *Citellus parryi nebulicola*; see Dufresne 136–37. Olaus J. Murie saw ground squirrels on Nagai in 1936 and 1937.

24. Wolves have rarely been sighted on the Shumagin Islands. Petroff re-

ported a single wolf pelt traded at Unga in 1850, but Edgar P. Bailey, a foremost authority on the wildlife of the Shumagins, pointed out to Frost that it could have been taken on the Alaska Peninsula. Andrew Gronholdt, a 72-year resident and local historian, writes that "in recent years three [wolves] were seen on Unga Island but only for a brief period" (letter to Frost, Dec. 29, 1985). Both Bailey and Gronholdt think Steller probably saw the footprint not of a wolf but of a land otter or bear cub.

25. In this short list of his sightings during two days on Nagai Island, Steller noted birds still abundant in the area today, together with a few surprises. Swans, for example, have infrequently been recorded in the Shumagins in recent years. Robert H. Day thinks that whistling swans (*Olor columbianus*), seen at King Cove, are "probably uncommon migrants through the area" ("Birds," 10). On the other hand, cormorants are widespread throughout the region. The two species Steller saw are probably the red-faced cormorant (*Phalacrocrox urile*) and pelagic cormorant (*P. pelagicus*), although the double-crested cormorant (*P. auritus*) has also been reported (on Simeonof Island in 1968) in much smaller numbers. By "auks" Steller may be referring to the common murre (*Uria aalge*) and thick-billed murre (*U. lomvia*). The ducks are almost certainly the harlequin duck (*Histrionicus histrionicus*), common today throughout the Shumagins. Steller's "snipes" are probably the black oystercatcher (*Haematopus bachmani*), which Bailey (p. 89) found nesting on most of the Shumagins. Sandpipers are infrequent in summer. Steller may have seen the western sandpiper (*Calidris mauri*), the least sandpiper (*C. minutilla*), or the rock sandpiper (*C. ptilocnemis*). The "various gulls" Steller saw certainly include the glaucous-winged gull (*Larus glaucescens*), which Bailey (p. 87) in 1977 found nesting on nearly all the Shumagins. L. W. Sowl, G. Divoky, and E. P. Bailey estimate a population of 6,400 on Nagai alone (unpublished field notes, U.S. Fish & Wildlife Service, 1973). Steller probably also saw the mew gull (*L. canis*), which Bailey found nesting on Bendel Island in 1976 (600 birds), and the black-legged kittiwake (*Rissa tridactyla*), which Bailey (p. 85) found in abundance on Near Island in 1977.

Steller's "divers" are very likely two species of loons, the common loon (*Gavia immer*) and the red-throated loon (*G. stellata*), both common in southcoastal Alaska. Of these two, the common loon may be the "very peculiar and unknown species" since it is not found in Eurasia (and, hence, was outside Steller's previous experience), and it seems to fit Steller's later description of "a very beautiful black pied diver never seen before" (see Chapter 5). The German here is "schwarz und bunten Mergum" (MS46), rewritten by Pallas "schwarz und weissbunten Taucher" (R76), or "black and white pied diver."

The Greenland pigeons are the pigeon guillemots (*Cepphus columba*), of which Bailey (p. 87) estimates 1,000 nest on Nagai, although densities in 1977 were low throughout the island. On the other hand, tiny Near Island, he reports, had 200 of these seabirds. The sea parrots are the horned puffin (*Fratercula corniculata*), which with the tufted puffin (*F. cirrhata*)—or "Mitschagatka" (MS32) as Steller calls them, using the Kamchadal name—are, says Bailey (p. 86), "the most abundant and widely distributed species in the Shumagin Islands." In 1977 Bailey estimated populations of 6,000 horned puffins on Nagai and an incredible 10,000 on Near, and of 4,750 tufted puffins on Nagai and 2,000 on Near.

Of the four land birds sighted by Steller, the raven is undoubtedly the common raven (*Corvus corax*), which Day ("Birds," 46) in 1977 reported as "a very common and prominent sight around all the islands the entire summer"; the flycatcher may be the water pipit (*Anthus spinoletta*); the "snowbirds" are probably the snow bunting (*Plectrophenax nivalis*); and the "Morast Hüner" (MS32), the willow ptarmigan (*Lagopus lagopus*) or rock ptarmigan (*L. mutus*).

26. A Dolly Varden or charr (*Salvelinus malma*) and red sculpin (*Hemilepidotus hemilepidotus*).

27. Steller may be counting Atka, Adak, Kiska, Buldir, two of the Semichi islands, and Copper Island (BV2: 82, *n*186).

28. Veniaminov, nearly a century later, noted another "main reason": the Aleutians "to judge by the soil layers, have begun to be clothed by vegetation not very long ago" (Veniaminov 31). Both Steller and Veniaminov fail to hit on the actual reason: low average soil temperatures combined with the strong winds.

29. Karaga Island, off the northeast coast of the Kamchatka Peninsula.

30. Two of the Semichi islands.

31. The only list among those duplicated by Golder in Russia in 1917 and based specifically on collections made on Nagai Island is entitled "Catalogus seminum anno 1741 in America septemtrionali sub gradu latitudinis 59 & 55 collectorum quorum dimidia pars d. 17 Nov. 1742 transmissa." Of the 25 species on the list, only 4 were not first gathered on Nagai during August 30 and 31, 1741.

32. The same "rothen Heidelbeeren" (*Vaccinium vitis-idaea*) and *Empetrum nigrum*, both scurvy berries, found on Kayak Island.

33. The *Cochlearia*, or scurvy grass, has leaves that "eaten raw or boiled . . . are a valuable antiscorbutic" (F499). Steller gathered *C. officinalis*, subspecies *oblongifolia*, found throughout south-coastal Alaska. The *Lapathum*, or

dock, is probably *Rumex graminifolius*, found on Kamchatka, whose "leaves are eaten raw by the Siberian Eskimo" (F376). The *Gentiana* is either *G. algida* or *G. amarella*, subspecies *acuta*, both found on Kamchatka. Among those who subsequently escaped the ravages of scurvy, Lepekhin, Plenisner, and Betge all possibly benefited from Steller's depleted stock of antiscorbutic plants and became the "scarcely four ablebodied men aboard." That Steller prescribed raw *Lapathum* for seamen with scurvy is evident from his own statement.

34. The officers probably scorned Steller's proposal out of ignorance, for scurvy was then very much a mystery, even to physicians. On Kamchatka, Steller independently identified scurvy with diet and thus achieved a significant medical discovery twelve years before Dr. James Lind, "the father of nautical medicine," published his landmark "Treatise of the Scurvy" in 1753. Lind's research, largely ignored when published, was occasioned by the disastrous voyage of Lord George Anson in 1740–42, when 1,051 out of 1,955 men on three ships died of scurvy. See the Introduction.

35. Why does this remark appear *after* Steller has already mentioned that his plants worked miracles with Bering and afflicted seamen? The contradiction suggests that in writing the manuscript journal, Steller used daily entries of his travel diary that reflected momentary bitter feelings rather than later compassionate deeds and that larger topics introduced in retrospect (e.g., Steller's success in treating scurvy) are not always editorially integrated into his day-by-day account.

36. Steller and Plenisner, accompanied no doubt by Lepekhin, had been collecting plants and seeds along the west coast toward the southern end of the island. At the time they were found, they must have been about five miles southwest of the landing site, where, during a second day, water was still being carried from the pond Steller calls "the preferred salty puddle."

37. Even on a relatively calm day, the surf along the shore of the landing site can be treacherous, as Frost discovered on May 12, 1985, in making a departure from the site by motorized Avon raft with Bailey in charge. At the southeast edge of a high rock cliff is a somewhat sheltered cove with a small sandy beach where the ship's mate, Andreas Hesselberg, and his water carriers probably landed, where the boat's painter was tied to a rock, and from which the northeast edge of the pond was about 100 fathoms or 200 yards away.

38. Nikita Shumagin's grave, unmarked today, is probably located on the gently rising grassy slope off the northeast end of the pond. Here, the sick could rest comfortably in the sun, be protected from northwesterly winds by

the hill rising steeply behind them, face the ship and the pond, and be close by the route taken by water carriers between pond and beach.

39. The third landing site of this expedition is located about one mile north of the first, off the northeast end of the large lake that Steller had recommended on Aug. 30 as a convenient second alternative to the salty pond from which 52 barrels were actually filled. Khitrov and his crew of five men landed here late in the afternoon of Aug. 31 after becoming caught in a rising storm on their return in the small jolly boat from the northwest end of Turner Island, the second landing site, where they had investigated the embers of a fire seen from the ship during the preceding night. For further particulars regarding Khitrov's ill-fated trip to and from Turner Island, see Waxell's journal (A109–12).

40. Khitrov had proposed that he investigate the fire (A109).

41. Steller is probably reflecting on Khitrov's role during the entire 1741–42 expedition. Certainly, to this point, Khitrov did not leave "the doing to others" but assumed leadership in reconnoitering unknown shores for signs of people.

42. This anchorage is indicated on Khitrov's sketch map.

43. Waxell says he ordered Khitrov to leave the jolly boat behind "if there was any difficulty about bringing the yawl back" (A112).

44. Near Island is a single huge rock projecting 1,289 feet out of the sea.

45. Bird Island in the Shumagin group.

46. MS37: "Boot" is again given instead of "Lot." See above, Chapter 3, note 1.

47. The ship anchored off a wide bay on the northwest side of Bird Island (see Khitrov's sketch map).

CHAPTER 5

1. Bird Island. The island trends northeast–southwest.

2. Steller later learned that these Aleuts had come from a small village on the northwest point of an island now known as Chernabura Island, located four miles across the strait from the northeast point of Bird Island. When did these Aleuts first see the Bering expedition? On the preceding day, which had been pleasant and clear with only passing clouds overhead, the ship's navigators, in passing to the north around Near Island before noon and heading toward Bird Island from the northwest, caught sight of what seemed to be a bay to the northeast around Bird Island. After dropping anchor in the afternoon and spending the night sheltered from southerly winds in the lee of Bird Is-

land, Kharlam Iushin, second mate and assistant navigator, reported in the ship's log that at 4:00 A.M., Sept. 4, "Put the boat into the water, and I was sent to examine what seemed a bay in NE in order to find shelter from whatever wind may come along." Three hours later he wrote in the log, "I returned to the ship and reported that what we sighted was not a bay but an open passage and that the depth was 15 and 16 fathoms" (BVI: 146). If Iushin did not see the Aleut village at the entrance to the open passage, it would seem likely that the Aleuts saw him, if not also the approaching ship the day before. While the ship vainly endeavored to put to sea off the west end of Bird Island, the Aleut party, in their kayaks hugging the shoreline around the northeast end of Bird Island, very possibly reached the bay and landed beneath the cliff just as the ship returned to its previous anchorage about four o'clock in the afternoon.

3. Steller means the cliff rimming the innermost part of the bay. See note 17 below.

4. Lev S. Berg, as reported by Waldemar Jochelson, remarks, "The Aleut without any doubt have taken the Russians for unearthly beings to whom they rendered divine homage" (Jochelson, *History*, 15).

5. No manuscript with this title has been found.

6. *Nouveaux voyages de M. le baron de Lahontan dans l'Amérique septentrionale* (p. 204) lists *nipi* for *eau* (water) in an appended "Petit dictionnaire de la langue des sauvages." It is clear that Lahontan's Huron or Algonquin word *nipi*, understood as *nitschi* (MS38) by Steller, could have been any word at all to the Aleuts. Note that, in Steller's account, they have, by scooping up water and pointing to the shore, established the concept of water before *nitschi* is even shouted to them. Waxell tells a story about a later, successful use of Lahontan's vocabulary: "I talked to them, using an English book, de la Hontan's description of North America, which I had with me. In it there is a whole number of American words in alphabetical order, with an English translation added. I questioned them about water and they showed me a little spring near by. Then I asked about wood because there wasn't a bush to be seen on the island, and in answer they pointed to another island where, as I myself could see, there grew a quantity of brushwood. I also asked them for meat and they brought me a large piece of whale-blubber. These and several other questions I put to them so as to learn whether or not they really were Americans, and as they answered all my queries to my satisfaction, I was completely convinced that we were in America" (A115). Müller questions, quite properly, both Lahontan's credibility and Waxell's claim that the words themselves were intelligible (*Bering's Voyages* 109).

7. MS38: "von fören Holz" (of pine wood).

8. Berg says the bird was presented "as an offering and not as a token of peace or friendship" (Jochelson, *History*, 15).

9. Waxell wrote, "I had a grapnel dropped some 20 fathoms from the shore and let the boat glide in between the rocks until it was scarcely 3 fathoms off" (A114).

10. Waxell identified the interpreter as a Chukchi and the other two as Russians (A114) and reported that they waded ashore "with the water right up under their arms" (A115).

11. Waxell added, "He was evidently the eldest and I am sure also the most eminent of them all" (A115).

12. *Amanita muscaria*, a highly toxic mushroom, used among Kamchadals and Koriaks (see B92, and Krasheninnikov 259–60). Chard (pp. 27, 139) doubted that Kamchadals were addicted to the extent of the Koriaks.

13. Waxell stated: "Night was approaching and it was beginning to grow dark. Also, a storm was brewing and rain on the way" (A115).

14. Waxell was more specific: "The savages let the two Russians go at once, but they did not want to release the interpreter. . . . He implored me not to abandon him" (A116).

15. Pallas (R67) omitted "mit englischen Beredungen" (MS40). The phrase literally means "with angelic persuasion"; "englischen" as the adjective form of "Engel" (angel) was still prevalent in the eighteenth century.

16. Waxell said he ordered two muskets to be fired (A116). The ship's log also reports the firing of two guns (BV1: 147).

17. Waxell wrote, "We were under a fairly high cliff" (A116). During Frost's visit to this site on May 11, 1985, he found that the cliff is between 100 to 120 feet high and extends about 100 feet along a pebbly beach; offshore below the cliff are the largest rocks standing anywhere in the bay. They are up to five feet in height above the surf. Around them is a broad expanse of sandy bottom.

18. Steller stated that the Aleuts were overwhelmed by the noise of the muskets, not by the flash of the explosion. Yet the Kamchadals thought of the Russians as "men of fire" because of these same muskets (Krasheninnikov 195).

19. Waxell recalled using signs to the Americans from the drifting longboat "for almost an hour" (A115).

20. Usually of sea lions.

21. Berg identified these pointed red sticks as "dart shafts for hunting sea-otters . . . colored red with mineral paint . . . which they dissolve in their own blood" (Jochelson, *History*, 25).

22. Mongoloid Siberian tribes living along the Arctic coast and the Ob and Enisei rivers.

23. Greenland Eskimos. For a historical, illustrated survey of the Aleut kayak, see Dyson 3–86.

24. Waxell said the knife he saw was "about eight inches long" (A117).

25. Questions regarding Aleut iron before Russian contact—what sort of iron it was and where it originated—are still much discussed in the twentieth century. It is generally agreed that the Aleuts did not smelt iron but obtained it from two possible sources, shipwrecks and trade. See Jochelson, *History*, 21–24; De Laguna, *Chugach Prehistory*, 62–63; and Black, "Some Problems," 59.

26. Little Diomede Island.

27. Steller was mistaken: there are no islands at this location.

28. Pallas omitted this phrase; see Introduction.

29. Black reports: "Aleuts related even recently that the long visor served to conceal a man's eye movement from his adversary. Aleut warriors, it is said, were trained from early childhood to scan the field of vision with the eyes only, without turning the head" (*Aleut Art*, 137).

30. MS44 "gramen paniculatum" is "buschigt Grass" (R73), or "tufts of grass" in the Pallas text.

31. Veniaminov supplied additional details: some of the "large, long visors . . . are adorned with sea-lion whiskers, trade beads, and bone [ivory ornaments]. The first [sea lion whiskers] are usually attached on the left side only [in order] not to interfere with spear-throwing" (Veniaminov 270).

32. The Kunstkammer, or "die Kunst und Naturalien kammer" (MS45), was a museum of natural history and ethnography founded by Peter the Great and transferred in 1728 to the Imperial Academy of Sciences.

33. Stone and bone ornaments in nose, ear, and lower lip had been abandoned by Veniaminov's time (Veniaminov 212–13).

34. Another Steller manuscript of which there is no other record.

35. Steller, of course, was mistaken. The Aleuts lived continuously on the islands. There, they had adequate food resources. Driftwood supplied their limited need for wood: most of what they ate was raw, and their underground homes were rarely heated (Jochelson, *History*, 21).

36. Bird and Chernabura.

37. At low tide, a sandy isthmus a quarter-mile long connects a rocky islet 200 feet high to the main island. This isthmus is not visible from sea, even a few miles away. One village site is located on the islet. A second village site is located on the main island near the other end of the isthmus. Here, near an eroding bank, R. D. Jones and E. P. Bailey in 1970 found the three human

skulls later reported by Nishimoto (p. 17). In 1984, L. Lewis Johnson, a Vassar College archaeologist, examined the eroding burials and began surface collecting and testing at the settlement site (see especially pp. 10–11, 14–15, 18). In 1986, Johnson excavated both "huge" sites, finding on the islet a "whale rib frame of at least one house on the periwinkle mound" as well as two skulls, one having a cranial index of 73 and the other of 84.5. Radiocarbon dating of sample site material indicates that "the barabara within the periwinkle mound was occupied shortly before 2,000 years ago" (see Johnson and Winslow 9–14).

38. Steller must mean "to the north on the southern side of this island." The ship is moving southward into open sea and the "northern side" of either island would no longer be visible. Moreover, Bird Island is so named because of the myriad sea birds nesting on high cliffs above the sea one mile west of Point Welcome, the southeast point.

39. Steller tells us that he sighted some of these birds earlier on Nagai (see Chapter 4). He probably saw here, off cliffs on the south side of Bird Island, justly known for its seabird colonies, the same red-faced and pelagic cormorants; Bailey (p. 87) in 1977 estimated 3,000 of the two species. The "auks" here would most likely be the common murre and the thick-billed murre, which Bailey (p. 86) in 1977 estimated to number 12,000 on Bird Island, "with the common murre greatly outnumbering the thick-bills." The gulls would be predominantly the black-legged kittiwake, of which Bailey (p. 85) counted 21,500 here in 1977, with the glaucous-winged gull present in much smaller numbers. Steller's "sea parrot," or horned puffin, which Jones (1970) considered to be "the fourth most common seabird on Bird Island" (Day, "Birds," p. 41), Bailey (p. 85) estimated to number 3,500 in 1977. On the other hand, the northern fulmar (*Fulmaris glacialis*), known to Steller as "Glupischen" (MS46), from the Russian word for "fool," is only occasionally sighted nowadays in the Shumagins (though Bailey found a new small colony on Bird Island in 1984), as is Steller's black snipe "mit einem rothen Schnabel und Füssen welcher beständig wie die Redschanka thut" (MS46), which is a good description for the black oystercatcher. Finally, the "black pied diver" that Steller admires is very likely the common loon.

CHAPTER 6

1. Of these three sea birds, the identification of only the first seems reasonably certain. Steller (MS47) used different names for birds he had already seen. What he calls "Seeparotten" in MS46 is here cited as "anates arcticas Clasii" (literally, "Clusius's arctic ducks"), which is reasonably close to John Ray's "Anas arcticas Clus." (*Synopsis* 120), identified as "Seepapagaien" by

Pallas (R77). What Steller calls "Meewen" in MS46 is here "Larum Joh. v. Rent dictum," the gulls called John of Ghent, and "Laros Wayel Anglis dictos," the gull called Wagel by the English. Pallas identified the former as "*Pelecan. bassanus* (R77), or gannet (*Sula bassana*). This bird, found only in the North Atlantic, has the same black wing tip as the black-legged kittiwake Steller has undoubtedly just seen in the Shumagin Islands. The second is Ray's "great gray gull" or "*Wagellus cornubiensium,*" the Wagel of the Cornish (*Synopsis* 130), whose counterpart in the Pacific is probably the glaucous-winged gull, already also seen in the Shumagins.

2. MS48: "288" is obviously erroneous. The Pallas text has "258" (R78), found in the ship's log for Sept. 14 (BV1: 157).

3. Open water between America and Asia (see Chapter 4, note 6).

4. MS48: in "ein Eule Sytsch," the last word is Russian for "owl." The only owl commonly seen throughout the Aleutians is the short-eared owl (*Asio flammeus*).

5. Steller supposed that the American continent was still close by to the north. There are no "river" gulls in the Aleutians, and Steller probably saw a smaller gull, such as the mew gull or the red-legged kittiwake.

6. MS48: "über 2. Stücke Swinky" differs from "bey sechs Stück Swinky oder Sturmfische" (R79). Russian *svinka* means "little sea pig," a name for porpoise. Note also the difference in numbers: "more than 2" and "sechs," or six. The "more than 2" is odd phrasing; it may be a copyist's error for a larger number (possibly 7 or 12).

7. The common snipe (*Gallinago gallinago*) is smaller (11 inches in length) than the black oystercatcher (17 inches), which Steller had been seeing.

8. Ellsworth P. Bertholf says, "The snow-covered mountain was the 5,000-foot peak on Great Sitkin Island. The land seen to the westward was the south shore of Adak Island or one of the small islands close by, and to the eastward they saw the shores of Atka Island" (BV1: 338). Both Khitrov's journal and the ship's log offer the opinion that the high volcanic peak is on the mainland (BV1: 168, *n*102).

9. The Pallas text has "Peilungen" (R80), bearings, instead of "Theilungen" (MS19), divisions. In a letter to Frost, dated Apr. 2, 1986, A. N. Stimson of the National Maritime Museum, London, writes: "In the 18th century a ship's position was expressed either in terms of latitude and longitude (observed or dead reckoning), or in bearings and distance from observed points of land." The ship's log indicates that three points of land were observed, two islands and the volcanic peak (BV1: 168).

10. See Chapter 1. Chirikov did not actually go ashore but anchored off

Adak Island on Sept. 9, obtaining fresh water from Aleuts in exchange for knives (BV1: 304–5).

11. The Pallas text has "Südosten," southeast (R81), for "Osten," east (MS50), a difference consistent with the ship's log (BV1: 168) and with "toward the southeast" just above under the date Sept. 25. However, "Osten" also conveys the same meaning of the ship's being driven farther away from Kamchatka.

12. MS51: "Prikaschtschiken," Russian *prikashchiki*, caretakers or estate managers.

13. The clouds reflect the glow from atmospheric electricity drawn to the ship's masts in stormy weather, considered a favorable sign from the patron saint of seamen (St. Elmo) or the appearance of the twin sons of Leda (Castor and Pollux), regarded as friends of seamen. The Latin means literally "flowing fires," or "fires that flow by."

14. The Pallas text has an abbreviated statement with a different meaning: "Man redete schon wieder von Kamtschatka, wohin uns doch Gott in diesem Jahre nicht lassen wollte" (R84), translated, "there was again talk of Kamchatka, which, however, God was not willing we should reach this year" (BV2: 117). In the MS, Steller is not making any such statement but alluding darkly to impending disaster.

15. The Pallas text has a slightly less effective simile: "wodurch die Gemüther aller wiederum so wankend wurden, als ihnen die Zähne vom Scorbut schon waren" (R84), translated, "so that the minds of all again became as shaky as were their teeth already from the scurvy" (BV2: 117).

16. MS52: "die Luft sehr kalt und ausserordentl. kalt [*sic*]" is in R84 "die Luft sehr klar." Doubtless one "kalt" should be "klar."

17. "Canes yaleos" (MS52), "Haien (*Canes Galeos*)" (R85) refers to topes (*Galeus*), or several species of smaller sharks with small, serrated teeth.

18. Bering's inactivity was no doubt an early sign of the disease. Waxell stated: "With us the disease first showed itself in a feeling of heaviness and weariness in all our limbs, such that we were all the time wanting to sleep and, having once sat down, were most reluctant to rise again" (A199).

19. MS53: "weil man doch die Ohnmöglichkeit vor Augen sehe" lacks an explanatory continuation; for clarity "of yet reaching Kamchatka" is added.

20. Bering's home in Finland.

21. MS53: "streit weise" should probably read "streif weise."

22. The MS is garbled here, but the meaning of the passage is reasonably clear.

23. MS55 reads "Meinung," opinion, instead of "Rechnung" (R88), reckoning.

24. Kiska Island.

25. Steller underestimated the distance by one-half (see BV2: 122, *n*276).

26. MS56: "a centro versus peripheriam."

27. MS56 has "Boot," boat, instead of "Loot" (R90). Scherer's manuscript French translation has "sonde," or sounding line (p. 184). "Boot" is, once again, a copyist's error.

28. Buldir Island.

29. MS57: "Taucher, Starik genannt" is in R91 "eine kleine Taucherant *Starik* genannt," translated "a small species of diver, known as *starik*" (BV2: 124). Russian *starik*, old man, is the ancient murrelet (*Synthliboramphus antiquus*), a nocturnal sea bird common throughout the Aleutian and Commander islands.

30. Probably two of the Semichi islands. Steller, of course, was mistaken in believing these to be "the first two Kuriles," some 600 miles away. How Steller could be so wrong in making his calculations seems hard to understand. To begin with, a course directly north of the first two Kurile islands would certainly have brought Cape Lopatka and, shortly thereafter, Avacha Bay into view.

31. MS58: "ewig werden schuldig bleiben" needs the addition of "die Antwort" in R93 to complete the sentence satisfactorily.

32. MS58: "verrathen und . . . verkauft" means utterly betrayed and sold (into slavery). The implication is that Waxell and Khitrov, for personal benefit, played Judas near the end of the voyage. Steller's suspicions, however, do not seem justified, considering the condition of the ship and crew. As Waxell stated in his official report of the voyage, "It became very difficult to run the ship because, in addition to those who died, 40 were ill and those who were still about were very feeble" (BV1: 275). In his journal written years later, Waxell was more graphic: "Our ship was like a piece of dead wood, with none to direct it; we had to drift hither and thither at the whim of the wind and waves" (A123).

33. Copper (Medni) Island.

CHAPTER 7

1. These are landmarks near Avacha Bay: Isopa (Povorotni) Cape is to the south; Cape Shipunski, to the north; and the lighthouse (MS59: "majak," or Russian *maiak*), on the north side of the entrance to Avacha Bay.

2. Dmitri Ovtsin surveyed the Arctic coast from the Ob to the Enisei in 1734–36. In 1738, because of his association with an exiled prince, he was demoted and sent to serve Bering. His rank of lieutenant was restored in

1741, and his name alone appears on a silver plaque donated to the chapel at Petropavlovsk by survivors of the voyage (see Chapter 11, note 9).

3. MS60: "Won—malschi—hundsfott, canaille!" Waxell and Khitrov speak in several tongues, at least when using epithets. "Won" is Russian *von*, out, away. "Malschi" is Russian *molchai*, be quiet. "Hundsfott" is German, scoundrel. "Canaille" is French, bastard, crook. Bering must have been ill indeed to tolerate such abuse of his adjutant.

4. MS61: "Nischna," i.e., Lower Kamchatka *ostrog*. It was from this settlement near the mouth of the Kamchatka River that Bering had sailed in 1728.

5. A very high estimate. Steller later writes (see "Physical Description" below) that the length of the island is 23.5 German miles (110 English miles). It is, in fact, only 56 English miles long.

6. MS61: "Boot" (boat), another error for "Lot."

7. MS62: "ausserhalb" is "innerhalb" in R99. The meaning can be read two ways: "outside the surf," i.e., first, into it, and later, out of it; or "inside," beyond the surf near the shore.

8. Steller is here alluding to Khitrov, whose appearance and behavior may be affected by scurvy.

9. Steller, Plenisner, and Lepekhin were among the few still healthy enough to scout the landing site. However, Waxell claimed that "at one o'clock of that 6th November, Adjunct Steller and I went ashore to look for a place to which we could transfer our sick" (A126). Stejneger thinks that Steller "had somehow confused the doings of the first two days" (G316).

10. MS63: "Gegend in naturalibus," the area in its natural particulars.

11. A distinct Commander Islands species, *Lagopus ridgwayi*.

12. MS63: "Bach Brung," *Veronica americana*. A succulent plant found along streams from the Aleutians to Kamchatka. Steller knew the European variety, *Veronica beccabunga*, or Bachbung.

13. MS63: "Pesci," Russian *pestsi*, foxes. The blue or Arctic fox, *Vulpes beringensis*, is also called the "stone" fox.

14. The North Pacific sea cow, *Hydrodamalis gigas*, known also as Steller's sea cow, is described more fully below in Chapter 10.

15. MS63: "Plebun oder Makoai." *Plevun* is Kamchadal for sperm whale, and *makoai* is Kamchadal for a large shark.

16. Henry Swanson of Unalaska, once a fox farmer in the Aleutians, says: "To kill a fox you have to tap 'em on the end of the nose, on top. On the nose, not the head. You can hammer them on the head all day and they won't die. . . . A little tap and they keel over and have a fit and while they are having their fit, you break their neck" (Swanson 71).

17. Russian for "little teeth."

18. MS65: "Conchyle," or conch.

19. Tooth shell, or scaphopod, a long tubular shell open at both ends, used as money by Pacific Coast Indians, but not present in Kamchatka.

20. Pallas reorganized large sections of the manuscript journal from this point, completely disregarding Steller's dating of events. Pallas continued with "depressing and terrifying sights," belonging to November 13, and moved them up to November 12, and placed events of November 12, e.g., Steller's going hunting for the first time with Plenisner and Betge, under the date November 14.

21. MS67: "Bobrowa Retschka," or Beaver Creek. Russian *rechka* is the diminutive of *reka*, river, and hence means "little river."

22. MS67: "Bobrowa Pohle," Russian *Bobrova Pole*.

23. I.e., Steller, Plenisner, Betge, Roselius, and Boris Sand, who joined the partnership on November 15 (see below). Steller's Boris Sand seems to have been Ivan or Johan Sind or Sint (see below, Apr. 1, and BV2: 151, *n*348), a son of Dr. Kaspar Feige, whom Steller replaced as Bering's physician. For additional biographical information on Steller's German "grave" companions, see G327–31.

24. MS68: "Petrusha," a diminutive, hence, condescending.

25. Stejneger quotes H. J. Snow as saying of sea otter meat, "a more disagreeable, ranker-tasting meat I have yet to find" (BV1: 150, *n*343). However, Henry Swanson, who once hunted the sea mammal, says: "Sea otter tastes like duck—coots or eider duck. See, they eat the same food as those ducks eat—shellfish" (Swanson 30). According to Steller, "Young sea otter meat is most delicious: it cannot easily be distinguished from meat of a nursing lamb, whether roasted or boiled" (D396).

26. MS68: "unterliess man nicht im bauen fortzufahren," literally, "we did not fail to continue to build."

27. MS69: "Lesaja Retschka," Russian *Lesnaia Rechka*.

28. On MS69 the last two sentences of this paragraph follow the fourth paragraph after this one. They are preceded by a "#," which might be an indication that they had been accidentally omitted and were to be inserted earlier. At any rate, their placement here clarifies "three parties."

29. Samson played a trick on the Philistines by catching 300 foxes, tying their tails together with a lighted torch, and turning them loose into the fields of the Philistines (see Judges 15: 4–5).

30. MS70: "Casarme," French *caserne*, German *Kaserne*.

31. According to Iushin's journal, the leader of the three men was "the as-

sistant constable Roselius, [who], with two men from Kamchatka, was sent north to examine the shore" (BV1: 229, *n*126).

32. MS71: "Feyerabend vor der Thüre," literally, the end of the workday in front of the door, a sarcastic way of saying "Done in!"

33. The night of Nov. 28, Waxell reported, "a violent ESE storm got up which broke the anchor cables and drove the ship on land, not far from the place where we had settled ourselves" (A130).

34. Steller's sentence in the MS is left incomplete, but the thought is taken up a few sentences later (see next chapter).

CHAPTER 8

1. According to Iushin's journal (BV1: 230, *n*127), Bering, on Dec. 1, sent the sailor Timofei Anchiugov out with the two men from Kamchatka who had gone out earlier with Roselius. This second party was away for four weeks.

2. MS71: "man noch imerdar, wie wohl mit wenigem Beyfall, bey sich selbst gedachte," or literally, "they were still thinking to themselves, though with little approval."

3. I.e., on Nov. 22. Steller's tribute is shorter in R113–14.

4. Actually, 32 men died. In his report, Waxell listed 31 dead, but overlooked Nikita Ovtsin, who died Nov. 19 (see BV1: 281–82).

5. The two following paragraphs are not found in the Pallas text.

6. Apparently an allusion to Khitrov.

7. Waxell, in his journal, provided this pathetic picture: "I cannot forbear to tell of the wretched state of the Captain Commander as he lay in his agony. The [lower] half of his body was already buried in the ground while he still lived, and even if it had been possible to pull him out again, it would have been against his wishes, for he said to us: "The deeper in the ground I lie, the warmer I am; the part of my body that lies above ground suffers from the cold" (A135).

8. In a letter to Gmelin, dated Nov. 4, 1742, Steller wrote: "The Captain Commander died miserably under the open sky on December 8, almost eaten up by lice" (BV2: 243).

9. MS74: "constrictiones artuum atoniae."

10. MS74: "ichorem lividum."

11. MS74: "gangrava" (gangraena).

12. MS74: "sphacelus."

13. Robert Fortuine, a physician and a writer on the early history of medicine in Alaska, commented in a letter to Frost, dated Jan. 21, 1986: "Steller's

215

description of Bering's last illness, though convoluted, is reasonably clear. He is probably correct in saying that Bering died 'more from hunger, cold, thirst, vermin, and grief than from a disease.' Certainly he was suffering from scurvy and the ill effects of cold and hunger. Vermin in the form of body lice was a terrible plague in those times. Certainly also he must have been worn out and depressed, circumstances which would probably lower his resistance.

"Beyond this, however, Steller is speculating as we must also. The swelling of the feet would most likely have been due to scurvy, but also could have resulted from congestive heart failure, kidney disease, or even 'trench foot.' What I cannot relate it to is a tertian fever, which is another word for malaria usually caused by *Plasmodium vivax*. The characteristic symptom of this disease is, of course, fever, not swelling.

"The 'atonic constriction of the joints' is a bit of a mystery, unless Steller is referring to the painful, swollen joints that occur with scurvy. Such symptoms could be aggravated by the cold, damp weather.

"The reference to 'internal and external parts of the fluid' may mean that Bering had ascites, which is an accumulation of fluid in the peritoneal cavity. This could again be caused by congestive heart failure, kidney disease, or even by liver disease (such as cirrhosis), but not from the cold.

"A fistula-in-ano (or ani) is an inflammatory tract which drains pus from an opening near the anus. It is usually caused by a chronic abscess in the neighborhood of the rectum. The discharge is usually dark and foul-smelling, due to the presence of anaerobic bacteria, and it is not surprising that Steller describes it as an internal gangrene. He would, however, have had no way of knowing, without an autopsy, whether such a condition existed. In any event, a fistula of this type is not a fatal condition. Usually, in fact, an abscess improves rapidly once it begins to drain."

14. I.e., the Lutheran Church. Waxell said in his journal that Bering's corpse "was tied fast to a plank and thrust down into the ground" and that "none of the other dead were buried with a plank" (A135).

15. Not Ovtsin, but Khotiaintsov, who died Dec. 9 (see above).

16. According to Berg, the location of Bering's grave is not known precisely: "In accordance with the description of Steller, the Russian-American Company put a cross on the supposed place of his grave" (Jochelson, *History* 30). In 1966, to commemorate the 225th year of Bering's death, a steel marker replaced the last wooden cross (see illustrations in Bondareva).

CHAPTER 9

1. In 1938, William S. Laughlin, accompanying Aleš Hrdlička, visited Commander Bay. "The housepits of Steller and others," he wrote, "were

clearly evident, dug down in the sandy soil, overgrown with deep grass" ("Russian-American Bering Sea Relations," 780).

2. Ivanov was the boatswain, and Alekseev the quartermaster and boatswain's helper.

3. Carrying wood and housekeeping are the other two chief tasks (see below).

4. MS76: "Statu naturali."

5. Waxell admitted in his journal that he was taken to task for allowing card playing (he said nothing about gambling), but he justified his tolerance (he said nothing about participating) with these words: "I was glad that they found something with which to pass the time and help them to overcome the melancholy from which most of them suffered badly" (A136).

6. Bancroft (p. 90, *n*15), using a Russian source, reported that Waxell and Khitrov, after Bering's death, "declared their willingness to temporarily resign their rank and put themselves on an equality with the men" but the men refused.

7. Pallas summarized in a single sentence the manuscript text of the five paragraphs ending here, and he removed the entire section on the sea otter, which follows, and added it, together with the section on the sea cow and other material, to Steller's appended description of Bering Island (see Introduction).

8. MS77: "Koslowa Reka," or Goat River; "Kitoba Reka," *Kitova Reka* or Whale River.

9. MS77: "Utaer" (Russian plural, *utsi*).

10. MS77: "Bolschaia Leida."

11. MS78: "lernten sie unsere Ohrenlöffel dergestalt kennen." "Ohren-löffel" (literally "ear spoon") means "ears." "Löffel" is hunter's language for rabbit ears because their shape resembles a spoon's; normally the word is used minus the "Ohren."

12. Müller, who got much of his information from Waxell, reported that on Bering Island the expedition accumulated "near 900" sea otter pelts (*Bering's Voyages* 120).

13. Pallas omitted this reference to Russians; perhaps it was too sensitive politically in the late eighteenth century (see Introduction).

14. Steller exaggerated if he was here comparing total body lengths. The maximum length of the sea otter is 58 inches; of the river otter, 50 inches. However, the tail of the former is only 25 percent of body length; of the latter, 40 percent. The weight of the sea otter (maximum, 100 lbs.) is more than three times that of the river otter (maximum, 30 lbs.). See Chanin 11–12, and Kenyon 9–29.

15. Steller previously reflected on sea otter migration (see Chapter 1).

16. Aerial surveys made along the north shore of the Alaskan Peninsula, and particularly between Port Moller (56° N) and Port Heiden (56°55′ N) during the winters of 1971 and 1972, indicate that very few otters can be expected to survive an average winter northeast of Port Heiden. Although the otters can survive cold and ice conditions, their survival depends upon having access to food through leads in the ice (Schneider and Faro 91–101).

17. I.e., the Shumagin Islands.

18. MS79: "auf der westl. Seite," an obvious error.

19. Pallas's reading is "Cariguebeju" (T283).

20. Ray's information came from Georg Markgraf, whose brief, distinguished career as a pioneer naturalist generally parallels Steller's. Born in Liebstadt, Germany, in 1610, Markgraf was largely self-taught in natural sciences and medicine when, at 26 years, he began studies at the University of Leiden. These he left in 1638 to join a military and scientific expedition to Dutch settlements in Brazil, then governed by the benevolent Dutch Count Maurice of Nassau. Despite the ongoing war against the Portuguese, Markgraf studied plants and animals, designed the new town of Mauritzstad (now part of Recife), made observations of the planet Mercury, started a botanical and zoological garden, and mapped much of northeast Brazil. When Count Maurice resigned as governor in 1644, Markgraf planned to return to Europe to publish his findings but took a detour to do fieldwork in Africa. He died of a fever in Angola in his 33d year; consequently, his published work, some of it badly jumbled, is all posthumous.

In any event, Markgraf's *ilya* or *carigueibeiu* is, as Pallas noted (T283), "ein ganz anderes Thier," or "an entirely different animal" from the sea otter. Pallas, however, did not identify it, and Stejneger (BV2: 219, *n*108) assumed uncritically that it is a giant otter (*Pteronura brasiliensis*). The otter Markgraf described and illustrated with a realistic woodblock print may not be Brazilian at all but an introduced species from Africa, the spotted-necked otter (*Hydrictis maculicollis*). It is significant that the specimen Markgraf observed was a pet that was fed mush ("Farina Mandiocae in aqua madefacta") like a rather young puppy ("ut catellus junior") and otherwise lived on fish, especially those it "caught" in a wicker fish trap ("ex nassis positis")!

In contrast to the sea otter and the giant otter (the average weight of each is about 60 lbs.), the spotted-necked is one of the smallest otters (about 10 lbs.), or, as Markgraf wrote, the size of an ordinary dog ("magnitudine mediocris canis"), with its tail but a foot long ("caudam ejusdem longitudinis cum pede"). Its chief identifying characteristic is its neck coloring. Whereas its body is entirely coal black and its head tawny, the neck is marked with yellowish spots; or, as Markgraf wrote, "in gutture maculam habet flavam"; hence, *maculicollis* or "spotted-necked" in the nomenclature.

On the other hand, Markgraf's otter may indeed be an orphaned giant otter juvenile.

21. Steller was comparing the sea otter to the river otter, the only otter known to Europeans.

22. MS80: "Medwedki."

23. MS80: "Koschloke."

24. MS81: "Bey der Furcht," in fright, is no doubt a spelling error for "Bey der Flucht," in flight, which appears in the Pallas text (T285).

25. In 1897, Frederick A. Cook, polar explorer and physician, advocated consumption of fresh seal meat as a method for combatting scurvy, but his captain, Adrien de Gerlache, took offense, and allowed seal and penguin to be served only to those who desired it. Few did. But Cook saved the *Belgica* Antarctic expedition by insisting on administering the meat as medicine to those who refused it as food, and scurvy at once subsided. Roald Amundsen, who was on the *Belgica*, later planned his own successful race to the South Pole in 1911–12 with a fresh meat diet as a part of his strategy, whereas Robert F. Scott and five companions died tragically of scurvy en route from the pole. See Huntford 70–72, 361–62, and 498–500.

26. *De bestiis marinis* (1751).

27. MS82: "tschamadoxen" (plural), Russian *chemodan*(?), suitcase, often padded.

28. Steller is saying that two or four hunted, two cooked, and four or six got wood.

29. MS82: "praedicat." Steller uses the spelling of the Latin verb form, but in the sense of German *Prädikat* (designation, title, label), i.e., as a noun.

30. I.e., Anchiugov and two men (see Chapter 8, note 1).

31. MS83: "nicht geringe Hoffnung," no slight hope.

32. MS83/84: "Leskaja," probably a copyist's error.

33. MS84: "Chalouppe" (French *chaloupe*).

34. Latinized Greek, meaning "couriers"; literally, "all-day runners."

35. Pallas summarized in two sentences (R123) the nine sentences ending here.

36. The Pallas text has two sentences about foxes that do not appear in the MS journal: "Bey unserem ersten Eintritt in diese Höhle, befanden sich viel Steinfüchse darinn, die sich rückwärts in eine Felsenkluft retirirten, durch welche sich nachmals, der Rauch von dem angelegten Feuer zog; wodurch ein solches Niesen und Räuspern unter ihnen entstand, dass wir genug zu lachen hatten. In der Nacht aber hatten wir keine Ruhe vor ihnen, da sie einem, nach

dem andern die Mütze abnahmen und andre Possen trieben" (R124), translated, "At our first entrance into this cave, we found many foxes in it; they retreated into a crevice in the rock through which afterwards the smoke passed from the fire we made so that there started among them such a sneezing and spitting that we had enough to laugh at. At night, however, they gave us no rest, as they pulled off the cap first of one and then of another and performed other tricks" (BV2: 173).

37. Waxell provided more information about the ship's carpenter: "His name was Sava Starodubtsov. What he knew of ship-building was just what he had seen of it in Okhotsk, when he was employed there as a labourer during the time our packet-boats were being built. He said that if I would give him the proportions of the new ship he would build it under my guidance and make her so solid that, with God's help, we should be able to put to sea in her without risk. . . . Later, when we were back in Siberia, he was on my recommendation appointed to a *syn boyarski*, or Siberian nobleman, by the provincial chancellery in Yeniseisk" (A147–48).

38. MS87: "durch den von den Gebürgen herab fallenden Schnee," by snow falling down from the mountains.

39. On this topic, see Introduction.

40. MS89: "Nieswurzel," *Veratrum album*, subsp. *oxysepalum* from Kamchatka, also known as false hellebore.

41. MS89: "Koslowa Pohle."

42. MS89: "Sibutsch."

43. Waxell, who in his journal seldom mentioned Steller by name, acknowledged his role in finding plants for food: "As soon as the snow was gone, and the green shoots came out of the ground, we collected and used quantities of herbs and plants. In this Adjunct Steller gave excellent assistance, for he was a good botanist. He collected and showed us many green herbs, some for drinking, some for eating, and by taking them we found our health noticeably improved. From my own experience I can assert that none of us became well or recovered his strength completely before we began eating something green, whether plant or root" (A142).

The botanical terminology Steller uses in the MS journal is listed below in the order given in the text, together with modern names (see also Stejneger's identifications, BV2: 178–79, *n*425). MS89: "Sphondylium," *Heracleum lanatum*. According to Hultén, "The marrow is eaten raw and the root boiled by the natives; the plant contains sugar and tastes much like licorice" (F707). Steller found this plant stored in the underground cache on Kayak Island (see Chapter 2). MS89: "lilium fl. reflexo atro purpureo," *Fritillaria camschatcensis*, also called Kamchatka fritillary or sarana. Hultén says: "The bulbs, which contain starch and sugar, were a staple food of prehistoric natives. Bulblets dug in fall, dried, used in stews or powdered into flour" (F308). The "celery-leaf and parsnip-root" plant is hemlock parsley, *Conioselinum chinense*. MS90: "Kutachschu" (Kamchadal), *Angelica lucida*, whose stem and petioles are edible. MS90: "Cerinthes," *Mertensia maritima*, subspecies *asiatica*, also called sea lungwort. MS90: "Chamnaerius Speciosus," *Epilobium angustifolium*. *Polygonum viviparum*, whose rhizome, "collected in early spring . . . can be eaten raw" (F385). MS90: "Thee boy," or "bohea tea." MS90: "Vitis idea buxi folio," *Vaccinium vitis-idaea*. MS90: "Pyrola," *Pyrola minor*. MS90: "Veronica humilis montana flore amplo," *Veronica aphylla*. MS90: "Cochlearia," *C. officinalis*, subspecies *arctica*. MS90: "beccabunga," *Veronica americana*. MS90: "Cardamine nasturtium," *C. beringensis*. Steller, of course, gathered the scurvy grass on Nagai Island (see Chapter 4, note 33) and the brooklime on arrival on Bering Island (see Chapter 7, note 12).

CHAPTER 10

1. It can be inferred from this statement and the following reference to "Greenland whaling" that Steller masterminded a change in strategy by recalling what he had once read in Adam Olearius about the way Greenland Eskimos hunt whales and then by adapting that learning to devise a new approach to overcome the sea cow. Olearius reported two stages in the Eskimo hunt for whales. First, the harpoon attached to a thong is cast at the whale; at the other end is a float (an inflated sealskin) to help hunters in *baidarkas* track the whale. Second, the pursuit begins with harpoons repeatedly cast into the whale "till such time as bloud and strength failing her, they come up, kill her, bring her ashore, and divide her" (Olearius 72).

2. Francisco Hernandez (1514–78) described the manatee in his *Nova plantarum, animalium et mineralium Mexicanorum historia* (pp. 323–24, with two pictures). A Spanish physician, he was a contemporary of the French naturalist Charles de Lécluse (Steller used his Latin name), who also described the "Manati Gomara" in the tenth book of his *Exoticorum libri* (pp. 132–35), using Hernandez or "Franciscus Lopez de Gomara" as his source. This is the same Hernandez whom Steller in his *De bestiis marinis* calls "Lopez Francisco Hernandes" (D322).

3. In his *New Voyage Round the World* (p. 33), Captain William Dampier wrote that he had seen the manatee in the northern hemisphere on Bluefield River (Nicaragua), in the Gulf of Campeche (Mexico), on the Darien River (Panama), and around the south keys of Cuba; and in the southern hemisphere around the island of Mindanao in the Philippines and along the coast of Australia. For information about the evolutionary history and distribution of

Steller's sea cow (*Hydrodamalis gigas*), see Whitmore and Gard, and Domning.

4. Hernandez (p. 323) simply noted "auriculae paruae" (tiny little.ears).

5. The figures in the MS journal ("1,200 pud or 480 short hundred-weight") are far in excess of those given in Steller's *De bestiis marinis*, in which he reported the weight of the adult to be "circiter 8000. libras 80. centenarios, seu 200. pud Russica" (D329), or "about 8,000 pounds, 80 short hundred-weight, or 200 Russian puds." It would appear that the initial "1" in "1,200" and "4" in "480" (MS94) may be copyist errors resulting from stray marks.

6. MS95: "dass es einen noch einmahl grösseren Raum einnimt als zu-vor," literally, "that it takes up a space once again larger than before."

7. Recently George V. Mann, professor of medicine, Vanderbilt University, analyzed the tissues of six samples of manatee flesh collected and frozen by biologists in Florida. He found that "these tissues have about twice the ascorbate content of fresh beef or chicken" (letter to Sheila Nickerson, editor, *Alaska Fish & Game* magazine, Mar. 19, 1987). Mann's sampling is suggestive but too small to be a reliable indicator, and he cautions that "we cannot know what the dietary intake of ascorbic acid was for the [Bering Island] sea cow" (letter to Frost, Apr. 6, 1987).

8. I.e., *De bestiis marinis*.

9. Juan Fernandez I.: actually, "der curieuse H. Dampier" (MS95) said nothing in his *New Voyage Round the World* about seeing two species of manatees near this island. However, Steller marveled at the self-educated Dampier: "Inter omnes, qui de Manati scripserunt, nemo pleniorem et curatiorem curiosissimo ac diligentissimo Capitaneo Dampiero concinnauit in itinerario suo Anglicano idiomate edito 1702. Londini" (D327), or "Among all who have written about the manatee, none has produced a more complete and painstaking description than the very inquisitive and industrious Captain Dampier in voyages published in English in London, 1702." The first edition of this work was issued in 1697.

10. Steller learned, after his return to Avacha Bay, that Kamchadals used the Russian word *kapustnik* (D328), or *krautfresser* (MS96) for the sea cow. The Russian *kapusta* means "cabbage," but the Kamchadals, who had never seen cabbage, used the word for the kelp on which the sea cow feeds (letter, dated Sept. 30, 1882, from Stejneger to Spencer F. Baird, p. 61).

CHAPTER 11

1. MS97: "Man unterlies die folgende Zeit über, nicht sowohl Tag als Nacht zu arbeiten," literally, "Subsequently we did not avoid working night and day."

2. The list of baggage of each survivor (BV1: 235) is revealing in that "Adjunct Steller" appears as the third name under "Officers" after "Lieutenant Sven Waxel" and "Master Sofron Khitrov." Steller was allowed ten puds, or 361 pounds of baggage, Waxell twenty puds, and Khitrov twelve.

3. The new *St. Peter* had a 12–foot beam and a depth of 5 feet, 3 inches (see BV1: 234).

4. The ship's log indicates that the anchor was weighed shortly before noon on Aug. 13 (BV1: 243).

5. The Pallas text inexplicably gives the distance between Bering and Copper islands as "fünf Werste" (R130), or five versts. Even five German miles, or 23.5 English miles, is a bit short since the two islands are 26 miles apart at the closest point.

6. Such kettles presumably keep debris out of the pumps when the hold begins to fill with water.

7. MS99: "unter den Pinnsen" is in R131 "unter den Pumpen."

8. MS99: "gegenseitigen," or "shared" does not make sense in the context; perhaps Steller meant "gegenteiligen," or "adverse" or "contrary."

9. Bancroft (p. 92, *n*19) stated that "in the church of Petropavlovsk there is still preserved a memorial of this event; a silver mounted image of the apostles Peter and Paul with the inscription, 'an offering in memory of our miraculous rescue from a barren island, and our return to the coast of Kamchatka, by lieutenant Dimitri Ovtzin, and the whole company, August 1741.'" Ovtsin had been restored to his former rank on Feb. 19, 1741, but did not learn of this good fortune until his return to Kamchatka from the voyage. The offering possibly resulted from Bering's order concerning a vow with money to be collected (see Chapter 6).

10. Waxell was promoted to captain of the second rank in 1744 and to captain of the first rank before he died in 1762. Khitrov became an admiral in 1753.

APPENDIX: PHYSICAL DESCRIPTION OF BERING ISLAND

1. Another name for "Vries Canal" (see Chapter 4) and "the channel" (used frequently). "Pico" is from "peak," or specifically from Captain Vries's Anthony Peak on Jeso.

2. Steller did not carry out this plan, but Pallas did so by transferring sections on the sea otter and sea cow and by adding other material; see Introduction.

3. MS100: "Ne Obkhodimyi Utes," literally, "Un-get-around-able Cliffs" or "cliffs that we could not get around."

4. MS100: "Sibutscha guba" and "Bobrowa utaes." See BV2: 192 for

Stejneger's location of these and other landmarks. In a letter of Sept. 30, 1882, to Spencer F. Baird, Stejneger stated (pp. 4–5) his purpose for going to Bering Island from Aug. 21 to Sept. 1, 1882: "to identify the places of which Steller speaks in order to compare his description with the facts of the present day."

5. MS100: "Sibirni Nos," also called Cape Waxell. Steller's estimates of distances are very inaccurate. Bering Island at its greatest width is 40 versts, not 23; from Northern Cape to Southeast Point, 67 versts, not 115; and from Northwest Point to Southeast Point, 84 versts, not 165.

6. Current thinking about the geography of Beringia is summed up by Hultén (Fxiv–xvi), using as his source *The Bering Land Bridge*, edited by D. M. Hopkins; namely, that the land bridge did *not* extend as far south as the Aleutian and Commander Islands during the Illinoian and Wisconsin periods of glaciation.

7. The highest mountain on the island is Mt. Steller, 2,200 feet high, named by Stejneger.

8. MS102 is unclear: "aus Süd Osten längst dem Lande gegen das Süd ostliche Ende, aus Nord westen aber gegen das Nord Westliche Ende (from the southeast along the land toward the southeast end, but from the northwest toward the northwest end).

9. MS102: "verstopfet," plugged up, stopped up, may be a copyist's error for *verstobt*, scattered, dispersed. See BV2: 195–96, *n*28.

10. MS103: "ne obgodimie Utaes." See note 3 above.

11. MS103: "Petschora," or Russian *peshchera*. Stejneger was unable to locate Steller's Cave (see BV2: 197, *n*35).

12. MS104: "Iuschnins Scherlop," most likely Russian *zherlo*, craterlike opening.

13. Louis Bourguet (1678–1742), a French naturalist, published a "Mémoire sur la théorie de la terre" (Memoir on a theory of the earth) as an appendix (pp. 177–220) to his *Lettres philosophiques*. Did Steller have this book at Bolsheretsk? If not (as seems likely), once again his memory regarding past readings of a half-dozen or more years before is truly remarkable. What Bourguet wrote—and Steller recalled—was "Le sommet des hautes Montagnes est composé de Roches, plus ou moins élevés, qui ressemblent, sur tout vûs de loin, aux ondes de la Mer" (p. 196), or "The summit of the high mountains is made up of rocks, more or less elevated, which resemble, above all when seen from afar, the waves of the sea."

14. Steller, of course, was describing Commander Bay.

15. Lissonkovaia Bay (see BV2: 201, *n*49).

16. The present-day site of Nikolski, the largest town on the island.

17. Saranna Lake in the north is considerably larger than Gavan Lake, which Steller describes here (see BV2: 202, *n*54). Steller's phrasing suggests that the river is flowing from the sea to the lake.

18. MS106: "Osernaja Reka."   19. Toporkov Island.

20. Probably Toporkov Island.   21. Ari Kamen.

22. Probably a cloud bank and certainly not the American continent (see Introduction).

23. These last two islands are almost certainly mirages.

24. Copper Island (Medni Ostrov).

25. Steller had spent the winter of 1740 on Kamchatka.

26. MS109 reads "dass sich Eiss in der See fande, und von dem festen lande hieher treiben könnte" (that ice occurred in the sea and could drift here from the mainland).

27. MS109 offers only "durch diesen Zufall" (through this accident), but it is clear that Steller is referring to avalanches.

Glossary

Terms below are defined as Steller used them.

ADJUNCT. Rank below professor, one of two ranks at the Imperial Academy of Sciences, St. Petersburg (e.g., Adjunct Steller).

AMBAR (Russian). Structure for storing supplies, including food. The underground structure Steller found on Kayak Island (Chapter 2) he also called a *cellar*. Underground dwellings on Kamchatka, the Aleutians, and along the Alaska coastline were called *barabara*s (Kamchadal).

ARSHIN (Russian). 28 inches.

BAIDAR (Russian). Large, open, skin-covered, wood-framed boat rowed with oars. The Aleut skinboat Steller described (Chapter 5) became known as a *baidarka* or *kayak* (Aleut); it is portable, has a deck with a hatch, and is propelled by a single paddle with a blade at each end.

CAPTAIN-COMMANDER. Russian naval rank below admiral and above captain.

COSSACK (Tatar). Any hired person, or soldier or sailor, on Russia's frontiers.

ELL (Old English). 21 inches, originally the length of the forearm from the tip of the elbow to the end of the middle finger.

FATHOM (English). 6 feet, sea measure; 7 feet, land measure.

FLEET MASTER. Russian naval rank below lieutenant (e.g., Master Khitrov).

GALLIOT (Latin). Broad, heavy cargo vessel with one or two masts and bowsprit sail.

GEODESIST (Greek). Land surveyor.

MILE, Dutch or German. 4.61 English statute miles, or 4 nautical miles.

NOS (Russian). Cape, peninsula; literally "nose."

OSTROG (Russian). Fortified settlement. In his *Beschreibung von dem Lande Kamtschatka*, Steller applied the term to any settlement, whether Russian fort or native village, on Kamchatka.

PACKET BOAT. Broad, heavy, two-masted ship, 60–80 feet long; originally, a ship designed to carry cargo, mail, and passengers on a fixed route.

PROMYSEL (Russian). A hunt. In Siberia and the North Pacific, a hunter, trapper, or trader was known as a *promyshlennik*.

PUD (Russian). 36 pounds.

SLUZHIV (Russian). Low-ranking government employee, civilian or military.

VERST (Russian). 0.66 English statute miles.

YAWL (Dutch). Ship's boat, or longboat. The *St. Peter* had two boats, a larger and a smaller, each equipped with oars, mast, and sail.

Bibliography

Amman, Johann. *Stirpium rariorum in Imperio Rutheno sponte provenientium icones et descriptiones*. St. Petersburg, 1739.

Anderson, Frank J. *An Illustrated History of the Herbals*. New York, 1977.

Andreev, Aleksandr I. *Russian Discoveries in the Pacific in the Eighteenth and Nineteenth Centuries*. Tr. Carl Ginsburg. Ann Arbor, 1952.

Arber, Agnes. *Herbals: Their Origin and Evolution. A Chapter in the History of Botany, 1470–1670*. 2d ed. Cambridge, 1953.

Bailey, Edgar P. "Breeding Seabird Distribution and Abundance in the Shumagin Islands." *Murrelet* 59 (1978): 82–91.

Bancroft, Hubert Howe. *History of Alaska, 1730–1885*. San Francisco, 1886.

Barratt, Glynn. *Russia in Pacific Waters: A Survey of the Origins of Russia's Naval Presence in the North and South Pacific*. Vancouver, 1981.

Bauhin, Gaspard. *Pinax theatri botanici*. Basel, 1671. [1st ed. 1623; Bauhin's *Prodromus theatri botanici* (1620) is added to the ed. of 1671.]

Beck, Hanno. "Einführung." In G. W. Steller, *Beschreibung von dem Lande Kamtschatka; Reise von Kamtschatka nach Amerika; Ausführliche Beschreibung von sonderbaren Meerthieren*, reprint ed., i–xxii. Stuttgart, 1974.

Beck, Lewis White. *Early German Philosophy: Kant and His Predecessors*. Cambridge, Mass., 1969.

Bell, Margaret E. *Touched with Fire: Alaska's Georg Wilhelm Steller*. New York, 1960.

Berg, Lev S. *Discovery of Kamchatka and Bering's Expeditions*. 3d ed. Moscow, 1946. [In Russian; 1st ed. 1924. Berg's information on Bering's voyage to America is also in Jochelson, *History* (q.v.), 13–39.]

————. "Russian Discoveries in the Pacific." In *The Pacific: Russian Scientific Investigations*, 1–26. New York, 1969.

Berkh, Vasilii N. *A Chronological History of the Discovery of the Aleutian Islands; or, The Exploits of Russian Merchants*. Tr. Dmitri Krenov. Kingston, Ont., 1974.

Beyreuther, Erich. *Geschichte des Pietismus*. Stuttgart, 1978.

Birket-Smith, Kaj, and Frederica De Laguna. *The Eyak Indians of the Copper River Delta, Alaska*. Copenhagen, 1938.

Black, J. L. *G.-F. Müller and the Imperial Russian Academy*. Kingston, Ont., 1986.

Black, Lydia T. *Aleut Art*. Anchorage, 1982.

————. "Some Problems in Interpretation of Aleut Prehistory." *Arctic Anthropology* 20, no. 1 (1983): 49–78.

Bogoras, Waldemar. "The Folk-Lore of Northeast Asia as Compared to That of Northwest America." *American Anthropologist* 4 (1902): 577–683.

Bondareva, Nina A. *Seven Weeks on the Commanders*. Petropavlovsk, 1966. [In Russian.]

Boorstin, Daniel J. *The Discoverers: A History of Man's Search to Know His World and Himself*. New York, 1983.

Bourguet, Louis. *Lettres philosophiques*. Amsterdam, 1729.

Catesby, Mark. *The Natural History of Carolina, Florida and the Bahama Islands*. London, 1731.

Chanin, Paul. *The Natural History of Otters*. London, 1985.

Chard, Chester S. *Kamchadal Culture and Its Relationship in the Old and New Worlds*. University of Wisconsin Archives of Archeology, no. 15. Madison, 1961.

Clusius, Carolus [Charles de Lécluse]. *Exoticorum libri decem*. Leiden, 1605.

Collins, Henry B., Austin H. Clark, and Egbert H. Walker. *The Aleutian Islands: Their People and Natural History*. Washington, 1945.

Cook, James. *The Journals of Captain James Cook on His Voyages of Discovery: The Voyage of the Resolution and Discovery, 1776–1780*. Ed. J. C. Beaglehole. Cambridge, 1967.

Coxe, William. *Account of the Russian Discoveries Between Asia and America*. 4th ed. London, 1803. [Chap. 2, pp. 30–101, is a summary translation of Steller's journal.]

Dall, William H. *Alaska and Its Resources*. Boston, 1870.

————. *Contributions to North American Ethnology*. Part 1, *Tribes of the Extreme Northwest*. Washington, 1877.

Dampier, William. *A Collection of Voyages.* Vol. 1, *A New Voyage Round the World.* London, 1729. [1st ed. 1697.]

Davidson, George. "The Tracks and Landfalls of Bering and Chirikof on the Northwest Coast of America." *Transactions and Proceedings of the Geographical Society of the Pacific* 1 (1901): 1–44.

Dawson, E. Yale. "A Guide to the Literature and Distributions of Pacific Benthic Algae from Alaska to the Galapagos." *Pacific Science* 15 (1961): 370–461.

Day, Robert H. "Birds of the Shumagin Islands, with Special Reference to the Koniuji Group." U.S. Fish and Wildlife Service, unpublished report. Anchorage, 1977.

———. "Mammals of the Shumagin Islands, with Special Reference to the Koniuji Island Group." U.S. Fish and Wildlife Service, unpublished report. Anchorage, 1976.

Debenham, Frank. "Bering's Last Voyage." *Polar Record* 3 (1941): 421–26.

De Laguna, Frederica. *Chugach Prehistory: The Archaeology of Prince William Sound, Alaska.* Seattle, 1956.

———. *Under Mount Saint Elias: The History and Culture of the Yakutat Tlingit.* Parts 1 and 2. Washington, 1972.

Dezhnev, Semen. *The Voyage of Semen Dezhnev in 1648.* Ed. Raymond H. Fisher. Cambridge, 1981.

Domning, Daryl P. "Sea Cow Family Reunion." *Natural History* 96 (1987), 64–71.

Dufresne, Frank. *Alaska's Animals and Fishes.* New York, 1946.

Dumond, Don E. *The Eskimos and Aleuts.* London, 1977.

Dyson, George. *Baidarka.* Edmonds, Wash., 1986.

Efimov, A. V. *Atlas of Geographical Discoveries of the Seventeenth and Eighteenth Centuries.* Moscow, 1964. [In Russian.]

Fisher, Raymond H. *Bering's Voyages: Whither and Why.* Seattle, 1977.

Ford, Corey. *Where the Sea Breaks Its Back: The Epic Story of a Pioneer Naturalist and the Discovery of Alaska.* Boston, 1966.

Förster, Johann Christian. *Übersicht der Geschichte der Universität zu Halle in ihrem ersten Jahrhunderte.* Halle, 1794.

Fortuine, Robert. "Georg Wilhelm Steller: Physician-Naturalist on the Bering Expedition to Alaska." *Alaska Medicine,* Mar. 1967: 2–7.

Francke, August Hermann. *Faith's Work Perfected; or, Francke's Orphan House at Halle.* Tr. William L. Gage. New York, 1867.

Fries, Wilhelm. *Die Stiftungen August Hermann Franckes.* Halle, 1913.

Frost, O. W. "Bering Expedition Landing Sites in the Shumagin Islands." U.S. Fish and Wildlife Service, unpublished report. Anchorage, 1985.

———. "Georg Steller: First Naturalist in Alaska." *Alaska Fish & Game*, Nov.–Dec. 1985: 6–9, 20–21.

———. "Georg Steller: First Physician in Alaska." *Alaska Medicine*, Sept. 1986: 61–66.

———. "Steller's Sea Cow." *Alaska Fish & Game*, Jan.–Feb. 1986: 8–9, 20–21.

Frost, O. W., and Karen E. Willmore. *Description of Unpublished Steller Papers in Smithsonian Archives and the Library of Congress*. Anchorage, 1983.

Gardner, Nathaniel Lyon. *The Genus Fucus on the Pacific Coast of North America*. University of California Publications in Botany, no. 10. Berkeley, 1922.

Gesner, Conrad. *Historia animalium*. 4 vols. in 3. Zurich, 1551–58.

———. *Icones animalium aquatilium in mari*. Vol. 1. Zurich, 1560.

Geyer-Kordesch, Johanna. "German Medical Education in the Eighteenth Century: The Prussian Context and Its Influence." In W. F. Bynum and Roy Porter, eds., *William Hunter and the Eighteenth-Century Medical World*, 177–205. Cambridge, 1985.

Gmelin, Johann Georg. *Flora Sibirica*. 4 vols. St. Petersburg, 1747, 1749, 1768–69. [Vols. 3 and 4 ed. Samuel Gottlieb Gmelin.]

———. *Reise durch Sibirien, 1733–1743*. 4 vols. Göttingen, 1751–52.

Golder, Frank A. *Bering's Voyages: An Account of the Effort of the Russians to Determine the Relation of Asia and America*. 2 vols. New York, 1922, 1925. [Vol. 2 is chiefly Steller's *Journal of the Sea Voyage from Kamchatka to America and Return on the Second Expedition, 1741–1742*, tr. Leonhard Stejneger.]

———. *Russian Expansion on the Pacific, 1641–1850: An Account of the Earliest and Later Expeditions Made by the Russians Along the Pacific Coast of Asia and North America*. Cleveland, 1914.

Grebnitzky, N. A. *Commander Islands*. Tr. Louise Woehlcke. St. Petersburg, 1902.

Gruening, Ernest. *The State of Alaska*. New York, 1954.

Haley, Delphine. "Great Northern Sea Cow." *Oceans* 13 (1980): 7–11.

Harnack, Adolf. *Geschichte der Königlich preussischen Akademie der Wissenschaften zu Berlin*. Berlin, 1901.

Hernandez, Francisco. *Nova plantarum, animalium et mineralium Mexicanorum historia*. Rome, 1651.

Hoffmann, Friedrich. *Opera omnia physico-medica.* 13 vols. in 6. Naples, 1754–63.

Hopkins, David M. *The Bering Land Bridge.* Stanford, Calif., 1967.

Hrdlička, Aleš. *The Aleutian and Commander Islands and Their Inhabitants.* Philadelphia, 1945.

Hultén, Eric. *Flora of Alaska and Neighboring Territories: A Manual of Vascular Plants.* Stanford, Calif., 1968.

———. *Flora of Kamchatka and the Adjacent Islands.* 4 vols. Stockholm, 1927–30.

———. *Flora of the Aleutian Islands and Westernmost Alaska Peninsula, with Notes on the Flora of Commander Islands.* 2d ed. Hafner, 1960.

———. "History of Botanical Exploration in Alaska and Yukon Territories from the Time of Their Discovery to 1940." *Botaniska Notiser,* 1940: 289–346.

Jenness, Diamond. "Prehistoric Culture Waves from Asia to America." *Journal of the Washington Academy of Sciences* 30 (1940): 383–96.

Jochelson, Waldemar. *Archaeological Investigations in the Aleutian Islands.* Washington, 1925.

———. *History, Ethnology, and Anthropology of the Aleut.* Washington, 1933.

Johnson, John F. C., comp. *Chugach Legends: Stories and Photographs of the Chugach Region.* Anchorage, 1984.

Johnson, L. Lewis. "An Archaeological Survey of the Outer Shumagin Islands, Alaska, 1984." National Geographic Society, unpublished report. Poughkeepsie, N.Y., 1984.

Johnson, L. Lewis, and Margaret A. Winslow. "Shumagin Island Prehistory: People in a Tectonically Unstable Environment." National Geographic Society, unpublished report. Poughkeepsie, N.Y., 1987.

Jones, R. D., and E. P. Bailey. "Aleutian Islands National Wildlife Refuge Annual Report." Cold Bay, Alaska, 1970. [Unpublished.]

Kenyon, Karl W. *The Sea Otter in the Eastern Pacific Ocean.* New York, 1975.

Kosven, Mark O. "Ethnographic Results of Bering's Great Northern Expedition, 1733–1743." *Siberian Ethnographic Collection,* n.s., 64 (1961): 167–212. [In Russian.]

Krasheninnikov, Stepan P. *Exploration of Kamchatka, 1735–1741.* Tr. E. P. Crownhart-Vaughan. Portland, Oreg., 1972.

Krusenstern, A. J. von. *Voyage Round the World in the Years 1803, 1804, 1805, and 1806.* Tr. Richard B. Hoppner. 2 vols. in 1. London, 1813.

LaBelle, Joseph C., and James L. Wise. *Alaska Marine Ice Atlas.* Anchorage, 1983.

Lahontan, Louis Armand, Baron de. *Nouveaux voyages . . . dans l'Amérique septentrionale.* 2 vols. La Haye, 1703.

Lantzeff, George V., and Richard A. Pierce. *Eastward to Empire: Exploration and Conquest on the Russian Open Frontier.* Kingston, Ont., 1973.

Laughlin, William S. "Aleuts: Ecosystem, Holocene History, and Siberian Origin." *Science* 189 (1975): 507–15.

———. *Aleuts: Survivors of the Bering Land Bridge.* New York, 1980.

———. "Russian-American Bering Sea Relations: Research and Reciprocity." *American Anthropologist* 87 (1985): 775–92.

Lauridsen, Peter. *Vitus Bering: The Discoverer of Bering Strait.* Tr. Julius E. Olson. Chicago, 1889.

Ley, Willy. *Dawn of Zoology.* Englewood Cliffs, N.J., 1968.

Lind, James. "Treatise of the Scurvy." In Christopher Lloyd, ed., *The Health of Seamen,* 6–25. London, 1965. [Originally published in 1753.]

Linnaeus, Carolus [Karl von Linné]. "Plantae Camschatcenses rariores." *Amoenitates Academicae* 2 (1750): 332–64.

McCartney, Allen P. "An Archaeological Site Survey and Inventory for the Alaska Peninsula, Shumagin Islands." U.S. Fish and Wildlife Service, unpublished report. Anchorage, 1973.

Makarova, Raisa V. *Russians in the Pacific, 1745–1799.* Tr. Richard A. Pierce and Alton S. Donnelly. Kingston, Ont., 1975.

Markgraf, Georg. *Historiae rerum naturalium Brasiliae.* Part 2 of W. Piso and G. Markgraf, *Historia naturalis Brasiliae,* ed. Johannes Laet. Leiden, 1648.

Mayr, Ernst. *The Growth of Biological Thought: Diversity, Evolution, and Inheritance.* Cambridge, Mass., 1982.

Merck, Carl Heinrich. *Siberia and Northwestern America, 1785–1795: The Journal of Carl Heinrich Merck, Naturalist with the Russian Scientific Expedition Led by Captain Joseph Billings.* Tr. Fritz Jaensch. Kingston, Ont., 1980.

Miyaoka, Osahito. "An Eskimo Tribe Near Mt. St. Elias (Alaska)" *Arctic Anthropology* 11 (1974): 73–80.

Morton, Henry Albert. *The Wind Commands: Sailors and Sailing Ships in the Pacific.* Middletown, Conn., 1975.

Mull, Gil, and George Plafker. "The First Russian Landings in Alaska." *Alaska Journal* 6 (1976): 134–45.

Müller, Gerhard Friedrich. *Bering's Voyages: The Reports from Russia.* Tr. Carol Urness. Fairbanks, 1986.

———. [?]. *Leben Herrn Georg Wilhelm Stellers.* Frankfurt, 1748. [Russian MS version in Manuscript Division, Library of Congress.]

———. *A Letter from a Russian Sea-Officer to a Person of Distinction at the Court of St. Petersburgh, Containing His Remarks upon Mr. de l'Isle's Chart and Memoir Relative to the New Discoveries Northward and Eastward from Kamtschatka*. London, 1754.

———. *Voyages from Asia to America for Completing the Discoveries of the North West Coast of America*. Tr. Thomas Jefferys. 2d ed. London, 1764. [1st ed. 1761.]

Murie, Olaus J. "Fauna of the Aleutian Islands and Alaska Peninsula." *North American Fauna* 61 (1959): 1–364.

Neatby, L. H. *Discovery in Russian and Siberian Waters*. Athens, Ohio, 1973.

Nishimoto, Mike. "A Survey of Selected Islands Along the Alaska Peninsula During the Spring of 1984." U.S. Fish and Wildlife Service, unpublished report. Anchorage, 1984.

Nordenskiöld, A. E. *The Voyage of the Vega Round Asia and Europe*. Tr. Alexander Leslie. New York, 1882.

Nordenskiöld, Erik. *The History of Biology: A Survey*. Tr. Leonard B. Eyre. New York, 1928.

Olearius, Adam. *The Travels of Olearius in Seventeenth-Century Russia*. Ed. and tr. Samuel H. Baron. Stanford, Calif., 1967.

———. *Vermehrte neue Beschreibung der muscowitischen und persischen Reysen*. Ed. Dieter Lohmeier. Tübingen, 1971. [Reprint of the 1656 ed.]

———. *The Voyages and Travels of the Ambassadors Sent by Frederick Duke of Holstein to the Great Duke of Moscovy and the King of Persia, Begun in the Year 1633 and Finish'd in 1639, Containing a Compleat History of Moscovy, Tartary, Persia, and Other Adjacent Countries*. London, 1662.

Orth, Donald J. *Dictionary of Alaska Place Names*. U.S. Geological Survey, Professional Papers, no. 576. Washington, 1967.

Pallas, Peter Simon. *Flora Rossica*. Parts 1 and 2. St. Petersburg, 1784, 1788.

———. *A Naturalist in Russia: Letters from Peter Simon Pallas to Thomas Pennant*. Ed. Carol Urness. Minneapolis, 1967.

Pasetskii, Vasilii M. *Vitus Bering, 1681–1741*. Moscow, 1982. [In Russian.]

Pekarskii, Petr. "Georg Wilhelm Steller." In *History of the Imperial Academy of Sciences, St. Petersburg* 1: 587–616. St. Petersburg, 1870. [In Russian.]

Pennant, Thomas, *Arctic Zoology*. 2 vols. London, 1784–85.

Petroff, Ivan. *Report on the Population, Industries and Resources of Alaska of the Tenth Census, 1880*. Washington, 1884.

Plieninger, G. H. T., ed. *Joannis Georgii Gmelini reliquiae quae supersunt commercii epistolici cum Carolo Linnaeo, Alberto Hallero, Guilielmo Stellero et aliis*. Stuttgart, 1861.

Raven, Charles E. *John Ray, Naturalist: His Life and Works*. Cambridge, 1950.

Ray, Dorothy Jean. *The Eskimos of Bering Strait, 1650–1898*. Seattle, 1975.

Ray, John. *Catalogus plantarum Angliae et insularum adjacentium*. 2d ed. London, 1777.

———. *Historia generalis plantarum*. 3 vols. London, 1686, 1688, 1704.

———. *Synopsis methodica avium et piscium*. London, 1713.

Ricketts, Edward F., and Jack Calvin. *Between Pacific Tides*. 3d ed., rev. Stanford, Calif., 1962.

Rowell, Margery. "Linnaeus and Botanists in Eighteenth-Century Russia." *Taxon* 29 (1980): 15–26.

Sachs, Julius von. *History of Botany, 1530–1860*. Tr. Henry E. F. Garnsey. Oxford, 1890.

Sarychev, Gavriil. *Account of a Voyage of Discovery to the North-East of Siberia, the Frozen Ocean, and the North-East Sea*. London, 1806.

Sauer, Martin. *An Account of a Geographical and Astronomical Expedition to the Northern Parts of Russia . . . in the Years 1785 etc. to 1794*. London, 1802.

Scherer, Jean Benoît. *Recherches historiques et géographiques sur le Nouveau-Monde*. Paris, 1777.

Schneider, Karl B., and James B. Faro. "Effects of Sea Ice on Sea Otters (*Enhydra lutris*)." *Journal of Mammalogy* 56 (1975): 91–101.

Schrader, Wilhelm. *Geschichte der Friedrichs-Universität zu Halle*. Berlin, 1894.

Shalkop, Antoinette, ed. *Exploration in Alaska: Captain Cook Commemorative Lectures*. Anchorage, 1980.

Sokol, A. E. "Russian Expansion and Exploration in the Pacific." *American Slavic and East European Review* 11, no. 2 (1952): 85–105.

Stejneger, Leonhard. "Contributions to the History of the Commander Islands." *Proceedings of the U.S. National Museum* 6 (1883): 58–89; 7 (1884–85): 181–89, 529–38; 12 (1890): 83–94.

———. *Georg Wilhelm Steller: The Pioneer of Alaskan Natural History*. Cambridge, Mass., 1936.

———. Letter to Spencer F. Baird, dated Sept. 30, 1882. Smithsonian Archives, Record Unit 7074, Box 13, Folder 8.

———. "A Trip to Kayak Island, Alaska." Unpublished MS, 13 pp. Smithsonian Archives, Record Unit 7074, Box 40, Folder 9.

———. "Witus Jonassen Bering." *American-Scandinavian Review* 29 (1941): 294–307.

Steller, Georg Wilhelm. *Beschreibung von dem Lande Kamtschatka*. Frankfurt, 1774.

————. "Catalogus plantarum in insula Beringi observatarum 1742." Unpublished MS, 18 pp. Manuscripts Division, Library of Congress.

————. "Catalogus plantarum intra sex horas in parte Americae septemtrionalis iuxta promontorium Eliae observatarum anno 1741 die 21 Iulii sub gradu latitudinis 59." In Stejneger, *Georg Wilhelm Steller* (q.v.), appendix E, 554–61.

————. "Catalogus seminum anno 1741 in America septemtrionali sub gradu latitudinis 59 et 55 collectorum, quorum dimidia pars die 17 Novembris 1742 transmissa." Unpublished MS, 7 pp. Manuscripts Division, Library of Congress.

————. *De bestiis marinis.* In *Novi Commentarii Academiae Scientiarum Imperialis Petropolitanae* 2 (1751): 289–398. [Tr. as *Ausführliche Beschreibung von sonderbaren Meerthieren* (Halle, 1753); also tr. in part by Walter Miller and Jennie Emerson Miller as "The Beasts of the Sea," in *The Fur Seals and Fur-Seal Islands of the North Pacific Ocean*, part 3 (Washington, 1899), 179–218.]

————. "Descriptiones L. plantarum rariorum in insula Beringi 1742 observatarum una cum catalogo plantarum omnium in dicta insula obviarum." Unpublished MS, 76 pp. Manuscripts Division, Library of Congress.

————. "Mantissa plantarum minus aut plane incognitarum." Unpublished MS, 14 pp. Manuscripts Division, Library of Congress.

————. "Report to the Imperial Governing Senate." In *Russian Expeditions Relating to the Study of the Northern Part of the Pacific Ocean in the First Part of the Eighteenth Century: Collection of Documents*, no. 157, pp. 170–73. Moscow, 1984. [In Russian; dated Nov. 16, 1742.]

————. *Tagebuch seiner Seereise aus dem Petripauls Hafen in Kamtschatka bis an die westlichen Küsten von Amerika und seiner Begebenheiten auf der Rückreise.* In *Neue Nordische Beyträge* 5 (1793): 129–236; 6 (1793): 1–26. [This journal was reprinted in book form from the same plates by Johann Z. Logan under the title *Reise von Kamtschatka nach Amerika mit dem Commandeur-Capitän Bering: Ein Pendant zu dessen Beschreibung von Kamtschatka* (St. Petersburg, 1793). The 1743 MS on which this publication is based has been reproduced as *Steller's Manuscript Journal: Facsimile Edition and Transliteration*, Alaska Historical Commission, Studies in History, no. 114, ed. O. W. Frost, with transliteration by Margritt A. Engel and Karen E. Willmore (Anchorage, 1984). A condensed French manuscript translation of Steller's MS by Jean Benoît Scherer, ca. 1770, entitled "Second voyage de Kamtschatka à Amérique," can be found in the Manuscripts Division, Library of Congress.]

————. "Topographische und physikalische Beschreibung der Beringsinsel, welche im östlichen Weltmeer an der Küste von Kamtschatka liegt." *Neue Nordische Beyträge* 1 (1781): 255–301.

Stöller, Johann Augustin. "Zuverlässige Nachricht von dem merkwürdigen Leben und Reisen Herrn Georg Wilhelm Stöllers." *Ergetzungen der vernünftigen Seele aus der Sittenlehre und der Gelehrsamkeit überhaupt* 5, part 4 (1747): 362–84.

Stürzbecher, Manfred. *Beiträge zur berliner Medizingeschichte.* Berlin, 1966.

Sutton, Ann, and Myron Sutton. *Steller of the North.* Skokie, Ill., 1961.

Swanson, Henry. *The Unknown Islands: Life and Tales.* Ed. Raymond Hudson. Unalaska, Alaska, 1982.

Thilenius, John F. "Steller's Journey on Kayak Island, Alaska, July 20, 1741: Where and How Far Did He Go?" Forestry Science Laboratory, unpublished report. Juneau, 1981. [Published in part in *Transportation in Alaska's Past* (Anchorage, 1982), 50–70.]

Tournefort, Joseph Pitton de. *Institutiones rei herbariae.* 2 vols. Paris, 1700.

Urness, Carol Louise. "Bering's First Expedition: A Re-examination Based on Eighteenth Century Books, Maps, and Manuscripts." Ph.D. diss., University of Minnesota, 1982.

Vancouver, George. *A Voyage of Discovery in the North Pacific Ocean.* 4 vols. London, 1798.

Vasilievskii, Ruslan S. "Problems of the Origin of Ancient Sea Hunters' Cultures in the North Pacific." In William Fitzhugh, ed., *Prehistoric Maritime Adaptations of the Circumpolar Zone,* 113–21. The Hague, 1975.

Veniaminov, Ivan. *Notes on the Islands of the Unalashka District.* Tr. Lydia T. Black and R. H. Geoghegan. Kingston, Ont., 1984.

Vucinich, Alexander. *Science in Russian Culture: A History to 1860.* Stanford, Calif., 1963.

Waxell, Sven. *The American Expedition.* Tr. M. A. Michael. London, 1952.

Whitmore, Frank C., Jr., and L. M. Gard, Jr. *Steller's Sea Cow (Hydrodamalis gigas) of Late Pleistocene Age from Amchitka, Aleutian Islands, Alaska.* U.S. Geological Survey, Professional Papers, no. 1036. Washington, 1977.

Winter, Eduard. *Halle als Ausgangspunkt der deutschen Russlandkunde im 18. Jahrhundert.* Berlin, 1953.

Index

In this index, "f" means a second mention on the next page; "ff" means separate mentions on the next two pages; two numbers with a dash between them mark a discussion spanning two or more pages; and *passim* denotes separate mentions on three or more pages in close but not necessarily consecutive sequence.

Library of Congress Cataloging-in-Publication Data

Steller, Georg Wilhelm, 1709–1746.
    Journal of a voyage with Bering, 1741–1742 / edited and with an intro-
    duction by O. W. Frost; translated by Margritt A. Engel and O. W.
    Frost.
       p.   cm.
    "First English translation based completely on a surviving copy of Stel-
    ler's manuscript, which was written in German and dated 1743"—
    Introd.
    "Published with the assistance of the Alaska Humanities Forum and the
    National Endowment for the Humanities"—T.p. verso.
    Bibliography: p.
    Includes index.
    ISBN 0-8047-1446-0 (cl.):   ISBN 0-8047-2181-5 (pbk.)
    1. Kamchatskaia ėkspeditsiia—Early works to 1800.   2. Bering, Vitus
Jonassen, 1681–1741—Journeys—Alaska—Early works to 1800. 3. Russians—Alaska—History—18th century.   4. Alaska—Discovery and exploration—Early works to 1800.   5. Steller, Georg Wilhelm, 1709–
1746—Journeys—Alaska—Early works to 1800.   I. Frost, O. W. (Orcutt
William), 1926–   .   II. Title.
F907.S734 1988
910'.0916451—dc19   87-36577
                                                               CIP

∞ This book is printed on acid-free paper.